Imagination and Idealism in John Updike's Fiction

Mind and American Literature

Edited by Linda Simon
(*Skidmore College*)

Imagination and Idealism in John Updike's Fiction

Michial Farmer

CAMDEN HOUSE
Rochester, New York

First published 2017
by Camden House

Camden House is an imprint of Boydell & Brewer Inc.
668 Mt. Hope Avenue, Rochester, NY 14620, USA
www.camden-house.com
and of Boydell & Brewer Limited
PO Box 9, Woodbridge, Suffolk IP12 3DF, UK
www.boydellandbrewer.com

ISBN-13: 978-1-57113-942-9
ISBN-10: 1-57113-942-7

Library of Congress Cataloging-in-Publication Data

Names: Farmer, Michial, 1982– author.
Title: Imagination and idealism in John Updike's fiction / Michial Farmer.
Description: Rochester, New York : Camden House, 2017. | Series: Mind and
  American literature | Includes bibliographical references and index.
Identifiers: LCCN 2016041258| ISBN 9781571139429 (hardcover : alk. paper) |
  ISBN 1571139427 (hardcover : alk. paper)
Subjects: LCSH: Updike, John—Criticism and interpretation. | Imagination in
  literature. | Idealism in literature.
Classification: LCC PS3571.P4 Z66 2017 | DDC 813/.54—dc23 LC record
  available at https://lccn.loc.gov/2016041258

This publication is printed on acid-free paper.
Printed in the United States of America.

world that Oberon creates—or that his imagination creates for him, without his input—is powerful and enticing, and by the time of the story, he has been beckoned into this secondary world of his own fashioning, such that he can no longer function in the world created by God, the world of nature and of society: "I have become ambitious of a bubble, and careless of solid reputation. I am surrounding myself with shadows, which bewilder me, by aping the realities of life. They have drawn me aside from the beaten path of the world, and led me into a strange sort of solitude—a solitude in the midst of men—where nobody wishes for what I do, nor thinks nor feels as I do. The tales have done all this" (331). The works of his hands have become almost literally diabolic, and he suggests "that there is a devil in this pile of blotted papers. You have read them, and know what I mean—that conception, in which I endeavored to embody the character of a fiend, as represented in our traditions and the written record of our witchcraft. Oh! I have a horror of what was created in my own brain, and shudder at the manuscripts in which I gave that dark idea a sort of material existence" (330–31). His imagination becomes his curse and his ruin.

For the storytelling narrator of "The Village Uncle" (1835), too, the imagination threatens to swallow up everything pleasant in life: "Oh! I should be loth to lose my treasure of past happiness, and become once more what I was then: a hermit in the depths of my own mind . . . a man who had wandered out of the real world and got into its shadows, where his troubles, joys, and vicissitudes were of such slight stuff, that he hardly knew whether he lived, or only dreamed of living."[9] This is the polar opposite of Hawthorne's hymn to the imagination in "Sir William Phips." Here, the world of the imagination corresponds to the lower Platonic realm, a shadowy and imperfect version of the world of human relationships. The imagination thus has, for Hawthorne, two sides, both intensely powerful, and two possible outcomes for those who devote their lives to it. For the Village Uncle, the imagination, properly focused, provides a way back into human connection. He speaks of his wife, Susan: I "dipp[ed] her image into my mind and color[ed] it of a thousand fantastic hues, before I could see her as she really was."[10] His language is ambiguous here. The word "before" suggests on the one hand that he had to discard the workings of his imagination before he could see her as she really was. But on the other hand, it also suggests that it was the application of those "thousand fantastic hues" that allowed him to see her as she really was. Imagination both obscures and clarifies her essence. Oberon, however, can escape the false world of the imagination only by destroying it—but when he burns his stories, his house catches on fire, as if he cannot destroy the world of his imagination without destroying himself too. Imagination, then, is powerful; perhaps human beings possess no force more powerful. But for that very reason it can be a temptation to solipsism, which for Hawthorne means a temptation to evil. Updike, I will argue in the pages that follow, shares this view of the potential of the human imagination for good and for evil, and many of his fictional works are explicitly or implicitly explorations of the issue.

The Structure of This Book

My first chapter will consist of an elucidation of the philosophical background through which I will examine Updike's fiction. By examining the aesthetics and metaphysics of the existentialist philosophers Jean-Paul Sartre, Maurice Merleau-Ponty, Martin Heidegger, and Søren Kierkegaard, I will construct a theory of the imagination that is implicit in Updike's work. I will argue that a major component of Updike's aesthetic project involves treating the balancing act of the human imagination. Imagination is, as I have said, among the most important and vital of human faculties; we need it in order to bestow a meaning on *l'être-en-soi* (being-in-itself), to re-present a universe that is habitable for human beings at all. And yet it is powerful enough to be dangerous, and many of Updike's most memorable characters are guilty of living in a falsified universe, of mistaking the order they bestow on the world for an order intrinsic to the world itself. He maintains his interest in this struggle throughout his career, but his emphasis shifts as the decades wear on.

I have divided the rest of this book into five parts. The first part (chapters 2–4) deals with two related early novels: 1963's *The Centaur* and 1965's *Of the Farm*. Both of these novels feature fictional presentations of the most painful event of Updike's childhood—his family's move from Shillington, Pennsylvania, to a farm a few miles away. In *The Centaur* and *Of the Farm*, he presents the move as the culmination of the long-time dream of his mother, Linda Hoyer Updike, who grew up on the farm. In these chapters, I discuss the way that characters representing Updike and his father become trapped in the dreams of characters representing his mother. The imagination—implicitly the aesthetic imagination, since Linda Updike wanted all her life to be a fiction writer—becomes a tool to create worlds that are then imposed on those closest to us.

In my second part (chapters 5–7), I examine the novel that made Updike a celebrity and then sealed his reputation as a chronicler of suburban adulteries: *Couples*. I read it in tandem with a much less popular novel, *Marry Me: A Romance*—which, as Adam Begley has made clear, was written before *Couples* but was shelved in order to keep Updike's marriage intact. I agree with Begley that *Couples* has not aged well and that *Marry Me* is a much more interesting and accomplished novel. But more importantly, both books feature characters who create imaginative worlds that then beckon their creators inward. The major difference between the approaches of the two novels is that *Marry Me*'s imaginative world is the product of two imaginations—those of Jerry Conant and Sally Matthias, who construct this world in order to facilitate their affair. Most of the novel's drama comes from the clash between the world of their imaginations and the world in which they must live with their flesh-and-blood spouses and children. The novel ends in a triple fantasy in which Jerry stays with Ruth or leaves her for Sally. This indecision defers the question of the viability of Jerry's relational imagination, pushing it onto the reader. *Couples*, on the other hand, is much less ambiguous in its ending—in which God removes the divine blessing from the adulterous society of partner-swapping couples and the society itself splinters. The couples, too, have been living in a world of almost pure sexual imagination—"the post-pill paradise," as one of them famously calls it—but it's a fantasy world built by corporate rather than dual effort, and when it cannot survive the realities of the world outside Tarbox, Massachusetts (most notably the Kennedy assassination), the imaginary world collapses. And here, as elsewhere in Updike's adultery fiction, children suffer from their parents' fleeing into their collective imagination.

Returning to the connections between Updike and Hawthorne that I sketched out at the beginning of this introduction, my third part (chapters 8–11) discusses Updike's trilogy of adaptations of Hawthorne's *The Scarlet Letter*: *A Month of Sundays*, *Roger's Version*, and *S*. In their reproduction of Hawthorne's love triangle—often described by Updike as a woman being torn between a man of science and a man of faith—these three novels explore the ways in which women are forced into the powerful fantasy lives of the men they love. This dynamic is clearest in *Roger's Version*, whose theologian protagonist constructs (either from whole cloth or from subtle clues) an affair between his wife and a young computer programmer. My analysis will thus focus on the world that Roger imagines—but this novel obviously has parallels, given its shared source material, in *A Month of Sundays* and *S*. The former's philandering clergyman is locked into a room with his thoughts, and he imagines (again ambiguously) a sprouting sexual connection between himself and the landlady of the facility to which he has been sent. In *S*. the male imagination becomes genuinely diabolic when a phony guru seduces an upper-class woman to his fraudulent religion. Here, because Updike's updated Hester Prynne narrates through postmodern epistles, we see the male imagination only from the outside. These three novels, then, do more than clarify their source material—they also demonstrate the destructive and dangerous power of an unchecked masculine imagination. I hope part 3 will suggest that, contrary to the popular image of Updike as a misogynistic celebrator of male sexual power, he is actually keenly aware of the damage that men inflict on women.

Building on my analysis of *S*. in the previous chapter, the first two chapters of my fourth part (12 and 13) examine another notably woman-centric novel from the 1980s: *The Witches of Eastwick*. But where *S*.'s

Sarah Worth suffers the effects of a demonic male imagination, the three women at the core of *Witches* are dreamers—aggressive and violent dreamers, at that—in their own right. Updike presents their magic as a particularly potent form of imagination, one that begins as their servant but quickly moves beyond their control, with disastrous and tragic results. Here, too, a clash between the genders is at play, as the literally diabolic Darryl Van Horne enters the witches' circle and becomes the sun around which they orbit, his imagination dictating the direction and the objectives of their own. In this way, *Witches* and *S.* have more in common than they may initially seem to. Their protagonists are connected by their destructive immersion in masculine mental spaces.

Chapters 14–16 deal with the complicated relationship of memory, history, and imagination. As the philosopher Mary Warnock notes, "whichever aspect of memory is chiefly emphasized, there are the closest possible links between it and imagination; indeed these two powers are impossible to separate."[11] And yet memory has ethical demands to it that other forms of imagination do not—when a person remembers, he must be true, in some sense, to the world outside of his own head. The same is true of the historian, who in some sense must construct and imagine the historical situation she writes about—and yet is duty bound by her profession not to construct it out of whole cloth. There is, as Warnock points out, an invisible line buried deep in the human practices of memory and history that the responsible imagination must not cross. I conclude this project, then, by discussing the way that Updike skirts up to the line in two books. In the 1989 memoir *Self-Consciousness*, the author—a strangely private man, given the autobiographical tenor of his fiction—attempts an act of self-concealment through an ostensible act of self-disclosure. In effect, these memoirs are imaginative works as much as they are autobiography—and the former manages, in some ways, to obscure the latter. Meanwhile, in *Memories of the Ford Administration* (1992), Alfred Clayton, a historian, simultaneously tells his own personal history and attempts a biographical defense of James Buchanan (a long-time interest of Updike's). But autobiography slithers into biography, and Clayton's fecund imagination begins to color his historical project, suggesting perhaps that no human activity can ever be free from the promise and the threat of the creative (and destructive) imagination.

Along the way—largely in the first chapter of each part—I dip into Updike's vast well of short fiction, poetry, and book reviews in order to demonstrate the ways that his concerns about reality and imagination infuse his career. I cannot, needless to say, touch on every instance in which this theme arises, but I have tried to pick out the most striking and important examples. The book concludes with a brief rumination on Updike's position in two competing aesthetic philosophies: literary realism and postmodernism.

Where's Rabbit?

Updike published more than sixty books in his lifetime, and several more appeared after his death in 2009. Of these, the most famous are certainly the *Rabbit* tetralogy: *Rabbit, Run* (1960), *Rabbit Redux* (1971), *Rabbit Is Rich* (1981), and *Rabbit at Rest* (1990), along with the novella-length sequel, *Rabbit Remembered* (2000), which takes place after Harry Angstrom's death. Updike is so deeply associated with these novels that very few book-length critical studies of his work fail to include chapters on the *Rabbit* novels. My book is an exception to this general rule, and my readers may rightly wonder why that is.

The answer is certainly not that Rabbit Angstrom is any less given to imaginative re-creation of the world than Updike's other protagonists. During his first night with the amateur prostitute Ruth, for example, he tries to turn her into the ideal wife. "Say," she asks him, exasperated, "do you think we're married or something the way you boss me around?" He is overcome by the thought: "The transparent wave moves over him again and he calls to her in a voice that is almost inaudible, 'Yes; let's be.' So quickly her arms don't move from hanging at her sides, he kneels at her feet and kisses the place on her fingers where a ring would have been."[12] This sort of imaginative transformation—of the world around Harry as well as of the women whom he seduces and beds—continues throughout the four novels, for better and for worse. Near the end of *Rabbit at Rest*, Harry has retreated to his and his wife's condo in Florida after having committed the unpardonable sin of sleeping with his daughter-in-law. There, too, he revisions the world: "The rooms and furniture of the condo in these days he's been living here alone have taken on the tension and menace of a living person who is choosing to remain motionless. At night he can feel the rooms breathe and think. They are thinking about him."[13] It goes without saying that this feeling represents an imaginative projection onto the world: Harry has attributed the processes of his mind to the world of things. And that world snaps him back into place when, a few pages later, he dies of a heart attack, the ultimate victory of *l'être-en-soi* that turns Harry himself into *l'être-en-soi* (at least as far as this material world is concerned).

There is, in other words, plenty to say about Harry Angstrom's imagination—so much, in fact, that doing justice to the topic would likely take up a book in its own right. I am therefore contenting myself to point to this future book, written by someone else. The seeds have already been planted in two commentaries on the *Rabbit* novels. Elizabeth Tallent argues in *Married Men and Magic Tricks* that "Rabbit, in his guise of Adam, has confiscated some of God's sleight of hand, and donated not only a single utilitarian rib but also an invaluable element of ease and delight to Eve's psyche. Newly loved, in Updike's work, means newly invented."[14] Later, she writes that Rabbit returns Ruth "to a woman's original functions, obedience and procreation, as chronicled in the admonitory tone of Genesis: 'in pain you shall bring forth children, yet your desire shall be for your husband, and he shall rule over you.'"[15] Reading the same scene, Mary Allen points out Rabbit's scrubbing-off of Ruth's makeup, connecting "this urge for the scrubbed nymph" with "Updike's use of the pastoral as one way of idealizing women, primarily for the wonder of their bodies."[16] Further, she points out that Rabbit, and by extension Updike, has little concern for Ruth's desires in this moment. In fact, though *Rabbit, Run*'s narration shifts at a few key points in the novel to Janice's and Ruth's consciousnesses, Allen argues that even these sections represent an imaginative male imposition on female experience: "Updike gives us the dreary aspects of the housewife's existence through the lyricism of his male point of view. This stylistic quality makes the reading of Updike at times enjoyable while it soothes the reader away from the fact that from a woman's viewpoint no such lyricism in describing her life would be possible."[17] With Updike standing behind him, then, it is clear that Rabbit has no less imagination than any of the other protagonists I discuss in this book—and, as is true of the men of the *Scarlet Letter* trilogy, the bodies of women (and "stupid" and talentless women, as Allen rightly points out) serve at least in part as the blank matter on which that imagination is stamped.[18] A book about Rabbit's imagination surely exists somewhere in the collective unconscious of Updike scholars, but I will content myself with reading it instead of writing it.

Notes

[1] Hawthorne, "Sir William Phips," in *Tales and Sketches*, 12. All Hawthorne stories cited hereafter are from the collection *Tales and Sketches*.

[2] Sidney, "A Defence of Poesy," 262–63.

[3] The philosopher does not appear directly in "Sir William Phips," but he is present by implication: Hawthorne, after all, has chosen to write historical fiction rather than philosophy, and thus is aware of the limits of the latter form.

[4] Hawthorne, "Sir William Phips," 12.

[5] Bloom, "Introduction," 7.

[6] It is tempting to say here, as many of his detractors do, that aesthetic power was all Updike was after; in fact, he claimed that he "thought of my novels as illustrations for texts from Kierkegaard and [Karl] Barth" ("Remarks Upon Receiving the Campion Medal," 852)—his fiction is undeniably more sensationalist than Hawthorne's, but it has a moral, or at least a theological, impulse behind it.

[7] Hawthorne, "An Old Woman's Tale," 25.

[8] Hawthorne, "The Devil in Manuscript," 331 (hereafter cited in text).

[9] Hawthorne, "The Village Uncle," 218.

10 Ibid., 218–19.

11 Warnock, *Memory*, 75.

12 Updike, *Rabbit, Run*, 67–68.

13 Updike, *Rabbit at Rest*, 449.

14 Tallent, *Married Men and Magic Tricks*, 4.

15 Ibid., 85. The quotation is of Genesis 3:16, English Standard Version.

16 Allen, "John Updike's Love of 'Dull Bovine Beauty,'" 76.

17 Ibid., 78. As a man, I hesitate to dispute Allen's point here, but I do find something distasteful about her implication that housewives lack the necessary imagination to elevate their daily experience to the level of poetry. Rabbit's life is, after all, hardly less dreary than Janice's at the beginning of *Rabbit, Run*, and few readers would disagree that Updike's narration successfully elevates Rabbit's life. To be fair, she does later argue that Janice's briefly presented interior monologue "is as poignant as it is unexpected" (85).

18 As Allen puts it, "The male wishes to impress his identity on the female's blankness, but she is often so blank that little impression can be made" (83)—hence Rabbit's leaving Janice for Ruth, only to discover that Ruth, too, cannot be reimagined totally.

1: John Updike and the
Existentialist Imagination

JUST A FEW YEARS BEFORE HIS DEATH, John Updike wrote a short essay for the National Public Radio series *This I Believe*. His remarks form the foundation of any theory about his treatment of the imagination. The essay's final paragraph reveals him as a man with split loyalties:

> Cosmically, I seem to be of two minds. The power of materialist science to explain everything, from the behavior of the galaxies to that of molecules, atoms, and their submicroscopic components, can scarcely be doubted. Such science forms the principal achievement of the modern mind; its manifold technical and medical benefits are ours to enjoy. On the other hand, subjective sensations, desires, and, may we even say, illusions compose the substance of our daily existence, and religion alone, in its many forms, attempts to address and placate these. We are part of nature, and natural necessity compels and in the end dissolves us; yet to renounce all and any supernature, any appeal or judgment beyond the claims of matter and private appetite, leaves in the dust too much of our humanity, as through the millennia it has manifested itself in art and altruism, idealism and *joie de vivre*.[1]

On the one side stands a material world whose every atom science can, or will be able to, account for; on the other stands human consciousness, which presents itself to itself as fundamentally inexplicable in materialist terms. The distinction, broadly speaking, belongs to Jean-Paul Sartre, who divides being into *l'être-en-soi* (being-in-itself) and *l'être-pour-soi* (being-for-itself).

Relatively scant critical attention has been paid to Updike's relationship to Sartrean metaphysics, although Jack de Bellis's *John Updike Encyclopedia* discusses Sartrean politics in relation to *The Coup* (1978), and numerous critics have applied Sartrean ethics to *Of the Farm* (1965), which features as its epigraph a quotation from "L'Existentialisme est un humanisme" (Existentialism Is a Humanism, 1946).[2] John Neary's *Something and Nothingness*, meanwhile, discusses Sartre, but pits him, along with John Fowles, as a foil to Updike and Kierkegaard. Ralph C. Wood's *The Comedy of Redemption* likewise contrasts Updike's *Midpoint* (1969) with the Sartrean position that existentialism's "absurd human freedom means the impossibility of a God who could command our loyalty and obedience."[3] It is true that Updike cannot endorse Sartre's atheism or the nihilism that lurks just beyond his celebration of humanity's radical freedom. But, as I hope to demonstrate in this chapter and in the rest of this book, he nevertheless uses Sartrean metaphysics as a jumping-off point for his own, more Kierkegaardian, reflections.

In the opening chapter of his book on the imagination, Sartre discusses the sheet of paper on which he is writing. Quite apart from any metaphysical speculations, "What is certain is that I cannot spontaneously produce the white of which I take note. This inert shape, which stands short of all spontaneities of consciousness, which must be observed and learned about bit by bit, is what we call 'a thing.'"[4] In its thingness, it is fundamentally different from Sartre himself: "Never could my consciousness be a thing, because its way of being in itself is precisely to be *for* itself; for consciousness, to exist is to be conscious of its existence" (1–2). Sartre thus distrusts any wholly materialist explanation of existence, any examination that "suppose[s], prior to all investigation, that the object in question is a combination of inert invariants in external relations" (20). Consciousness cannot be ignored for Sartre—just as, in Updike's account of his beliefs, he holds out for something "beyond the claims of matter."

Sartre provides a fuller explanation of the differences between *l'être-en-soi* and *l'être-pour-soi* in his magnum opus, *L'être et le neant* (Being and Nothingness, 1943). Here, he argues that *l'être-en-soi* is utterly beyond the reaches of human consciousnesses, utterly independent of it: "It is itself so completely that the perpetual reflection which constitutes the self is dissolved in an identity. That is why being is at bottom beyond the *self*, and our first formula can be only an approximation due to the requirements of language. In fact being is opaque to itself precisely because it is filled with itself. This can be better expressed by saying that *being is what it is*."[5] *L'être-en-soi* is thus opaque. By contrast, *l'être-pour-soi* is transparent; it always looks through itself toward whatever *l'être-en-soi* it happens to be looking at. To put it another way, *l'être-pour-soi* has a self in a way that *l'être-en-soi* simply does not. This self, or consciousness, is precisely what makes *l'être-pour-soi* capable of looking in the first place. Sartre notes that "the term in-itself, which we have borrowed from tradition to designate the transcending being, is inaccurate. At the limit of coincidence with itself, in fact, the self vanishes to give place to identical being. The *self* can not be a property of being-in-itself" (123). *L'être-pour-soi*, on the other hand, is always self-conscious; to have consciousness at all means to have consciousness of one's consciousness. But this self-consciousness splits *l'être-pour-soi* in a way that *l'être-en-soi* is not split. Whereas *l'être-en-soi* is always what it is, *l'être-pour-soi* is marked by its alienation from itself: It is not what it is. The human being is made up of both *l'être-pour-soi* and *l'être-en-soi*—both "transcendence" and "facticity," as Sartre puts it in an existentialist spin on Cartesian dualism.[6]

A human being's confrontation with *l'être-en-soi*—whether external or internal to the person—can be an anxiety-producing process, as it
clearly was for Updike. In Sartre's first novel, *La nausée* (Nausea, 1938),
his protagonist, Roquentin, confronts a chestnut tree, to horrifying effect:

> My eyes only encountered completion. The tips of the branches
> rustled with existence which unceasingly renewed itself and which
> was never born. The existing wind rested on the tree like a great
> bluebottle, and the tree shuddered. But the shudder was not a
> nascent quality, a passing from power to action; it was a thing; a
> shudder-thing flowed into the tree, took possession of it, shook
> it and suddenly abandoned it, going further on to spin about
> itself. All was fullness and all was active, there was no weakness
> in time, all, even the least perceptible stirring, was made of exis-
> tence. And all these existents which bustled about this tree came
> from nowhere and were going nowhere. Suddenly they existed,
> then suddenly they existed no longer; existence is without mem-
> ory; of the vanished it retains nothing—not even a memory. Exis-
> tence everywhere, infinitely, in excess, for ever and everywhere;
> existence—which is limited only by existence. I sank down on the
> bench, stupefied, stunned by this profusion of beings without ori-
> gin: everywhere blossomings, hatchings out, my ears buzzed with
> existence, my very flesh throbbed and opened, abandoned itself to
> the universal burgeoning. It was repugnant.[7]

What repulses Roquentin here—what brings about his titular nausea—is
the separation of *l'être-en-soi* from human consciousness. Consciousness
seeks meaning, but *l'être-en-soi*, by its very nature, is meaningless, "in
excess . . . without origin." It is this same nausea that Updike describes
in his "This I Believe" essay: When materialist science accounts for every
atom and sub-atom of the universe, in effect, it reduces all of existence to
that excessive, originless *l'être-en-soi*. Updike desires such a reduction and
recoils from it in equal measure. Repeatedly in his fiction, his characters
struggle with the thingness of the universe, the thingness of their own
lives. The young David Kern, for example, has "an exact vision of death"
in which his consciousness will be stilled and he will become a thing forever: "a long hole in the ground, no wider than your body, down which
you are drawn while the white faces above recede. You try to reach them
but your arms are pinned. Shovels pour dirt into your face. There you will
be forever, in an upright position, blind and silent, and in time no one
will remember you, and you will never be called."[8] He can hope to escape
this everlasting thingness only through the eternal survival of *l'être-pour-
soi*, the Christian promise of an afterlife. And yet the authority figures in
David's life cannot affirm this promise—not even the Lutheran minister,
Reverend Dobson, who, when asked if Abraham Lincoln is still conscious

after his death (still maintains *l'être-pour-soi*, in Sartrean terms), answers, "I would have to say no; but I don't think it matters."[9] Dobson cannot understand the existential crisis that takes place when *l'être-pour-soi* confronts *l'être-en-soi*. Updike clearly means for us to condemn him for this failure. David's horrible visions continue into his adult life; one night, after lusting after a friend's wife, he lies awake in his bed, tortured by the encroaching materialist universe:

> The universe that so easily permitted me to commit adultery became, by logical steps each one of which went more steeply down than the one above it, a universe that would easily permit me to die. The enormities of cosmic space, the maddening distension of time, history's forgotten slaughters, the child smothered in the dumped icebox, the recent breakdown of the molecular life-spiral, the proven physiological roots of the mind, the presence in our midst of idiots, Eichmanns, animals, and bacteria—all this evidence piled on, and I seemed already eternally forgotten. The dark vibrating air of my bedroom seemed the dust of my grave; the dust went up and up and I prayed upward into it, prayed, prayed for a sign, any glimmer of all, any microscopic loophole or chink in the chain of evidence, and saw none.[10]

His language here is the language of mechanism that Sartre condemns in *Imagination*. Because, in David's midnight vision, no God holds him back from committing sins, the universe itself becomes a Rube Goldberg device by which every action inevitably sets off another action, which inevitably sets off a third. Human beings, like Charlie Chaplin in *Modern Times*, get ground to pieces in the cogs of the mechanistic and materialist universe.[11] *L'être-pour-soi*, for Updike, is a fragile thing, and *l'être-en-soi* always threatens, horribly, to subsume it into itself. And Sartre agrees: "But, if we know that we are directors of being, we also know that we are not its producers. If we turn away from this landscape, it will sink back into its dark permanence. At least, it will sink back; there is no one mad enough to think that it is going to be annihilated. It is we who shall be annihilated, and the earth will remain in its lethargy until another consciousness comes along to awaken it."[12] Human consciousness is a mere blip on the radar of the vast, meaningless, perhaps eternal field of *l'être-en-soi*.

The Creative Imagination

Given this state of affairs, Sartre suggests that the human imagination—and in particular the aesthetic imagination—can be a way to fight against meaninglessness. In Susan Sontag's memorable phrase, Sartre proposes "the philosophical rite of cosmophagy, . . . the devouring of the world by consciousness." Only through such a rite can the human imagination deal with "the brute reality of things."[13] Art is a fine example. "One of the chief motives of aesthetic creation," he writes in *Qu'est-ce que la littérature?* (What Is Literature?, 1948), "is certainly the need of feeling that we are essential in relationship to the world" (28). In painting a picture of or writing a description of the things around me,[14] "I am conscious of having produced them by condensing relationships, by introducing order where there was none, by imposing the unity of mind on the diversity of things. That is, I feel myself essential in relation to my creation" (28). The work of art becomes a way to kick against the meaningless mechanism of *l'être-en-soi*: "So that, through the various objects which it produces or reproduces, the creative act aims at a total renewal of the world. . . . For this is quite the final goal of art: to recover this world by giving it to be seen as it is, but as if it had its source in human freedom" (42–43). The work of art takes the universe—wrapped up in the absurdity of its thingness—and creates order within it: not the mechanistic order of the scientist, but the personal and subjective order of the imaginative writer. And then, because writing is a discipline that demands a reader other than the writer, the reader also bestows his or her emotions on the work of literature—"Raskolnikov's waiting is *my* waiting which I lend him. Without this impatience of the reader he would remain only a collection of signs" (33)—even as the work of literature transforms the emotions of the reader.

Writing—and particularly writing prose—thus alters the world of *l'être-en-soi* by an act of the imaginative will. Writing draws attention to things and actions and, in so doing, fixes them in place. To describe a man's gesture, for example, is to allow it to "begin[] to exist beyond all measure, to exist for everybody; it is integrated into the objective mind; it takes on new dimensions; it is retrieved" (13). The man's gestures change because he becomes conscious of them in a way that he was not before the presence of the writing. The very act of speaking, of writing, therefore attempts to change existence: "Thus, by speaking, I reveal the situation by my very intention of changing it; I reveal it to myself and to others in order to change it; I strike at its very heart, I transfix it, and I displace it in full view; at present I dispose of it; with every word I utter, I involve myself a little more in the world, and by the same token I emerge from it a little more, since I go beyond it towards the future" (13–14). In this sense the writer is the creator of a world—or, perhaps more accurately, of a communicable stance toward the world. This is an enormous responsibility, and the writer has a duty to communicate appropriately, to create worlds that promote rather than restrict freedom among those who encounter them. And in this sense, the artist conceives a more intense version of something that all human beings do in all their interactions with the world. Perception, for Sartre, is imagination, because "each of our perceptions is accompanied by the consciousness that human reality is a 'revealer,' that is, it is through human reality that 'there is' being, or, to put it differently, that man is the means by which things are manifested. It is our presence in the world which multiplies relations. It is we who set up a relationship between this tree and that bit of sky. Thanks to us, that star which has been dead for millennia, that quarter moon, and that dark river are disclosed in the unity of landscape" (27). This revelation takes place whenever we look at some swath of our world, but turning that swath into a painting cements the revelation. The interaction of *l'être-pour-soi* and *l'être-en-soi* will always involve an act of the imagination—but the work of art makes this explicit and thus more powerful.

Sartre's contemporary Maurice Merleau-Ponty separates the process a bit more than Sartre does. For him, perception and imagination are two related but distinct operations. Art, for Merleau-Ponty, "is not imitation, nor is it something manufactured according to the wishes of instinct or good taste. It is a process of expressing. Just as the function of words is to name—that is, to grasp the nature of what appears to us in a confused way and to place it before us as a recognizable object—so it is up to the painter, said Gasquet, to 'objectify,' 'project,' and 'arrest.' Words do not look like the things they designate; and a picture is not a trompe-l'oeil."[15] In other words, art does not show us the world exactly as it is. Instead, art organizes the world, and then it expresses this organization. It is precisely a re-presentation, a taking-in of the objects of perception and a putting-out of an expression of them. "The painter," Merleau-Ponty writes, "recaptures and coverts into visible objects what would, without him, remain walled up in the separate life of each consciousness: the vibration of appearances which is the cradle of things" (242–43). But the end result is the same for Merleau-Ponty as for Sartre. When we encounter an artist's work, it can show us the world for the first time. This re-presentation requires immense, almost superhuman ingenuity from the artist, who must take the world of *l'être-en-soi* and, in effect, turn it into the world of *l'être-pour-soi*. Works of art hang between these two realms of being: "They are the inside of the outside and the outside of the inside, which the duplicity of feeling makes possible and without which we would never understand the quasi presence and imminent visibility which make up the whole problem of the imaginary."[16] Art's re-presentation of the world is a perfection of the world, albeit a heuristic one that is performed infinitely by an infinite number of artists. The painter's eye "sees the world, sees what inadequacies keep the world from being a painting, sees what keeps a painting from being itself, sees—on the palette—the colors awaited by the painting, and sees, once it is done, the painting that answers to all these inadequacies just as it sees the paintings of others as answers to other inadequacies" (259). Thus art has a spiritual function for Merleau-Ponty, in that "it gives visible existence to what profane vision believes to be invisible" (259). *L'être-en-soi* impresses the artist—and the artist in turn presses his own *l'être-pour-soi*, his own vision, upon *l'être-en-soi*.

Martin Heidegger, in his long essay *Der Ursprung des Kunstwerkes* (The Origin of the Work of Art, 1936), shares Merleau-Ponty's emphasis on the spiritual function of art. He, like Merleau-Ponty, positions the work of art midway between *l'être-en-soi* and *l'être-pour-soi*, pointing out that, whatever elevated experience the work of art offers, it is also always a thing, that "there is something stony in a work of architecture, wooden in a carving, colored in a painting, spoken in a linguistic work, sonorous in a musical composition."[17] However, at the same time, "the art work is something else over and above the thingly element," and this transcendence "constitutes its artistic nature" (19). The work of art points beyond the world of things and thus has a dual nature: *l'être-en-soi* that has been transformed, if only partially, into *l'être-pour-soi*. The work of art, as Heidegger sees it, reveals the thing as what it is. It uncovers the essence of things—an essence that depends on their being more than just things. "To be a work," he says, "is to set up a world" (44), a world quite different from the collection of things that constitutes *l'être-en-soi*: "World is never an object that stands before us and can be seen. World is the ever-nonobjective to which we are subject as long as the paths of birth and death, blessing and curse, keep us transported into Being" (44). A world requires consciousness, requires imagination, and so inanimate objects, plants, and animals do not have a world but instead "belong to the covert throng of a surrounding into which they are linked" (45). An imaginative work thus carves out a space in *l'être-en-soi* for *l'être-pour-soi*. And yet this process also transforms *l'être-en-soi*. The work of art "causes it to come forth for the very first time and to come into the Open of the work's world" (46). As Sartre and Merleau-Ponty also point out, a new order is bestowed on *l'être-en-soi* by the creation of the aesthetic work.

For Heidegger, a genuine work of art is always a battle. It sets up a world, yes, but it also "sets forth the earth." His language here, as in so many other places, is difficult—but he seems to be arguing that by the very act of creating an aesthetic world, the work of art accentuates, by contrast, everything that does not belong to the imagination. Thus art instigates an eternal war "between world and earth," such that "the repose of the work that rests in itself thus has its presencing in the intimacy of strife" (49–50). So whatever the direct subject of a work of art, it has an additional subject to those with eyes to see and ears to hear: the clash between world and earth—between the human imagination and the mute collection of things that crowd it from the wings. Updike describes just this clash in his "This I Believe" essay, and at many notable places in his fiction directly represents it.

I suspect, however, that the major source of this aesthetic concept in Updike comes not from Sartre, Merleau-Ponty, and Heidegger, but rather from the Danish protoexistentialist Søren Kierkegaard. Kierkegaard was first being published into English at a formative time in Updike's intellectual development, and the autobiographical narrator of "The Astronomer" describes buying a different Kierkegaard book every week the summer of his twenty-fourth year:

> They were beautiful books, sometimes very thick, sometimes very thin, always typographically exhilarating, with their welter of title pages, subheads, epigraphs, emphatic italics, italicized catchwords taken from German philosophy and too subtle for translation, translator's prefaces and footnotes, and Kierkegaard's own end-less footnotes, blanketing pages at a time as, crippled, agonized by distractions, he scribbled on and on, heaping irony on irony, curse on curse, gnashing, sneering, praising Jehovah in the privacy of his empty home in Copenhagen. The demons with which he wrestled— Hegel and his avatars—were unknown to me, so Kierkegaard at his desk seemed to me to be writhing in the clutch of phantoms, slap-ping at silent mosquitoes, twisting furiously to confront presences that were not there. It was a spectacle unlike any I had ever seen in print before, and it brought me much comfort during those August and September evenings.[18]

We can easily imagine the David Kern of "Pigeon Feathers" and "Packed Dirt" avidly reading the opening paragraph of Kierkegaard's *Sygdommen til Døden* (The Sickness unto Death, 1849). "A human being," Kierkeg-aard writes, "is a synthesis of the infinite and the finite, of the temporal and the eternal, of freedom and necessity."[19] These are religious terms for just the striving later described by Sartre, Merleau-Ponty, Heidegger, and Updike—and Kierkegaard, too, notes the struggle: "Looked at in this way a human being is not yet a self" (43). To be a self is to manage a balance of the infinite and the finite—in Sartrean terms, to learn to live as *l'être-pour-soi* surrounded by *l'être-en-soi*. The self is thus not a stable thing but an eternal struggle: "Yet a self, every moment it exists, is in a process of becoming; for the self κατα δυναμιν[20] is not present actually, it is merely what is to come into existence" (60). When a person cannot manage this synthesis, he or she is in despair.

One form of despair comes from being immersed in finitude, which Kierkegaard connects with fatalism. "The fatalist," he writes, "is in despair, he has lost God and thereby his self; for a person who has no God has no self either. But the fatalist has no God, or, what is the same, his God is necessity. Since for God everything is possible, then God is that everything is possible. The fatalist's worship of God is therefore at most an interjection, and really it is muteness, mute submission, he is unable to pray" (70). We should think of David Kern here, suffocating in the middle of the night, having lost all ability to cry out to the God he wants to believe in. The chain of physical causes belonging to *l'être-en-soi* has mired him in necessity. Kierkegaard connects this sort of despair with middle-class complacency and blames it on a failure of imagination: "For to be aware of his self and of God, a man's imagination must whirl him up higher than the dank air of the probable, it must tear him out of that and, by making possible what exceeds the *quantum satis* [measure of sufficiency] of all experience, teach him to hope and fear, or fear and hope. But imagination is what the petty bourgeois mentality does not have, will not have, shrinks from with horror" (71). Without imagination, then, selfhood cannot be achieved, and human beings will be bound to necessity and the finite—to *l'être-en-soi* and the materialist universe. We need imagination for our spiritual health. All of us possess this faculty, "which is the first condition determining what a man will turn out to be; for the second condition is the will, which in the final resort is definitive. . . . For the imagination is itself more perfect than the sufferings of reality, it is timelessly qualified, soaring above the sufferings of reality, it is capable of presenting perfection admirably, it possesses all the splendid colors for portraying it."[21] Imagination, for Kierkegaard, becomes a kind of faith, a way of transcending the merely physical and integrating the infinite with the finite.

John Updike, a diligent reader of Kierkegaard, particularly in the early stages of his career, largely adopts this vision of the human imagination. It is, for him, the definitive human characteristic—something absolutely necessary to make it past the despair brought on by the "materialist science" he describes in his "This I Believe" essay and elsewhere. As he says in a 1986 interview, "Science has made human beings feel less significant: It has diminished our faith. How could it not? It tells us that we're specks of organic matter on an obscure planet in the middle suburbs of a galaxy that's one among millions. Just the scale of the universe that has been revealed to us is truly daunting. If you try for a moment to internalize these numbers, it's very hard to see yourself as a hero or heroine of a cosmic drama—which is, after all, what the great religions tell us we are."[22] Art and religion alike bring the imagination to bear on this depressing physicalist landscape. As Kristiaan Versluys points out, the incredible physical detail of Updike's prose "cannot be reduced to pure *chosisme* or description for description's sake. On the contrary, in many stories mere accumulation of detail is depressing for the protagonist. Objects piled onto objects make for melancholy or despair." The blank material of the physical world must be made hospitable for human life, and so "the Updike protagonist seeks, through memory and imagination, to align objects along a vector so that they become meaningful and accessible."[23] This is also Updike's job as a fiction writer and poet. The writer, he says in the 1974 lecture "Why Write?," is given the task of reproducing the world; writing itself is at its best "an imitation of the life we know, however narrow."[24] His aesthetics in this lecture has two major points. First, "mimesis demands no replacement" (33). In other words, writing creates, but the creations that it offers do not compete with real-life objects for their existence or sustenance. And second, "the world called into being . . . admit[s] of connections." Writing thus follows a human urge "to make collections, to assemble sets" (34). Art must therefore organize *l'être-en-soi*, as Sartre, Merleau-Ponty, and Heidegger argue. It is for this reason that Updike finds the *nouveau roman* of Alain Robbe-Grillet and others dissatisfying. For Updike, Robbe-Grillet's theories have to them

> a hollow ring of Thomism. Robbe-Grillet's concept of thereness looks like the medieval *quidditas*; the attempt to treat existence itself as a quality that can be artistically emphasized seems a formal confusion, a scholastic bottling of the wind. Robbe-Grillet's key concept—of "purely external and superficial" things—takes no account of the vast area of mobile and animate phenomena that mediate between *Homo sapiens* and inert matter, or of the difference between raw material and artifacts already imbued with human intention, or of the fact that to one man another is as much a "thing" as a chair or waterfall.[25]

The more appropriate metaphysics on which to base one's aesthetics, Updike argues, is the split "between the single ego and the external world."[26] Such a split would allow for the infinite gradations of the human imagination in its workings on the material world, from which Robbe-Grillet would exclude it. For this reason, Updike finds the work of Robert Pinget, another practitioner of the *nouveau roman*, more satisfying (if still difficult). Reading Pinget's book *Le Libera* (1969; *The Libera Me Domine*, 1978), he writes, "we do feel we have lived in a provincial French village and experienced its tedium and its entertainments . . . at a bone-deep level no logic-bound tale could have reached."[27] What is realistic about Pinget's work is precisely the haze into which *l'être-en-soi* settles: "For in fact human events, whether they be Kennedy's assassination or Watergate or how we spent the day before yesterday, have a permanently unsettled shape once past the instant in which they occur, and Pinget's reverberations of hearsay are less anti-realistic than they appear."[28] The genuine artist must organize *l'être-en-soi*, even if that organization is inchoate, heuristic, and hazy. And yet this organization is aesthetic rather than philosophical. As he puts it elsewhere, "a work of fiction is not a statement about the world; it is an attempt to create, out of hieroglyphs imprinted by the world upon the writer's inner being, another world."[29] This world is holistic and imagistic, and it is informed by the world of things—but it is fundamentally an organization of those things and must not be confused with the real world that it re-presents. Even so, artists "must sit down in the expectation that the material will speak through us, that certain unforeseeable happinesses of pattern and realization will emerge out of blankness as we write."[30] The world of things must guide the world of the imagination—Updike says in an interview that his work tries "to capture . . . the wonder of the real which is very easy to ignore"[31]—but at the same time, the world of the imagination, in creating patterns, is not itself the world of things.

A number of Updike's short stories also function essentially as brief essays on aesthetic theory. Take the strange monologue "The Sea's Green Sameness" (1960), for example. It is a plotless rumination on the role of the imagination and of art in re-creating the world. Its narrator suggests that the world has become disenchanted and impoverished by the reign of *l'être-en-soi*: "This is a rude age. Nothing is hidden."[32] One thinks of his later declaration that "the power of materialist science to explain everything, from the behavior of the galaxies to that of molecules, atoms, and their submicroscopic components, can scarcely be doubted."[33] And yet he does doubt it: "Yet everything is [hidden]. In a sense a person *observed* walking to a closed door is *less* 'there' than someone being forcibly imagined to be invisible" ("The Sea's Green Sameness," 159). He holds out hope that the human faculty of the imagination cannot quite be explained away by merely physical means.

"The Sea's Green Sameness" has a good deal in common with Wallace Stevens's poem "The Idea of Order at Key West." Stevens's poem, like Updike's story, is a difficult philosophical meditation on the relationship of the human imagination to the material world around it. He describes a woman singing at the edge of the ocean; in so doing, she in some sense creates that ocean. "She was," he writes, "the single artificer of the world" of her song.[34] And yet this meaning that the artist brings to the world is always an artificial meaning. Stevens has already told us that "it was she and not the sea we heard."[35] As for Sartre, then, there are two worlds: the imagination (*l'être-pour-soi*, or at least one faculty of it) and the world outside the imagination (*l'être-en-soi*). Updike, as well, "posit[s] a world of two halves: the ego and the external object. I think it is a fair representation of the world, a kind of biform Parliament, where two members sit, and speak for all parties" ("The Sea's Green Sameness," 160). Meaning resides always in the former and never in the latter. And yet we must interact with the world through our imagination. We must bring to a fundamentally meaningless world a meaning created by ourselves and thus always a little false—or at least always preliminary, always alterable.

"The Sea's Green Sameness" extends this philosophy. After informing us that he is a writer sitting on a beach in the Caribbean, Updike proceeds to describe the ocean that lies before him: "Its receding green surface is marked everywhere by millions of depressions, or nicks, of an uncertain color: much as this page is marked. But this page yields a meaning, however slowly, whereas the marks on the sea are everywhere the same. That is the difference between Art and Nature" (159). Nature no less than art calls out to be interpreted, but it is fundamentally uninterpretable: "And I seem to see, now and then, running vertically with no regard for perspective, veins of a metallic color; filaments of silver or gold—it is impossible to be certain which—waver elusively, but valuably, at an indeterminate distance below the skin of the massive, flat, monotonous volume" (160). *L'être-en-soi* defies our ability to make meaning from it; it remains excessive, as Roquentin recognizes in *La nausée*.

We do have one hope for meaning, however. In these paragraphs, Updike has turned the uninterpretable ocean into interpretable art. He does so in characteristic Updike fashion, with long sentences of descriptions, but he wonders about the validity of this approach—not for its own sake, or for his, but for ours: "It is a chronic question, whether to say simply 'the sea' and trust to people's imaginations, or whether to put in the adjectives. I have had only fair luck with people's imaginations; hence tend to trust adjectives" (160). The commonplace imagination, he suggests, needs help in re-presenting the world around it; it needs the urgings of the artistic imagination. Thus Updike creates the world for us as well as for himself, just as the woman singing by the sea in "The Idea of Order at Key West" creates it for the first-person plural poetic voice that narrates the poem. The problem is that language is not inherently trustworthy: Updike wonders of adjectives, "Are they to be trusted? Are they—words—anything substantial upon which we can rest our weight?" (160). Language is shrouded in mystery and thus cannot allow for real precision: "The source of language, the spring from which all these shadows (tinted, alliterative, shapely, but still shadows) flow, is itself in shadow" (160). How can we ground the meaning of our lives in something as shifty as language? To view the world through language is to be an idealist, interacting with our own thoughts rather than with the world itself.

But a writer like Updike has no other choice. He comes to language, to literature, rather late in the game and feels the pressure of the true masters of the form before him. "Were Proust and Joyce," he wonders, "an ending or a beginning? They seemed, from their newness, a beginning, but as time passes does not their continued newness make it clear that they are the opposite, that everything since comprises a vacuum in which the surfaces of these old works, that should be cracked and sunken, are preserved like fresh pigment?" (161–62). The imagination has scarcely progressed since the high modernists, and our postmodern attempts at making meaning fail. All of this returns, perhaps, to his earlier notion that he lives in a vulgar age that shows too much and thus destroys the role of the artistic imagination. Thus, "Perhaps all of us latter-day writers are like the priests that the peasantry continued to supply to the Church long after the aristocracy acknowledged that the jig was up" (162–63). The imagination has been replaced, most of all, by the disenchanting reign of science. The role of the writer is thus reduced: "No longer am I permitted to conceive charming legends about how it came to be salt, for this is known. Its chemistry, its weight, its depth, its age, its creatures so disturbingly suggestive of our own mortality—what is not known of these things, will be known. The veins of silver (or gold) in it are all mapped and will be mined tomorrow. This leaves, you say, its essence, its ens. Yes, but what, really, can we hope for in this line, after Plato, after Aquinas, after Einstein? Have not their brave fancies already gone the way of Poseidon?" (160). Under the sway of science, then, Updike doubts the ability of the artistic imagination to provide access to the essence of things. The story enacts the struggle that Heidegger demands of great art, the struggle between earth and world, between science and imagination, between *l'être-en-soi* and *l'être-pour-soi*. The piece ends with a weakened faith in the power of the imagination—but not an utter loss of faith:

> I have reverted, in my art (which I gaily admit I have not mastered), to the first enchanters, who expected their nets of words to imprison the weather, to induce the trees to bear and the clouds to weep, and to drag down advice from the stars. I expect less. I do not expect the waves to obey my wand, or support my weight. I am too tired; my modesty, perhaps, damns me. All I expect is that once into my blindly spun web of words the thing itself will break: make an entry and an account of itself. Not declare what it will do. This is no mystery; we are old friends. I can observe. Not cast its vote with mine, and make a decree: I have no hope of this. The session has lasted too long. I wish it to yield only on the point of its identity. What is it? Its breadth, its glitter, its greenness and sameness balk me. *What is it?* If I knew, I could say. (164)

He does not wish, in other words, fully to create the world using his imagination. He does not even really wish to *enchant* the world using his imagination. He wants to use his imagination to *re-present* the world, to bestow an order on the unordered mass of things.[36]

Updike returns to the sea and the imagination in "Lifeguard," whose protagonist is a divinity student who spends his summers lifeguarding at a Massachusetts beach. As in "The Sea's Green Sameness," he notes that our age has been disenchanted by a materialist science that has all the answers: "That the sea, with its multiform and mysterious hosts, its savage and senseless rages, no longer comfortably serves as a divine metaphor indicates how severely humanism has corrupted the apples of our creed. We seek God now in flowers and good deeds, and the immensities of blue that surround the little scabs of land upon which we draw our lives to their unsatisfactory conclusions are suffused by science with vacuous horror."[37] As a divinity student, he believes in the afterlife that David Kern hopes for in "Pigeon Feathers," the afterlife that will infuse *l'être-en-soi* with *l'être-pour-soi* eternally: "My own persistence beyond the last rim of time is easy to imagine; indeed, the effort of imagination lies the other way—to conceive of my ceasing" (218). But he runs into trouble when he expands the world beyond himself:

> But when I study the vast tangle of humanity that blackens the beach as far as the sand stretches, absurdities crowd in on me. Is it as maiden, matron, or crone that the females will be eternalized? What will they do without children to watch and gossip to exchange? What of the thousand deaths of memory and bodily change we endure—can each be redeemed at a final Adjustments Counter? The sheer numbers involved make the mind scream. The race is no longer a tiny clan of simian aristocrats lording it over an ocean of grass; mankind is a plague racing like fire across the exhausted continents. (218)

Even so, the lifeguard longs to bring a kind of immortality to the crowd by the exertion of his imagination—presented, as in "The Sea's Green Sameness," as a detailed description of the material world, a bestowing of order on the orderless mass: "My chief exercise, as I sit above the crowd, is to lift the whole mass into immortality" (217). The story itself becomes the agent of immortality, an imaginative force against the materialist disenchantment of God's world.[38] And Updike does not stand alone in this; as he explains in a 1968 essay on meeting other authors, "writers, like everyone else, see a world their personalities to some extent create."[39] Thus it is that "a room containing Philip Roth, I have noticed, begins hilariously to whirl and pulse with a mix of rebelliousness and constriction that I take to be Oedipal. And I have seen John Cheever, for ten days we shared in Russia, turn the dour world of Soviet literary officials into a bright scuttle of somehow suburban characters, invented with marvelous speed and arranged in sudden tableaux expressive, amid wistful neo-Czarist trappings, of the lyric desperation associated with influence. As if transported to the moon, people in Cheever's neighborhood lose half their bodily weight."[40] Literary writers—men and women of tremendous imaginative power—create the worlds they live in as surely as they create the worlds their characters live in. This is part of the glory of their calling.

Updike's fullest exploration of the clash between *l'être-en-soi* and *l'être-pour-soi*, however, appears in his 1969 collection *Midpoint and Other Poems*—most evidently in the title poem, but also in several other poems in the collection.[41] In these poems, as in the "This I Believe" essay, Updike conceives of himself as a subjective imagination struggling against a materialist universe. Even as a child, he points out, "I feared myself an epiphenomenon"[42]—feared, that is, that the materialist conception of the universe, and the nihilism to which it necessarily leads, is accurate. In an echo of Pascal, who writes that "the eternal silence of these infinite spaces frightens me,"[43] Updike tells us that

> Sickened by Space's waste, I tried to cling
>
> to the thought of the indissoluble:
> a point infinitely hard
> was luminous in me, and cried *I will*. ("Midpoint," 1.39–42)

This point is his selfhood, which cannot be reduced to mere material, as much as modern thinkers might try to do so. And yet materialism always beckons, always threatens. The third canto of "Midpoint" is a light-verse hymn to the atomic structure of the world, based on a description from *Scientific American* and first published in the same magazine. "All things are atoms," it begins, and atoms resist our attempts at making magic of them:

> Swiss *Paracelsus*, in's alchemic lair,
> Saw Sulphur, Salt, and Mercury unfold
> Amid Millennial hopes of faking Gold. (3.3–5)

This materialist universe is fundamentally godless: "*Nature* alone / Of Collagen and Apatite compounded bone" (3.53–54). Later, he will write that "the Demi-urge expands up to a rim / Where calculable cold collapses Him" (5.35–36). This universe, in other words, is made only of material stuff, and in it "Elegant Formulations sever Chance / From Cause, and clumsy Matter learns to dance" (5.29–30). This is *l'être-en-soi*—pure matter, unconcerned with human consciousness. It confounds the imagination: "Textbooks and Heaven only are Ideal; / Solidity is an imperfect state" (3.73–74). Likewise, in the poem "Fireworks," Updike fears that human life, human emotions, are only a temporary event in the empty eternity of materialism. The fireworks that represent our mental faculties are "followed, after an empty bang, / by an ebbing amber galaxy, despair."[44] Only science, it seems, can discover the nature of reality: "How nicely microscopic forces yield, / In Units growing visible, the World we wield!" ("Midpoint," 3.98–99). And yet we cannot help but impose our imagination on this blank world, as Updike cannot help but allegorize throughout the third canto. The imagination thus undermines the materialist vision of the universe, it makes matter "dance."

The stubborn midpoint of a self that he praises in the opening canto is heavily connected with this undermining imagination. As a boy, he imagined art

> as descending, via pencil, into dry
> exactitude. The beaded curtain
> of Matter hid an understanding Eye. (1.46–48)

There is a ghost in the machine, a mystical imagination at the center of the physical world, just as there is an immaterial self hidden in the folds of Updike's physical body. For this reason, Jeff Campbell argues that "Midpoint" affirms "a dualistic world-view which recognizes the interpenetration and interdependence of mind/spirit and body/matter."[45] The imaginative self becomes a spot of *l'être-pour-soi* that illuminates the darkness of *l'être-en-soi*; it becomes the midpoint of the universe:

> the night sky, with a little luck,
> was a camera back, the constellations
> faint silver salts, and I the crux
>
> of radii, the tip of two huge cones,
> called Heaven and Earth,
> that took their slant and spin from me alone. (1.94–99)

The imagination is in constant struggle with the nihilism that materialism ultimately implies. Updike recounts

> having waited out numerous dead nights with lis-
> tening and with prayer
> having brought myself back from the dead with
> extravagant motions of the mind (4.286–89)

And he imagines a material world onto which human consciousness asserts itself:

> I was so happy I stuttered
> perhaps Creation is a stutter of the Void
> (I could revise the universe if I just knew math)
> I think it may all turn out to be an illusion
> the red shift merely travel fatigue
> and distance losing its value like inflated currency
> (physicists are always so comfortably talking
> about infinite flashlight beams
> and men on frictionless roller skates)
> and the atom a wrinkle that imagines itself
> and mass a factor of our own feebleness (4.299–309)

Likewise, in "Dream Objects," the products of the human imagination are given a quasi-material existence all their own:

> Strangest is their reality,
> their three-dimensional workmanship:
> veined pebbles that have an underside,
> maps one could have studied for minutes longer,
> books we seem to read page after page.[46]

So real are they, in fact, that they elude our total concentration, our total assimilation. The products of the human imagination actually become more powerful than the imagination that created them:

> Fine
> as dandelion polls, they surface and explode
> in the wind of the speed of our dreaming,
>
> so that we awake with the sense
> of having missed everything.[47]

Art, then, becomes a dreamlike means of transcending and re-creating the material world. Updike praises the artists of the past—composers, painters, and authors—who spend their afterlives

> lavishing measures of light down upon us,
> telling us, over and over, there is a realm
> above this plane of silent compromise.[48]

Their works thus transcend their material elements—as Heidegger says great art must—and stand,

> waiting larger than life in shadowy galleries
> to whisper that edges of color
> lie all about us innocent as grass.[49]

Updike's task as an artist is to join in this process: "Dance, words!" he instructs ("Midpoint" 4.334), recalling the dance of the atoms in the previous canto. For ultimately his words make the atoms dance, the imagination that makes a pattern out of the endless material world.

Some of the same ideas appear in a 1963 review of a collection of Max Beerbohm poems. Here, Updike presents light verse—generally not a genre taken seriously as a vehicle for aesthetic theory—as a fundamentally imaginative and powerful genre. "Language," he writes, "is finite and formal; reality is infinite and formless. Order is comic; chaos is tragic."[50] Thus the very artificiality of light verse—its firm insistence on rhyme, its comedic tone—makes it a powerful tool for imposing order on a chaotic *l'être-en-soi*. Updike explains further in a footnote added upon the 1965 publication of *Assorted Prose*: "I think I meant that order is comic in the sense that it is deathless. The essence of a machine is its *idea*; though every part is replaced, the machine persists, as the (successful) embodiment of certain abstract notions. There is something Platonic about machines. . . . Likewise, a poem is a verbal machine infinitely reproducible, whose existence cannot be said to lie anywhere or to depend upon any set of atoms" (206n). The very artificiality of light verse gives it its power: We know, when we read Max Beerbohm's work (or Updike's own light verse, which he implicitly defends here), that we are reading a false order on material reality—and yet the order, in some sense, prevails. Novels, he suggests, are harder: "Our mode is realism, 'realistic' is synonymous with prosaic, and the prose writer's duty is to suppress not only rhyme but any verbal accident that would mar the textural correspondence to the massive, onflowing impersonality that has supplanted the chiming heavens of the saints" (207). That Updike's own prose is not prosaic is thus an important fact. He does not suppress the "verbal accidents" that separate poetry from prose; his prose leaps forth with alliteration and rhyme intact, and in so doing he shoots for an imaginative realism, a presentation of the material world that lifts it into the world of the imagination. He suggests as much in his acceptance speech for the National Book Awards fiction prize, which *The Centaur* won in 1963: "Fiction is a tissue of literal lies that refreshes and informs our sense of actuality. Reality is—chemically, atomically, biologically—a fabric of microscopic accuracies."[51] His job as a fiction writer, as he presents it here, is to use his powerful imagination, and the language that makes up its currency, to falsify the material world, to bestow on it an order that does not properly speaking belong to it, but in bestowing that order to preserve and re-present it. The imagination thus counts among the highest and most important human faculties. To live without it is to live in materialist, mechanistic despair, a world without meaning.

The Falsifying Imagination

Kierkegaard, as we have seen, presents the imagination as a way out of a certain kind of despair—despair brought on by the individual's being mired in necessity and finitude. But despair, for Kierkegaard, comes from an imbalance of the elements that make up the human self, and it is possible to swing too far in the opposite direction. The imagination that lifts a person out of the despair of finitude and necessity can lead her to the despair of infinitude and possibility. This sort of despair comes from what Kierkegaard refers to as the fantastic, which "is, of course, most closely related to the imagination, but the imagination is related in its turn to feeling, understanding, and will, so that a person's feelings, understanding and will may be fantastic. Fantasy is, in general, the medium of infinitization. It is not a faculty like other faculties—if one wishes to speak this way, it is the faculty *instar omnium*. What feelings, understanding and will a person has depends in the last resort upon what imagination he has—how he represents himself to himself, that is, upon imagination. Imagination is the infinitizing reflection" (*Sickness*, 60–61). A too-powerful or improperly used imagination can deliver a person over to a kind of drunkenness by which he separates from the material world altogether: "But to become fantastic in this way, and therefore be in despair, although usually obvious, does not mean that a person may not continue living a fairly good life, to all appearances be someone, employed with temporal matters, get married, beget children, be honoured and esteemed—and one may fail to notice that in a deeper sense he lacks a self. Such things cause little stir in the world; for in the world a self is what one least asks after, and the thing it is most dangerous of all to show signs of having" (62). He enters the realm of pure possibility, and the despair that goes along with it:

> Thus possibility seems greater and greater to the self; more and more becomes possible because nothing becomes actual. In the end it seems as though everything were possible, but that is the very moment that the self is swallowed up in the abyss. Even a small possibility needs some time to become actual. But eventually the time that should be spent on actuality gets shorter and shorter, everything becomes more and more momentary. . . . Just when one thing seems possible some new possibility arises, and finally these phantasms succeed one another with such speed that it seems as though everything were possible, and that is the very moment the individual himself has finally become nothing but an atmospheric illusion. (66)

We have, then, a balancing act. Living without imagination mires us in *l'être-en-soi*, in a purely material reality in which human beings cannot truly be at home. So we must exert our imaginations on the world around us in order to create order and possibility. But in doing so, we always risk asserting too much and too strongly, risk forgetting that the order we create is always heuristic, always, in Kierkegaard's terms, becoming rather than being. If we move too far in either direction, the result is despair.

Merleau-Ponty makes a similar point in the preface to his *La phénoménologie de la perception* (1945; *Phenomenology of Perception*, 1996). The phenomenologist differs from the transcendental idealist, he says, in that he recognizes that "the real has to be described, not constructed or formed. Which means that I cannot put perception into the same category as the syntheses represented by judgements, acts, or predications."[52] Thus, my experience of the world cannot be built, as an idealist would have it, on "representations" that come from real objects on the one hand and imaginary objects on the other hand. If it were, "I ought to be ceaselessly taking apart misleading syntheses, and reinstating in reality stray phenomena which I had excluded in the first place. But this does not happen. The real is a closely woven fabric."[53] To reduce *l'être-en-soi* to merely the product of *l'être-pour-soi* is to make a serious error—an almost impossible error in Merleau-Ponty's eyes. The real world must not be confused with the world of the imagination—even though imaginative works organize the real world.

In "Midpoint," Updike insists on the existence and importance of *l'être-en-soi*. Jeff Campbell points out that Canto 3, "The Dance of the Solids," "makes specific the allusions to the solidity and importance of matter offered in the first two cantos while providing a foundation for the insights in the next two cantos. By removing the I/eye from the center of the poem, Updike is able to find firmer ground for the Archimedean point of his conclusion."[54] Indeed, the imagination cut loose from the reality of the material world would be a childish disaster. Updike's self is tied to a body, and "I am disarmed / to think that my body has mattered," since

> I did not expect it; humble
> as a glow-worm, my boneless ego asked
> only to witness, to serve as the hub
>
> of a wheeling spectacle that would not pass.
>   ("Midpoint," 1.113–14, 118–21)

The imagination must always be referred back to the material world it seeks to reorder. Human life exists in no other form. And, just as in the fifth canto Updike praises Kierkegaard, Karl Barth, and his other heroes, he

> Praise[s] IBM, that boils the brain's rich store
> Down to a few electric either/ors;
> Praise Pointillism, Calculus, and all
> That turn the world infinitesimal;
> The midget of the alphabet is I;
> The Infinite is littleness heaped high. (5.21–26)

For the imagination to triumph, then, the material world must be real, must be reducible to *l'être-en-soi*. Then and only then can "The Archimedean point, however small / . . . serve to lift th' entire terrestrial Ball" (5.3–4). Human life is always a balancing act between the imagination that seeks to make sense of the world and the material world that resists our sense-making. Thus, in a review of Italo Calvino's *Il castello dei destini incrociati* (1969; *The Castle of Crossed Destinies*, 1977), Updike lays out a means for material reality to correct human flights of fancy:

> Every moment is, in a sense, a dealt hand. The combinations that the human mind invents are relatively facile and unmagical compared to reality's dovetailed richness. Behind the artist's transformative sorcery lurks, like a sheepish apprentice, an irrational willingness to view the accidents of the actual as purposeful and the given as sacred. We are all artists insofar as we take the inexorable and quite unchosen data of our own circumstances and philosophically internalize them, give

them a significance to match their awful centrality, and thus lend our lives a "meaning." Narrative and metaphysics alike become flimsy and frivolous if they venture too far from the home base of all human-ism—the single, simple human life that we all more or less lead.[55]

We must, therefore, approach the world of *l'être-en-soi* as a given—but at the same time, Updike's language suggests that we must impart meaning to its objects, meaning that does not adhere to them naturally. The imagi-nation corrects the material world, which then corrects the imagination; to go too far in either direction is a grave mistake. Thus, as Kristiaan Ver-sluys shows, the typical Updike story presents both sides simultaneously: the flat, barren world of *l'être-en-soi* is transformed by *l'être-pour-soi*, but it always lurks beneath the filigree. Any metaphysical closure the story offers "is always considered to be temporary—a provisional halt in the meaning-making apparatus—and is arrived at only after many narrative loops and dialectical digressions."[56] It is a double dialectic; the author himself is imposing meaning on a material world that resists it, and his characters are largely doing the same thing.[57]

Updike's fiction frequently reflects this balancing act, learned from the existentialists who make up the better part of his philosophical back-ground. His protagonists frequently are driven by despair to impose an imaginative order on the universe—but they also frequently go too far and are psychologically and spiritually damaged by the foundering of their imaginations on the jagged rocks of *l'être-en-soi*—and on other charac-ters' imaginative impositions. The 1964 story "Leaves" is a good exam-ple. Its narrator defines the natural world in strikingly Sartrean terms. Nature appeals to him, he tells us, because it "exists without guilt. Our bodies are in Nature; our shoes, their laces, the little plastic tips of the laces—everything around us and about us is in Nature, and yet something holds us away from it."[58] To Sartre's description of *l'être-en-soi* Updike has added that, in lacking self-consciousness, the world of objects also lacks guilt. It is for this reason that the narrator is able to take some com-fort in the natural world—whereas he is guilty (of adultery), *l'être-en-soi* is innocent. But he wants to explain his adultery. This act of the imagina-tion attempts to move the unpredictably human into the predictably nat-ural and thus remove the guilt of the situation: "And once the events are sorted out—the actions given motivations, the actors assigned psycholo-gies, the miscalculations tabulated, the abnormalities named, the whole furious and careless growth pruned by explanation and rooted in history and returned, as it were, to Nature—what then? Is not such a return spu-rious? Can our spirits really enter Time's haven of mortality and sink com-posedly among the mulching leaves?" (54). The answer, of course, is no. The natural world cannot offer an explanation for human guilt, which is all-consuming and inexhaustible.

Furthermore, though the narrator would like to ground his relationship with his lover in the world of the merely natural, it is doomed, like all other human endeavors, to belong to the imagination: "And I, satisfied at last, divorced, studied my children with the eyes of one who had left them, examined my house as one does a set of snapshots from an irrevocable time, drove through the turning landscape as a man in asbestos cuts through a fire, met my wife-to-be—weeping yet smiling, stunned yet brave—and felt, unstoppably, to my horror, the inner darkness burst my skin and engulf us both and drown our love. The natural world, where our love had existed, ceased to exist" (54–55). His guilty idealism has become complete; the natural world has been replaced by the world of the imagination, and this world is run through with guilt. The implications for art are not good. The narrator, as in "The Sea's Green Sameness" and "Lifeguard," wants to re-present the world through description. He describes a blue jay: "See him? I do, and snapping the chain of my thought, I have reached through glass and seized him and stamped him on this page. Now he is gone. And yet, there, a few lines above, he still is, 'astraddle,' his rump 'dingy,' his head 'alertly frozen.' A curious trick, possibly useless, but mine" (53). But this moves the bird from the realm of Nature to the realm of the imagination, and since the imagination is guilty in this story, the bird is soiled: "And what are these pages but leaves? Why do I produce them but to thrust, by some subjective photosynthesis, my guilt into Nature, where there is no guilt?" (56). Art has become not a divine act but a diabolic one.

A less serious examination of the overreaching imagination comes in the short story "A Madman." The story is, in its way, an expanded version of Updike's early poem "English Train Compartment." In the poem, as Updike's fellow travelers look out the window, they see a world created by art rather than by God, an unpainted landscape in which "Sheep elegant enough for any eclogue / browse under Constable clouds."[59] It is as though once the art—the poetry or the painting—has entered the world, we can no longer see the world without seeing it through the art. The same thing happens for the visiting American narrator of "A Madman," for whom "England itself seemed slightly insane . . . The meadows skimming past the windows of the Southampton-London train seemed green deliriously, seemed so obsessively steeped in the color that my eyes, still attuned to the exhausted verdure and September rust of American fields, doubted the ability of this landscape to perform useful work. England appeared to exist purely as a context of literature."[60] Everything he sees in London "seemed too authentic to be real, too corroborative of literature to be solid" (36). And Oxford is the same: "But looking back toward the center of town, we were treated to the storybook view of Oxford, all spires and silhouette and flaking stone, under a sky by John Constable, R.A." (42). The impression is confirmed by Mr. Robinson, an elderly man who is staying at the same lodging-house as the narrator and his wife. He greets the couple academically: "Welcome to Oxford . . . 'That home of lost causes, and forsaken beliefs, and unpopular names, and impossible loyalties.' That's Matthew Arnold; if you want to understand Oxford, read Arnold" (38). But what this titular madman demonstrates, as the story progresses, is how little he understands Oxford. He is unable to procure the narrator even a place to stay, and his presence quickly becomes grating and even dangerous. He is a man who lives entirely in text, as his copy of Arnold, loaned to the narrator, demonstrates:

> Right there, on the jostling pavement, I opened it, and nearly slammed it shut in horror, for every page was a spider's web of annotations and underlinings, in many pencils and inks and a wild variety of handwritings. "Cf.," "videlicet," "He betrays himself here," "19th cent. optmsm."—these leaped at me out of the mad swarm. The annotations were themselves annotated, as his argument with the text doubled and redoubled back on itself. "Is this so?" a firm hand had written in one margin, and below it, in a different slant and fainter pencil, had been added, "Yes it is so," with the "is" triple-underlined; and below this a wobby ball-point pen had added, without capitals, "but is it?" (45–46)

This midrash-in-microcosm is proof of Robinson's madness, proof of his inability to exist in the world of flesh and blood, the world of things and rooms to be let—and it is also, perhaps, the cause of it. His imagination is so incredibly potent that it lifts him out of *l'être-en-soi* altogether. The effect may be charming at first, but eventually his presence becomes noxious to the narrator and his wife, and they are glad to escape him. And Robinson is not the only Don Quixote figure in Updike's fiction, as I hope the chapters that follow will demonstrate. Updike's characters are forever confusing the products of their imagination with the world of things that they must live in—a world that eventually snaps them back into place, painfully.

Notes

[1] Updike, "This I Believe," 671.

[2] See, for example, Samuels, *John Updike*; Hamilton and Hamilton, *The Elements of John Updike*; Taylor, *Pastoral and Anti-Pastoral Patterns in John Updike's Fiction*; Galloway, *The Absurd Hero in American Fiction*; Greiner, *John Updike's Novels*; and Newman, *John Updike*.

[3] Wood, *The Comedy of Redemption*, 198.

[4] Sartre, *Imagination*, 1 (hereafter cited in text).

[5] Sartre, *Being and Nothingness*, 28. Hereafter cited in-text.

[6] Sartre's ontology also has quite a bit in common with Immanuel Kant's, which divides the world into the noumenal (things as they exist in and of themselves) and the phenomenal (things as we experience them). Kant's "Copernican revolution" in metaphysics was his declaration that the noumenal is off-limits to human consciousness. The Galileo to Kant's Copernicus is surely Edmund Husserl, the founder of the phenomenological school in philosophy out of which Sartrean existentialism springs. The phenomenological innovation is to declare the noumenal realm of little interest, focusing instead on direct human experience.

[7] Sartre, *Nausea*, 132–33.

[8] Updike, "Pigeon Feathers," 123.

[9] Ibid., 133.

[10] Updike, "Packed Dirt," 260–61.

[11] It could be argued that this determinist, materialist conception of the universe is just as much a projection of human consciousness as sunnier visions are, and in fact, Kant suggests in the *Prolegomena zu einer jeden Künftigen Metaphysik* (Prolegomena to Any Future Metaphysics, 1783) that causality itself belongs to the phenomenal rather than the noumenal realm: "The sensible world is nothing but a chain of appearances connected according to universal laws; it has therefore no subsistence by itself; it is not the thing in itself, and consequently must point to that which contains the basis of this appearance, to beings which cannot be cognized merely as appearances, but as things in themselves" (354). But this is not Updike's view—he consistently presents materialist atheism as a lack of imagination, a failure to adequately project human consciousness onto the meaningless slate of the material world.

[12] Sartre, *What Is Literature?*, 28. Hereafter cited in-text.

[13] Sontag, "Sartre's *Saint Genet*," 97.

[14] Sartre limits himself, in this essay, to painting and writing as art forms. I see no particular reason why his aesthetic theory cannot be transferred to music, architecture, or any other type of art.

[15] Merleau-Ponty, "Cézanne's Doubt," 242. Hereafter cited in-text.

[16] Merleau-Ponty, "Eye and Mind," 258. Hereafter cited in-text.

[17] Heidegger, *The Origin of the Work of Art*, 19. Hereafter cited in-text.

[18] Updike, "The Astronomer," 179–80.

[19] Kierkegaard, *The Sickness unto Death*, 43. Hereafter cited in-text.

[20] Alastair Hannay glosses this Koine Greek term as *potentially*—that is, the self that is not actually in existence but that might be. See Hannay's Introduction to *Sickness unto Death*.

[21] Kierkegaard, *Training in Christianity*, 185.

[22] Sanoff and Updike, "Writers 'Are Really Servants of Reality,'" 181.

[23] Versluys, "Nakedness," 31.

[24] Updike, "Why Write?" 32. Hereafter cited in-text.

[25] Updike, "Grove Is My Press," 354–55.

[26] Ibid., 355.

[27] Updike, "Robert Pinget," 421.

[28] Ibid.

[29] Updike, "Should Writers Give Lectures?" 145.

[30] Updike, "How Does the Writer Imagine?" 136.

[31] Orr and Updike, "Interview with John Updike," 159.

[32] Updike, "The Sea's Green Sameness," 159. Hereafter cited in-text.

[33] Updike, "This I Believe," 671.

[34] Stevens, "The Idea of Order at Key West," ll. 37–38.

[35] Ibid., line 4.

[36] Edward Vargo reads "The Sea's Green Sameness" as suggesting "Updike's understanding of his task as a quest for the unseen and elusive ambiguity behind life, as a search for the means to help his readers experience the transcendent realities of life" (*Rainstorms and Fire*, 6). This reading, I would argue, ignores the stated impossibility of reaching those transcendent realities—at the very least, Updike can never be sure that he is not imposing an order on the orderless, although I think his language in this piece suggests precisely that imposition, as opposed to Vargo's discovery.

[37] Updike, "Lifeguard," 213. Hereafter cited in-text.

[38] I will return to "Lifeguard" in my discussion of imaginative lust in chapter 4.

[39] Updike, "On Meeting Writers," 7.

[40] Ibid., 5–6.

[41] The fullest critical examination of "Midpoint" comes in the first chapter of Jeff Campbell's *Updike's Novels: Thorns Spell a Word*, and my analysis here owes a good deal to Campbell's work. My hope is that my analysis will be both narrower and broader than Campbell's—narrower in the sense that Updike's "dualistic world-view" (31) is only one of the aspects of the poem Campbell discusses, and broader in the sense that I will look at several other poems from the collection.

[42] Updike, "Midpoint," canto 1, l. 33. Hereafter cited in-text.

[43] Pascal, *Pensées*, section 206.

[44] Updike, "Fireworks," ll. 10–11.

[45] Campbell, *Updike's Novels*, 31.

[46] Updike, "Dream Objects," ll. 1–5.

[47] Ibid., ll. 8–12.

[48] Updike, "The Angels," ll. 4–6.

[49] Updike, "The Angels," ll. 12–14. Interestingly, not all art manages to transcend its physical origins. This is the case in the poem "Roman Portrait Busts." Updike confesses that "I / am drawn like a maggot to meat / by their pupilless eyes / and their putrefying individuality" (ll. 2–5). The choice of words is important, for these are works of art that fail to be anything but "meat," that fail to be anything other than their material components. "Never has art," he writes, "so whorishly submitted / to the importunities of the real" (ll. 8–10). He is fascinated and

repelled in equal measure: "It is vile, / deliciously, to see them so unsoftened by history, such / indigestible gristle" (ll. 16–20).

[50] Updike, "Rhyming Max," 206. Hereafter cited in-text.

[51] Updike, "Accuracy," 17.

[52] Merleau-Ponty, *Phenomenology of Perception*, x.

[53] Ibid.

[54] Campbell, *Updike's Novels*, 30.

[55] Updike, "Card Tricks," 469.

[56] Versluys, "Nakedness," 33.

[57] The word *dialectic* is an important one for Updike; as Marshall Boswell points out, Updike's two favorite theologians, Søren Kierkegaard and Karl Barth, "share . . . a dialectical approach to religious issues in which defining oppositions do not resolve into a satisfying synthesis but rather remain in sustained tension and ambiguity" ("Updike, Religion," 43). Boswell points out that Updike's theology follows this same pattern; my point is that his metaphysics does too.

[58] Updike, "Leaves," 52. Hereafter cited in-text.

[59] Updike, "English Train Compartment," ll. 10–11.

[60] Updike, "A Madman," 35. Hereafter cited in-text.

Part I. The "Mythic Immensity" of the Parental Imagination

2: "Flight," "His Mother Inside Him," and "Ace in the Hole"

ONE OF JOHN UPDIKE'S MOST BRUTAL early stories is "Flight" (1959). Its protagonist, Allen Dow, is a recognizable type in Updike's fiction—virtually indistinguishable, in fact, from later, more famous narrators like David Kern and Peter Caldwell—and "Flight," like so much of Updike's fiction, is thinly veiled autobiography. It is not the first story explicitly set in Olinger, Pennsylvania—a stand-in for Updike's native Shillington—but it is one of the most fully realized of that group. Allen feels like an outsider in his small town because "consciousness of a special destiny made me both arrogant and shy."[1] The idea of Allen's "special destiny," as it turns out, comes largely from his mother. One day the two of them sit on a hill overlooking Olinger.

> Suddenly she dug her fingers into the hair on my head and announced, "There we all are, and there we'll all be forever." She hesitated before the word "forever," and hesitated again before adding, "Except you, Allen. You're going to fly." A few birds were hung far out over the valley, at the level of our eyes, and in her impulsive way she had just plucked the image from them, but it felt like the clue I had been waiting all my childhood for. My most secret self had been made to respond, and I was intensely embarrassed, and irritably ducked my head out from under her melodramatic hand. (50)

This announcement throws Allen's life into disarray—even more so because his mother "continued to treat me like an ordinary child" in an apparent "betrayal of the vision she had made me share. I was captive to a hope she had tossed off and forgotten" (50). But when he attempts to act like something other than an ordinary boy, she responds violently: "once she did respond to my protest that I was learning to fly, by crying with red-faced ferocity, 'You'll never learn, you'll stick and die in the dirt just like I'm doing. Why should you be better than your mother?'" (50). In other words, Mrs. Dow creates an incredibly powerful, if only potential, future for her son, and then she both expects and does not expect him to live in it. The contradiction has a profound effect on Allen; the story presents this hilltop scene as the pivotal episode in his boyhood, and since he presumably narrates it to us from the higher vantage point of adulthood, we can assume that it is in some ways the pivotal event of his entire life. The parent-child relationship portrayed in "Flight," furthermore, typifies a whole category of Updike's early fiction: Before he became the cataloguer of suburban adultery, he was the cataloguer of the effects of the parental imagination—particularly the imagination of the mother—on the child. Mothers, in Updike's early fiction, tend to create imaginative worlds for their sons to live in, and these worlds, when confronted with the world of mere things, tend to crush the sons for whom they were created.

Tellingly, Allen Dow describes his mother as a maker of myths. "My mother's genius," he reports, "was to give the people closest to her mythic immensity. I was the phoenix. My father and grandmother were legendary invader-saints, she springing out of some narrow vein of Arab blood in the German race and he crossing over from the Protestant wastes of New Jersey, both of them serving and enslaving their mates with their prodigious powers of endurance and labor" (58–59). She succeeds wildly at this imaginative project, at least as far as her son is concerned. Allen notes: "The entire town seemed ensnarled in my mother's myth, that escape was my proper fate. It was as if I were a sport that the ghostly elders of Olinger had segregated from the rest of the livestock and agreed to donate in time to the air; this fitted with the ambiguous sensation I had always had in the town, of being simultaneously flattered and rejected" (67). Allen's language here suggests that he always already approaches the town of Olinger, with its varied inhabitants, through the filter of his mother's mythic imagination: She has already told him the story by which he can relate himself to the town, and unsurprisingly, everything he encounters in the town confirms the truth of that story.

The Oedipal tragedy of "Flight" takes place when the confirmation fails. While participating in an out-of-town debate with some classmates, Allen begins a relationship with Molly Bingham—a relationship that his mother opposes from the very beginning, using her mythic imagination to present poor Molly as a succubus. "Why," she announces, "when she stepped off the train from the way her chins bounced I thought she had eaten a canary. And then making my poor son, all skin and bones, carry her bag" (65). Allen himself presents the scene of their getting off the train quite differently, but that does not matter. His mother's imagination is more powerful than his own, and soon he finds himself wondering why Molly is so ugly, "despite the fact that she often, especially in intimate moments, looked beautiful to me" (68). His mother controls his vision and thus his actions: "Every time I saw my mother cry, it seemed I had to make Molly cry" (68). Mrs. Dow does not try to end their relationship outright, but what she does—controlling his romantic imagination by machinations that are all the more powerful for being subtle—is much more insidious.

Allen eventually decides that this is the way that generations respond to each other. The older generation creates the younger and then destroys it with its expectations, its refusals, and its blessings. His mother hates her own father, for example, because he forbade her, at a crucial time in her life, from going to New York City; as Allen explains, "the great moist weight of that forbidding continued to be felt in the house for years, and when I was a child, as one of my mother's endless harangues to my grandfather screamed toward its weeping peak, I could feel it around and above me, like a huge root encountered by an earthworm" (55). It is, he tells us, "as if each generation commits atrocities against their children which by God's decree remain invisible to the rest of the world" (53)—invisible because the scars of those atrocities exist on the child's imagination rather than her body. One can escape only by a more powerful assertion of one's own imagination, which in "Flight" takes the form of Allen's sexual desire toward Molly.[2] Their first kiss is strikingly predatory: "Molly came forward with a prim look and kissed me. With clumsy force I entered the negative space that had been waiting. Her lipstick smeared in little unflattering flecks into the skin around her mouth; it was as if I had been given a face to eat, and the presence of bone—skull under skin, teeth behind lips—impeded me" (63). This scene symbolizes their entire relationship, in which he uses and wounds her repeatedly as a way of striking back against his mother. After they lose their debate, he uses her to forget his pain: "For the first time, on that ride home, I felt what it was to bury a humiliation in the body of a woman. Nothing but the friction of my face against hers drowned out the echo of those boos. When we kissed, a red shadow would well under my lids and eclipse the hostile hooting faces of the debate audience, and when our lips parted, the bright inner sea would ebb, and there the faces would be again, more intense than ever" (63–64). Their physical contact becomes, in its strange way, an act of Allen's imagination, as his elevated poetic language suggests.

He tells us that they "never made love in the final coital sense. My reason was a mixture of idealism and superstition; I felt that if I took her virginity she would be mine forever" (69), feeling, no doubt, that since he is destined to fly away from Olinger, Molly would be nothing but dead weight. But, as an adult, he recognizes that his teenage self miscalculated the degree to which he took her away from herself: "She gave herself to me anyway, and I had her anyway, and have her still, for the longer I travel in a direction I could not have taken with her, the more clearly she seems the one person who loved me without advantage. I was a homely, comically ambitious hillbilly, and I even refused to tell her I loved her, to pronounce the word 'love'—an icy piece of pedantry that shocks me now that I have almost forgotten the context of confusion in which it seemed wise" (69). That confusion, of course, arises from the battle of imaginations that these passages recount: In order to escape the mythic world his mother has created for him—paradoxically, a world that demands his escape from the town of Olinger, and presumably from his mother—Allen turns his own imagination on Molly Bingham, who, if we can trust him as a narrator, is torn to pieces by it. He holds some of these pieces in his imagination to this day, and yet the ultimate triumph is Molly's, for she has seen into his soul in a way that no one else has. And Mrs. Dow has also triumphed, for the relationship does not last, and it does not last specifically because Allen has accepted the myth of escape and flight that she has created for him. He becomes incapable of viewing his life as anything but a flight out of the birdcage of home: "Frightened by my father's tales of nervous breakdowns he had seen, I kept listening for the sounds of my brain snapping, and the image of that gray, infinitely interconnected mass seemed to extend outward, to become my whole world, one dense organic dungeon, and I felt I had to get out; if I could just get out of this, into June, it would be blue sky, and I would be all right for life" (69). Thus Mrs. Dow must be dissatisfied with her own triumph—she becomes just another thing for Allen to escape, even if he views that escape through her imaginative framework. Allen, too, must be dissatisfied with his escape, for in accomplishing it, he fulfills his mother's plans for him.[3]

In 1992's "His Mother Inside Him," in fact, we learn that Allen never made it out of his mother's mythology. Its opening reiterates the central fact of "Flight," that Allen grew up in his mother's enormous shadow. He spent his childhood "fearful . . . of his mother's unhappiness, which would vent itself in sudden storms of temper that flattened the other occupants of the house into the corners and far rooms."[4] As an adult, he believes himself to have escaped her influence, and so "he resented it, . . . when, after her death, people (second cousins, Lutheran ministers) fondly remarked on how much he, as he approached sixty, resembled his mother" (235). He sees a few superficial physical resemblances but would like to deny any deep similarities. He wants to believe that he exists fully apart from his mother's dominating presence. But he discovers, to his chagrin, that his mother "had implanted him with a set of images that entwined, flourishing and fading, among those he had acquired with his own senses" (236). The fact that the story features a third-person narrator instead of the earlier story's first-person account suggests that Allen has actually lost his personal voice with the death of his mother. And the myth-making tendency so central to "Flight" continues to control his imagination long after his mother dies. During an argument with his second wife about how much to pay for a house, "he felt his mother inside him itching to embark on a discourse as to the small- and mean-mindedness of taking anything as simple as a single side, this being the root of all wars and exploitation. . . . Yet in some sense, too, he was arguing *against* his mother, for she had been, in her rural realm, a considerable acquirer of acreage" (236–37). Even breaking away from his mother's imagination, then, involves a return to her. Even arguing against her means arguing as her—just as fleeing Olinger in "Flight" is both an escape from her imagination and a reification of it. He is in an impossible situation in which "within him his mother was battling his mother" (237). His personality scarcely exists except in relation to her.

Even in her old age and death, he is helpless in the face of her superior imagination, her superior power. Updike tells us that "all of Allen's ideas came from her, save the male, boyish idea of *getting away*, of getting out into unheated, unmediated space" (238). And, as readers of "Flight" are only too aware, "even that, in truth, had been her idea" (238). His marriages, he realizes, are reiterations of that primal relationship: "It seemed to be his circular fate to settle one woman after another on a sizable property and then move on, momentarily free, until the next female real-estate developer locked him into her plans" (237). Mrs. Dow is the dominant figure in his own imagination: "She was in him not as he had been in her, as a seed becoming a little male offshoot, but as the full tracery of his perceptions and reactions; he had led his life as an extension of hers, a superior version of hers, and when she died he became custodian of a specialized semiotics, a thousand tiny nuanced understandings of her, a once commonplace language of which he was now the sole surviving speaker" (239). The imaginative world he lives in is, in a real sense, her world, created by the myths she filled his childhood with. Even her drives become his drives—at the end of the story, Allen, who has carefully guarded his relationship with food after watching his mother get fat young, finds himself unable to stop eating, the food pouring into his gut. This, too, is a victory for his mother, who "had reached this point at the age of thirty, whereas he was all of sixty. As they tell you in seventh-grade health class, girls develop more rapidly than boys" (241). Allen is doomed to follow the path traced out for him by his mother.

Updike's early fiction, as I have suggested, is replete with images like this:[5] Powerful mothers, no doubt modeled on Linda Hoyer Updike, cut paths through their sons' lives, and yet this very cutting creates enmity between them. The seeds are planted as early as "Ace in the Hole," Updike's second published story. Ace Anderson—an early model for Updike's most famous protagonist, Rabbit Angstrom—is, as Robert Detweiler puts it, "the sad product of maternal domination."[6] Mrs. Anderson is apparently incapable of seeing him as doing anything wrong. For example, when Ace reports that he has been fired from his job at a used-car lot for damaging a car, his mother replies, "Good for you . . . I always said he never treated you right."[7] She even attempts to talk him into abandoning his wife and child:

> "Well, I don't dare think what Evey will say, but I, for one, thank dear God you had the brains to get out of it. I always said that job had no future to it—no future of any kind, Freddy."

> "I guess," Ace admitted. "But I wanted to keep at it, for the family's sake."
>
> "Now, I know I shouldn't be saying this, but any time Evey—this is just between us—any time Evey thinks she can do better, there's room for you *and* Bonnie right in your father's house." (16)

But Ace cannot bear his oppressively positive mother any more than his oppressively negative wife, and he lumps them both into the feminine domestic sphere that he feels he must flee: "He hoped [Evey] wouldn't get too mad, because when she was mad he wondered if he should have married her, and doubting that made him feel crowded. It was bad enough, his mother always crowding him" (19). Nothing in the story suggests that either Ace or his mother have the imaginative power of the Dows—but their relationship is much the same, if pitched at a lower aesthetic level.

Notes

[1] Updike, "Flight," 49. Hereafter cited in-text.

[2] Male lust, as I will argue in part 3, often serves in Updike's fiction as a particularly virulent form of imagination.

[3] The telling of the story itself represents an additional layer of Allen's ambivalence; as D. Quentin Miller argues, "the story of Allen's life, following the myth of his youth, is a story of flight from his stultifying home town; yet the story he tells us from a mature perspective is a kind of flight back to his past" ("Updike, Middles," 18).

[4] Updike, "His Mother Inside Him," 234. Hereafter cited in-text.

[5] So much so that Aristi Trendel has suggested that "the cycle of mother-son-related stories rearranged from Updike's thirteen story collections could be read as a sort of *Famielienroman*, a family romance" ("Resurgence of the Repressed," 163) and suggests publishing a dedicated volume of them akin to 1964's *Olinger Stories*.

[6] Detweiler, "The Same Door," 170.

[7] Updike, "Ace in the Hole," 16. Hereafter cited in-text.

3: *The Centaur*

WE SEE THE WORKING OF THE parental imagination in Updike's 1963 novel, *The Centaur*, in which Cassie Caldwell—the name given this time to the Mrs. Dow character—features, more or less, as a distant threat. *The Centaur* is primarily a novel about fathers and sons, after all, not about mothers and sons, but the relationship between George and Peter Caldwell is scarcely imaginable without Cassie's spectral presence. Her most important role in the novel is as the force that made George give up his dreams of city living; before the action of the novel, she has followed her own dreams of moving to a farmhouse a few miles away from Olinger. This detail parallels Updike's own life. His mother, Linda Hoyer Updike, moved her entire family, by sheer force of will, to her childhood farmhouse in Plowville, a few miles outside of Shillington, when her son was thirteen. She would later write John Updike a letter suggesting that she would not have been courageous enough to make such a move if she had known how disruptive it would be for him, but Adam Begley is skeptical:

> My guess is that she would in fact have found the courage—after all, she rode roughshod over the resistance of her eighty-two-year-old father, who had to endure a humiliating return to the farm he thought he'd put behind him a quarter of a century earlier. And she brushed aside the complaints of her husband (a "man of the streets" who liked to say that he wanted to be buried under a sidewalk); Wesley had to surrender to what he considered rural imprisonment. Only Linda's habitually silent mother voiced no objection to leaving Shillington. So why insist on imposing this relocation on the rest of the family? "I was returning to the Garden of Eden and taking my family with me. I thought I was doing them a great service," she told a television interviewer.[1]

The force of Linda Updike's imagination clearly exerted itself powerfully on her son. "Why is it," he wonders in "Cemeteries," "that nothing that happens to me is as real as these dramas that my mother arranges around herself, like Titania calling Peaseblossom and Mustardseed from the air?"[2] And in an early autobiographical piece, "The Dogwood Tree," Updike describes "waiting with her by a window for my father to return from weeks on the road. It is in the Shillington living room. My hands are on the radiator ridges, I can see my father striding through the hedge toward the grape arbor, I feel my mother's excitement beside me mingle with mine."[3] It is the sort of childhood memory that most of us have, "but she says this cannot be; he had lost his job before I was born" (124). Updike's supposed memory, then—vivid even in his re-creation of it—is actually a reconstruction of his mother's memory, an artifact he constructs out of the materials of the stories his mother tells him. And the move from town to country represented, in his life, the word made flesh—his mother's rural idealism beget the actual material conditions of her son's boyhood.

In *The Centaur*, then, the tension between city and country will be a major sticking point between George and Peter on one side and Cassie on the other. The two men see the city as a place of life, as opposed to the stifling deathliness of the country. Peter "wonder[s] if any man ever enjoyed walking in the small ugly cities of the East as much as my father"[4] and notes George's discomfort with the supposed pleasures of both the country and the small town. Peter clearly allies himself with his father. His mother, on the other hand, almost worships Firetown, the unincorporated area where their farm sits; as Peter says, "the country represented purity to her but I couldn't take her seriously. As far as I could see, the land was built on rot and excrement" (59). The division sets up a metaphysical conflict—Cassie imparts a spiritual purity to the farm, whereas Peter can see it only as basely material—that will become even more important a few years later in *Of the Farm*. For Peter, the country represents both extreme innocence and extreme defilement, as represented by the leering eyes of the 4-H group his mother forces him to join: "The dull innocence of some and the viciously detailed knowingness of others struck me as equally savage and remote from my highly civilized aspirations" (74). For Peter, as for George, the city is not debased—the way it is for, say, Rabbit Angstrom, who codes his own flight in the early pages of *Rabbit, Run* as an escape from Philadelphia's noxious influence.[5] Instead, in *The Centaur*, the city is the Aristotelian polis, a place where a man can pursue the civilized middle ground. It is also, not coincidentally, a place free from the influence of Cassie Caldwell, a place free from the imagination that has dragged George and Peter into the countryside.

The city thus gives Peter, in particular, a place in which to exercise his own imagination and to set himself free from his mother's. We see his imagination at work most strongly when he and his father are forced, by their broken car, to spend the night at the shabby New Yorker hotel in Alton. Alone in the strange room, Peter crawls into bed, and a strange transformation takes place: "As the sheets warmed, I enlarged to human size, and then, as the dissolution of drowsiness crept toward me, a sensation, both vivid and numb, of enormity entered my cells, and I seemed a giant who included in his fingernail all the galaxies that are. This sensation operated not only in space but in time; it seemed, as literally as one says 'a minute,' an eternity since I had risen from bed, put on my bright red shirt, stamped my foot at my mother, patted the dog through the frosted metal mesh, and drunk orange juice" (166). This strange sensation distances Peter from his mother's power. An entire eternity, after all, seems to have passed since the last time he saw her. In this sense, it is a destructive force, tearing down the walls she has built around him. But there is something constructive in it, too, and I think the best way to understand that constructiveness is in terms of what Updike calls *egotheism.*

He coins the term for a concept found in Walt Whitman's poetry, in which "the obligatory optimism of American enterprise has found its theology, a panoramic egotheism."[6] The egotheistic soul expands to fill every contour of the universe, as in Whitman's poem "Crossing Brooklyn Ferry," where the poet announces that

> It avails not, neither time or place—distance avails not;
> I am with you, you men and women of a generation, or ever so
>   many generations hence;
> I project myself—also I return—I am with you, and know how it is.[7]

Peter's egotheism allows him to imagine—or, more accurately, to project—a world for himself. It is not a coincidence that this scene takes place in the New Yorker hotel, for though the hotel itself is dilapidated and pulsing with insects, New York is for Peter, as for so many other budding young artists, the site of ultimate personal and aesthetic freedom. George, meanwhile, experiences this same egotheism by his immersion in astronomy, a field of study that "transfixed him; at night sometimes when he lay down in bed exhausted he felt that his ebbing body was fantastically huge and contained in its darkness a billion stars" (38). These egotheistic activities, however, grind uncomfortably against the merely natural, the merely material, as when Peter prays that his father does not have cancer:

> The prayer was addressed to all who would listen; in concentric circles it widened, first, into the town, and beyond, into the hemisphere of sky, and beyond that, into what was beyond. The sky behind the eastward houses already was purple; above, it was still deep daylight blue; and behind me the sky beyond the houses was aflame. The sky's blue was an optical illusion that, though described to me in General Science class by my father himself, my mind could only picture as an accumulation of lightly tinted crystal spheres, as two almost invisibly pink pieces of cellophane will together make rose; add a third, you have red; a fourth, crinkling crimson; and a fifth, such scarlet as must blaze in the heart of the most ardent furnace. If the blue dome beyond the town was an illusion, how much more, then, of an illusion might be what is beyond that. (124)

Peter sees Cassie Caldwell's beloved farm, we must remember, as suffocatingly material in just this way; it thus stands in the way of his religious and imaginative transcendence and must be escaped. But when he does escape, he finds that the life he has always imagined for himself in New York is constricting in its own way: "I consider the life we have made together, with its days spent without relation to the days the sun keeps and its baroque arabesques of increasingly attenuated emotion and its furnishings like a scattering of worn-out Braques and its rather wistful half-Freudian half-Oriental sex-mysticism, and I wonder, *Was it for this that my father gave up his life?*" (270). By utterly abandoning the natural world—Peter sleeps during the daytime and creates his nonrepresentational paintings at night—he has lost the ability for sacrifice that so defines George Caldwell in this novel. He has escaped his mother's imagination, but at the cost of leaving his father behind. The novel itself becomes an act of penance, albeit a necessarily incomplete one.[8]

Given Allen Dow's characterization of his mother's imagination as "mythic" in "Flight," the experimental structure of *The Centaur* is important. The novel alternates between openly mythological sections, wherein Olinger characters are reconstituted as figures from Greek legend, their everyday activities thereby given new importance, and straightforward sections of Updike's typical literary realism. Critics have, in fact, complained about this feature of the novel. Frederick R. Karl, for example, argues that *The Centaur* is "incoherent," not because of "Updike's ambitious reach, which is admirable," but because "he had no way of integrating mythological references to daily characters. Words betrayed him. He had to make the characters artificial in their daily lives and speech so as to permit transitions to their mythological selves. Realistic foreground and mythical background struggle against each other, a monistic mind trying to be dualistic."[9] Likewise, although Martin Prince admires the character portrait of George Caldwell, he says that "the mythical dimension hardly seems to deepen it. The myths, as Updike uses them, are too fluid to give form to the novel. They keep before us suggestions of a profound life that takes on the improbable incarnation of Olinger High, and they remind us that the actual is always in some sense improbable."[10] For Prince, the mythology succeeds only inasmuch as it throws the realistic portrait of George Caldwell into relief.

But Updike by no means included the mythology as an afterthought; he clearly saw it as central to his aesthetic project in this novel. He claims that the novel "began as an attempt to publicize [the] myth" of Chiron's sacrifice and suggests that he uses mythology for a number of purposes in the novel: "a correlative of the enlarging effect of Peter's nostalgia, a dramatization of Caldwell's sense of exclusion and mysteriousness around him, a counterpoint of ideality to the drab real level, an excuse for a number of jokes, a serious expression of my sensation that the people we meet are *guises*, do conceal something mythic, perhaps prototypes or longings in our minds."[11] The novel's mythic underpinnings, the grandiose divinities that cannot help but erupt to the surface from time to time, thus operate as a counterforce against Cassie Caldwell's own presumptive mythologizing tendencies. Peter, who narrates the realist sections of the novel, is attempting to do for himself what Allen Dow's mother did for him: to connect his daily life with some higher imaginative force. In another interview, Updike says that "I don't think that without the myth you'd have a book,"[12] and this sentiment holds true for both author and narrator: Updike needed the mythological framework to write the book, and Peter Caldwell needs it to find a voice free of his mother's imagination. He tells us early on that "her voice was so often expressive of what I wanted to hear that my own brain sometimes thought in her voice" (47). The mythology allows him to think in his own voice, as it were. (It is interesting that he has to do so by moving from first-person narration—narration that is literally in his own voice—to third-person narration in a mythological voice. Perhaps this move suggests that the third-person narration of "His Mother Inside Him" represents Allen Dow's own attempts to remove his mother's voice by removing his own.) As Edward Vargo points out, the mythological function of the novel is to "infuse[ ] all of Peter's memories with a new and deeper significance,"[13] turning the entire novel into a type of ritual by which Peter Caldwell tries to make sense of his universe—to make sense of it, I would add, outside the imaginative and mythic structure imposed on him by his mother.[14]

Notes

1 Begley, *Updike*, 33.

2 Updike, "Cemeteries," 61.

3 Updike, "The Dogwood Tree," 124. Hereafter cited in-text.

4 Updike, *The Centaur*, 145. Hereafter cited in-text.

5 As Rabbit makes his attempt at escape in the early pages of the novel, Updike notes: "He hates Philadelphia. Dirtiest city in the world, they live on poisoned water, you can taste the chemicals" (*Rabbit, Run*, 23).

6 Updike, "Whitman's Egotheism," 112.

7 Whitman, "Crossing Brooklyn Ferry," ll. 21–23.

8 See my article "An Existentialist *Ars Moriendi*."

9 Karl, *American Fictions*, 170.

10 Prince, "A Note on Character in *The Centaur*," 133.

11 Samuels, "The Art of Fiction XLIII," 35.

12 Rhode, "John Updike Talks," 51.

13 Vargo, *Rainstorms and Fire*, 84.

14 Updike also has, of course, a personal reason for this most personal of his novels. In 1984, he wrote that much of his adult success has been in vindication of

his father, who was an unhappy outsider in Shillington: "Leaving Pennsylvania, where my father had been pinned by necessity, was another such reversal on my part, a spurning on his behalf. Life had given my father a beating, beginning with his hard childhood peddling papers in Trenton; his own father's failures and sorrow and early death had poured through him like rain through a broken window. And his, in turn, through me" ("Soft Spring," 33). In this sense, *The Centaur* is Updike's ultimate act of vindication; he turns his poor benighted, besieged, beaten father into George Caldwell, probably the most heroic character in his entire catalogue. Again myth improves on the world of bare facts.

4: *Of the Farm*, "A Sandstone Farmhouse," and "The Cats"

NOWHERE IS THE POWER OF THE parental imagination clearer in Updike's work than in his farewell to Olinger, the 1965 novel *Of the Farm*. It covers some of the same ground as *The Centaur*, but whereas the earlier novel was expansive and grandiose, *Of the Farm* is modest almost to the point of claustrophobia. Updike wrote it after a period of writing short stories, and in an introduction to the Czech edition of the novel, he says that, like a short story, "it has continuous action, a narrow setting, a small cast. I thought of it as chamber music, containing only four voices—the various ghosts in it do not speak, and the minister's sermon, you will notice, is delivered in close paraphrase, without the benefit of quotation marks. The voices, like musical instruments, echo each other's phrases and themes, take turns dominating, embark on brief narrative solos, and recombine in argument or harmony."[1] The novel is unusual in Updike's fiction in its isolation from the outside world: We get no popular culture, no time markers, not even the name of the president. This aesthetic decision allows the reader to observe all the more closely the effects of the parental imagination. The four voices of the novel are Joey Robinson, a businessman in his midthirties; his mother, whose farm he is visiting for the weekend in order to mow the fields, a task she cannot do herself after the death of her husband; Peggy, his new second wife; and Richard, her preteen son. The novel carries over many of the themes and settings from *The Centaur*. Updike himself says that "this novella is *The Centaur* after the centaur has died; the mythical has fled the ethical, and a quartet of scattered survivors grope with their voices toward cohesion."[2] George W. Hunt rightly corrects Updike on this point, however, suggesting that "the farm is already a mythic place when [Joey] arrives because of his conscious recognition of his mother's genius for mythologizing everything connected with it."[3] In fact, in some ways, *Of the Farm* may be even more mythologized an environment than *The Centaur*, for Joey Robinson, unlike Peter Caldwell, does not have his father to stand between him and the imaginative force of his mother. His diminutive first name suggests that he lacks the requisite maturity to stand up for himself, even though he lives his life, in some ways, in defiance of her: "I work for a firm which arranges educational programs for corporations on such matters as tax minimization, overseas expansion, federal contract acquisition, and automation. My specialty is advertising dollar distribution, which is to say, broadly, corporate image presentation. My mother wanted me to be a poet, like Wordsworth."[4] And yet her desires have nevertheless shaped his entire life.

Early in the novel, Joey encounters a series of photographs of himself in his mother's house and notes that "each time I returned I more strongly resented how much of myself was already here" (15), as if his mother were some sort of ancient witch able to catch and imprison his soul through the act of photography. He will later suggest that they destroy the photos, and she will refuse: "Don't you touch them. Those pictures are my son. Those pictures are the only son I have" (119). His very existence, as she sees it, belongs to her imagination; as Jeff Campbell argues, Mrs. Robinson is trying "to keep her son alive in the saga of her own mythology" rather than by treating him as a flesh-and-blood person.[5] Indeed, his mother holds to a kind of rural idealism, believing most strongly in her own power to create worlds. She belongs, in other words, to the same aesthetic category as Mrs. Dow and Cassie Caldwell. But we spend much more time with Mrs. Robinson and thus get much more of a sense of how she operates. The peculiar quality of her imagination is revealed by a painting that hangs in her living room. It is

> an idyllic little landscape, a much-reduced print of an oil, that had ornamented my room as a child, when we lived in my grandparents' house in the town. . . . The pentagonal side of a barn was diagonally bisected by a purple shadow cast by nothing visible, and a leafless tree of uncertain species stood rooted in lush grass impossibly green. Beyond, I revisited, bending deeper into the picture, a marvelous sky of lateral stripes of pastel color where as a child I had imagined myself treading, upside-down, a terrain of crayons. The tiny black V of one flying bird was planted in this sky, between two furrows of color, so that I had imagined that if my fingers could get through the glass they could pluck it up, like a carrot sprout. (18)

The painting is, from this description, hardly great art, but "this quaint picture, windowing a fabulous rural world" (18), does some heavy thematic lifting in the novel. It physically embodied Joey's mother's dreams when she lived in Olinger. After all, "the great effort of her life had been to purchase this farm and move us all to it" (8). The painting, despite its kitchiness, is powerful enough to draw Joey into it, both when he is a child and in the present day. What is more, because this painting has hung in the bedrooms of Joey, his father, and now Richard, it suggests that "Mrs. Robinson has tried, with only modest success, to communicate this vision to three generations."[6] It is clear that the world on display in the painting is the world that his mother lives in, and it expands to fill the physical world outside the farmhouse. "Her spirit had acquired a troubling resonance," Joey explains, "a murky subtlety doubly oppressive out of doors—as if in being surrounded by her farm we had been plunged into the very territory of her thoughts" (13). And Joey criticizes her for "read[ing] into the animate world, including infants and dogs, a richness of motive that could hardly be there—though, like believers everywhere, she had a way of making her environment supply corroboration" (23). The natural world and the world of art thus become one in the externalized consciousness of Joey's mother.

Joey, understandably, is disturbed by the effect. When his mother talks about his relationship with his ex-wife, Joan, "It startled me to hear how Joan and my earlier self had become part of my mother's saga of the farm" (25). His mother's power of imagination is so strong, in fact, that it acts as a vacuum for the less-powerful personalities around her. And, though Joey introduces us to his mother's inner world by means of visual art, it is words—stories—that are the tool by which she exerts her imagination most powerfully on the world around her:

> Talk—it seemed throughout my growing-up that there was no end of talk. Talk was everything to us—food and love, money and mud, God and the Devil, confession, philosophy, and exercise. And though my grandfather's sculpturally spaced utterances, given additional dignity and point by many judicious throat-clearings and heavenward gesticulations of his dry-skinned hands, had ceased, and my father's humorous prancing whine had fallen silent forever, yet my mother's voice alone, rising and falling, sighing itself away and wishing itself reborn, letting itself grow so slack and diffuse it seemed the murmur of nature and then abruptly narrowing into swift self-justification, managed, for all the distention of her heart and lungs, to maintain almost uninterrupted the dense vocal outpouring in which I had been bathed and raised. (28–29)

We see here the incredible power of Mrs. Robinson's imagination—combining art with nature once again ("food and love, money and mud"), it becomes the world itself, the background to Joey's growing up and the implicit background to his adult life as well. His psyche, then, pressed on nearly all sides by his mother's, is as claustrophobic and narrow as the novel itself. He feels incredible, almost unbearable, pressure: "My mother within the mythology she had made of her life was like a mathematician who, having decreed certain severely limited assumptions, performs feats of warping and circumvention and paradoxical linkage that an outside observer, unrestricted to the plane of their logic, would find irksomely arbitrary. And, with the death of my father and my divorce of Joan, there was no inside observer left but myself—myself, and the adoring dogs" (31). She lives almost entirely inside her own mind, and Joey's filial obligation forces him into that same strained space.

His second marriage, to Peggy, works as a counterpunch of sorts, an attempt at escaping his mother's imagination. After all, he blames her for the existence and the breakdown of his first marriage. She had wanted him to become an artist, and though he ultimately rejected poetry as a career, his marriage to Joan suggests a capitulation to his mother's vision. Joan is, as Alice and Kenneth Hamilton put it, "a poetic image belonging to the world his mother wishes to him."[7] He marries her, he admits "because, when I first saw her wheeling her bicycle through the autumnal dusk of the Yard, she suggested, remote and lithe and inward, the girl of 'The Solitary Reaper' and close-up, seemed a cool Lucy who might give me cause to sing" (109). He uses the language of aesthetic idealism here, praising her inner life—an imagination, perhaps, matching his mother's, though since we never encounter Joan directly, we can never know—as well as her Wordsworthian quality. Surely Joey's mother owes some of her self-conception to Wordsworth's "The Solitary Reaper":

> Behold her, single in the field,
> Yon solitary Highland Lass!
> Reaping and singing by herself;
> Stop here, or gently pass!
> Alone she cuts and binds the grain,
> And sings a melancholy strain;
> O listen! for the Vale profound
> Is overflowing with the sound.[8]

And indeed, the poem more clearly suggests Joey's mother's role in his life than his first wife's role. The song sung by the maiden worms its way into the poet's imagination until he can think of nothing else:

> I saw her singing at her work,
> And o'er the sickle bending;—
> I listened, motionless and still;
> And, as I mounted up the hill,
> The music in my heart I bore,
> Long after it was heard no more.[9]

This may as well be a poetic description of Joey's mother's continuing influence over his life. Long after he has moved to Boston and New York, far away from the family farm in Firetown, he continues to hear the "song" of his mother's imagination; it haunts his every action. Her fingerprints are thus all over his first marriage; he marries Joan because she is the sort of woman his mother would approve of, even though she does not actually approve of her and even though there was always enmity between the two. And Joan proves too ideal for Joey to hold on to for very long. He describes her as being almost incorporeal.[10] When she tells him to leave, "I realized that she had not been applauding my victory over my love for her but was herself that love, knew herself only in my love for her and saw herself abolished, saw us not meeting forever in a dwindling eternal width, which I then realized that I had not . . . envisioned" (86). The vision, presumably, belongs to Mrs. Robinson, whose imagination has shaped Joey's without his realizing it. Joan is his Platonic ideal, a woman of soul and spirit rather than of flesh, and when his marriage to her fails, he turns to a woman who is sheer corporeality—she even wears a bikini when she gardens. His blazon of Peggy's body early on in the novel acts as a counterpoint to the landscape that hangs in his mother's living room:

> Peggy was wearing, the straps a little awry on her shoulders, a loose orange nightie I liked, and as she bent forward to call to me through the screen her smile was wonderful; she was so happy here, so full of delight in the strangeness of this place, so in love with the farm and so eager to redeem, with the sun of her presence, the years of dismal hours I had spent here. Her smile told me to come up; its high bright note assumed and summed up our history of fear and sorrow and considered ruthlessness; it knowingly conveyed, through itself from elsewhere, forgiveness—and it was so gay. Never had the farm been so gay. (48)

The problem is that the dream signaled by this blazon is no more an objective and material reality than is the landscape painting. He may be unaware of it, but Joey engages in the same sort of imaginative reconstruction as his mother: Both of them would like the world to be more beautiful, more idyllic and graceful, than it is. The difference between them is that Mrs. Robinson pushes her imagination against the natural world, whereas Joey pushes his against his wife's body; as David Galloway points out, "Peggy is the landscape that Joey embraces, choosing not the earth but the earth mother herself."[11] But both visions, tellingly, reconstruct the farm in the image of the imaginer. Thus, Joey—despite his abandoning of poetry and his vocational capitulation to the world of commerce—is more of an idealist, more of an aesthete, than he thinks he is. Larry Taylor argues that "Joey, while contemptuous of his mother's idealization and love of the farm, participates in a form of mythologizing very similar to his mother's. As his mother has centered her life around a personal myth about her land, Joey has centered his life around his sexy new wife."[12] As Allen Dow's attitude toward Olinger both reinforces and rebukes his mother's mythology, so Joey's limning of Peggy's limbs stays within his mother's idealist orbit even as it attempts to break free of it. More to the point, he has turned from the nearly incorporeal Joan to the aggressively embodied Peggy without turning away from his own idealism.

He has idealism in common not just with his mother but also with his stepson. Their first morning on the farm, Joey asks him about a familiar sensation: "Richard, do you ever at night, just before dropping off, feel yourself terribly huge? Your fingers feel miles thick" (53). Peter Caldwell experiences a similar sensation at the New Yorker Hotel in *The Centaur*, and it suggests an imaginative expansion of individual consciousness. But Richard attempts to give it a scientific rather than an aesthetic or religious explanation: "I often do . . . It's uncanny. I've read somewhere a rational explanation, I forget where. Maybe in *Scientific American*" (54). And yet Richard is drawn to idealism of certain kinds. He spends much of the novel reading Joey's old collection of science fiction stories, and even relates the plot of a particular story. A boy "reinvents geometry with bits of colored cloth when he's three years old and then reinvents all mathematics and finally asks somebody how long it will be for a line pointed straight up to come back from underneath to where it started. You see, that's relativity" (107). This story seems to be an imaginative retelling of Plato's *Meno*, in which all learning is figured as the remembering of ideal forms. Socrates has a slave boy perform a series of geometrical operations that he should have no way of knowing; that the boy is able to perform them suggests that he "always possessed" the requisite knowledge.[13] His conclusion is universal rather than particular: "Then if the truth about reality is always in our soul, the soul would be immortal so that you should always confidently try to seek out and recollect what you do not know at present—that is, what you do not recollect."[14] Richard is unable or unwilling to follow Plato the entire way; after all, the power to "reinvent" (not "recollect") geometry belongs not to an illiterate slave (and thus presumably to all human beings), but to a boy with an exceptionally high IQ. Even so, the similarities between the story and the *Meno* suggest that something in Richard leans toward idealism.[15] Peggy pushes against this leaning, however; a thoroughly unimaginative person, she resists her new mother-in-law's efforts at getting through to her son: "He's not going to manage anything for you. He's not going to be another Joey" (92). She asks if Mrs. Robinson wants him to be a farmer, and the older woman's response is telling: "I think it would take more imagination than you'll permit him to have." Peggy's response is equally telling: "I can't imagine what you mean" (111). Peggy's entire life is marked by just such a failure of imagination—at least the way Joey's mother sees it.[16]

Peggy's most notable acts of the imagination, after all, do not belong to her; she is instead the catalyst for some of her husband's most powerful imaginative flights of fancy. At one point, he tells Peggy to go to the store in Galilee, for example, and she repeats the town's name as a question: "Her repetition cast a spell. The world became a cup running over with light. I looked up and was shocked to see the meadow and the intervening trees (a young locust, a black walnut, a blue spruce that had once been no taller than I) and the grass of the lawn drenched in a glistening stillness, an absolute visual silence like an eighth-note rest in the flow of circumstance, each waxen leaf and silvered blade receiving the hazed August sunlight so precisely my heart beat double, as if pierced" (77). This is closer to the way his mother sees the farm than Joey might like to admit; as Judie Newman argues, visions like these are an "attempt to insert Peggy into his mother's myth."[17] But he cannot find a way to reconcile the ideal world with the material world, and so he allows physicality to intrude and break him from his epiphany: "Then my vision was gently eroded by awareness of the insect and bird song that form a constant undercurrent to country silence" (77). He cannot maintain his spiritual vision; his imagination cannot compete with his mother's, for good or for ill.

The same is true of his imaginative reconstruction of Peggy. He eventually realizes that he has failed to see her for what she really is, that he, like his mother, has fallen in love with the product of his own mind. Mrs. Robinson recognizes his failure well before he does. He admits, "She *is* stupid," and when his mother suggests that he knew this all along, he disagrees: "No . . . I threw myself into her. I gave her credit for everything I thought. I couldn't believe that anything so beautiful could be less intelligent than I. I must have thought she had made herself" (141)—when in fact it is he who has made her. From a woman all but created by his mother's imagination, he has turned to a woman whom he must create with his own imagination, and when the clouds of his mind have been swept away, he is left with a sheerly physical being. This could be an opportunity for Mrs. Robinson to claim her final victory: her son has recognized that his own imagination cannot be trusted, that he has made a grave mistake in legally binding himself to Peggy. And yet, although the conversation ends uneventfully a few pages later, the novel continues, and Mrs. Robinson's imaginative power over her son will be, at the very least, mitigated.

Joey and his mother go to church the next morning, and the sermon—paraphrased over the course of five pages—deals with gender and marriage. The preacher, drawing from the work of Karl Barth, Updike's favorite theologian, affirms the ontological differences between the sexes, and assigns to them separate roles: "So Woman, if I have not misunderstood these verses, was put on earth to help Man do his work, which is God's work. She is less than Man, and superior to him. In designating her with his own generic name, Adam commits an act of faith: 'This is *now* bone of my bones, and flesh of my flesh.' In so declaring, he acknowledges within himself a responsibility to be kind" (153). Joey is clearly moved by this sermon, even though his mother dismisses it. And yet she then, quite unexpectedly, blesses his new marriage. He need not worry about creating a local scandal, she tells him: "They met Joan. They could see she wasn't right for you. . . . This one's more your style" (155–56).

And just as unexpectedly, she blesses his independence: "Blood must flow. You have a streak of your father in you, you tend to be too obliging. You were becoming something very tame before I brought us to the farm. That's why I did it. That's what you went back to when you married Joan" (156). This little speech is one of the most important in the novel. It is not at all clear whether Mrs. Robinson is telling the truth about her long-ago motives for moving to the farm, or whether she is subjecting Joey to another imaginative reconstruction, a new mythology; in fact, I rather suspect that the latter is true. But this new myth is one in which both of them can comfortably live, unlike the previous one—and, when combined with the sermon Joey has just responded to, it gives him a way to live in a marriage that is not ideal. He has exercised his freedom in rejecting Joan in favor of Peggy, only to discover that Peggy is not entirely the woman he would like her to be. The solution is to take the pressure off the higher ideal of righteousness in favor of the lower virtue of kindness. As Joey reports the sermon as saying, "Kindness differs from righteousness as the grasses from the stars. Both are infinite. Without conscious confession of God, there can be no righteousness. But kindness needs no belief. It is implicit in the nature of Creation, in the very curves and amplitude of God's fashioning" (154). Kindness, in other words, is not creation itself but the product of creation—it belongs to the natural world that Mrs. Robinson approaches through the farm and that Joey approaches through Peggy, and it is a way to weather the clash between the imagination and physical reality. It is a kind of glue that could hold Joey's marriage together, and it is a sustaining force that will allow Mrs. Robinson to live alone on the farm, having released her son as an act of that same kindness.

The novel ends with Joey, Peggy, and Richard preparing to leave the farm. Joey's life lies stretched out before him: "New York, the city that is always its own photograph, the living memento of my childish dream of escape, called to me, urged me away, into the car, down the road, along the highway, up the Turnpike. I was ashamed of my desire yet confirmed in it" (174). In this passage, Joey manages to unite the ideal and the real: New York is both at once, as perhaps his mother's farm is both at once in her own imagination. In a certain way, he has broken free of that imagination—and yet, in another way, this is a reification of it, if only because he is openly exercising his own imagination in a way parallel to hers. And as a result, he is able at last to embrace the farm, even as he leaves it. "*Your* farm?" he asks her in the novel's final line. "I've always thought of it as our farm" (174). They have come, at last, to respect each other's mythologies.

Larry Taylor suggests that the novel ultimately means us to condemn Mrs. Robinson for hypocrisy in her treatment of Peggy; her "pastoral idealizing has led to her possessiveness of her son, her inability to accept his spiritual first wife, and her attacks on the new wife Peggy. But Peggy, the very embodiment of earthiness and sexuality, is ironically *like the land*; thus the mother's rejection of Peggy . . . is a rejection of her (the mother's) most fundamental beliefs."[18] But Peggy is "like the land" only in that both of them serve as blank *l'être-en-soi* ready for imaginative projection; we can no more blame Mrs. Robinson for not seeing Joey's idealization of Peggy than we can blame Joey for not seeing Mrs. Robinson's idealization of the farm. The novel moves, in fact, toward "separate spheres" of idealization—Mrs. Robinson will have her myths, and Joey will have his, and the two will come to peace by acknowledging each other's without accepting them. For Joey, it is "our farm" in the sense that Mrs. Robinson has "approved" of Peggy in the preceding scenes; he will always resist the parental imagination that held him hostage, just as she will resist his insistence that Peggy is the proper woman for him. The farm belongs to both of them just as Peggy belongs to both of them—but neither belongs to both of them in the same way. As Joey puts it, "We were striking terms, and circumspection was needed. I must answer in our old language, our only language, allusive and teasing, that with conspiratorial tact declared nothing and left the past apparently unrevised" (174). But only apparently; the tension exists but no longer threatens their relationship. Joey's change in attitude, and Mrs. Robinson's, reveal that they have broken the spells that kept them both captive to the imagination of others. Earlier in the novel, after all, Mrs. Robinson reveals the degree to which her own imagination has been shaped by her father's:

> "With Joan, you still had the space to be a poet. That's who you love, the poet you can never become now."
>
> "Poet. It was you who wanted to be the poet."
>
> "No. I wanted to be a farmer. My father, who was a farmer, wanted to be an orator."
>
> I laughed at the ease with which she, short of breath and recumbent, could weave these patterns. "And now," I said, "you've become the orator and me the farmer." (139)

In the novel's closing pages, however, mutual freedom has been bestowed. As Jeff Campbell points out, "Each has granted the other his or her freedom, has voluntarily surrendered any false claims on the other. In granting freedom to the other, each has found new freedom for him/herself."[19] In being left alone with the farm, Mrs. Robinson is free to become the farmer she wanted to be, and Joey is free from the unwanted obligation to be a poet, even though there is something of the orator in Mrs. Robinson's endless speeches and something of the poet in Joey's recording these episodes for posterity. The parental imagination has not been destroyed, it has merely been put into its proper place. And Updike, in this ending, must have made a sort of peace with the parental imagination as well, for *Of the Farm* is his last major treatment of it until after his mother's death in October 1989, at which point a few stories return to the theme, presumably as a way of processing his own grief.

Joey Robinson and his mother return, for example, in "A Sandstone Farmhouse." Joey's marriage to Peggy has ended, as has a brief third marriage. His children have grown up, and he seems to have only his mother left in the world. He thinks quite a bit about her powerful mythologizing imagination; we are told that "she loved the old house; she loved the *idea* of it. For most of her life, except for the twenty years of exile in her young womanhood, . . . she happily inhabited an idea."[20] This attitude is familiar to readers of the novel, but the story reveals the degree to which young Joey was also an idealist. As a boy, "He clung to civilization by reading; huddled in the brown stove's aromatic aura of coal oil, he read anything—P. G. Wodehouse, Ellery Queen, John Dickson Carr, Thorne Smith—that savored of cities and took him out of his damp, cold little stone house" (108). He too inhabits an idea, albeit an idea diametrically opposed to his mother's, and we see more fully where the conflicts in *Of the Farm* originated. We are also shown a moment in which Joey nearly accepts his mother's mythic vision of the farm. He and his mother are clearing a field shortly after moving to the farmhouse:

> The work seemed hopeless. Yet, when the afternoon breeze came up, he heard a purity of silence that didn't exist in his beloved street of semi-detached houses. Perhaps one car an hour passed, the people staring at this woman and boy dressed in clothes suitable for neither country nor city. And he felt a kind of heroism in his periodic trudge, with the empty sprinkling can, for the half-mile along the edge of the cornfields to the empty house, with its rusty iron pump on the back porch, and then the long haul back, the sloshing can as heavy now as a stone. (110)

This is as close as Joey has ever come to adopting his mother's mythic vision, as opposed to merely having it forced on him. "He felt heroic to himself," Updike says. "Space for heroism existed out here; his being had been transposed to a new scale" (110–11). But this cannot last, as *Of the Farm* demonstrates; among other things, Joey, in moving to the farm, "encountered something she apparently loved as much as she loved him" (111), and this fact is too difficult to accept. While his mother has tried to make him live in the world she has created, that world excludes him even as it traps him; he realizes that "his own self, which he had imagined she cherished for qualities all his own, was lovable to her above all as a piece of her body, as a living proof of her own womanhood" (119). In other words, his very existence is meant to prove hers; the existence of the son makes the mother a mother. Once again he exists within her conception of the world rather than as a being in his own right.

Her death allows him breathing room. He cries only once, we are told, during the funeral, when an image of her running down the Olinger street comes into his head. He realizes at this moment, "This was the mother . . . that he had loved, the young woman living with him and others in a brick semi-detached house, a woman of the world, youthfully finding her way" (127). This is the myth he has made—as his mother wished her whole life to return to her idealized farm, Joey has wished for his whole life to return to his idealized town. As he considers this, he encounters

> the maternal enactments of those misty years when he was a child—crayoning with him on the living-room floor, sewing him Halloween costumes in the shape of Disney creatures, having him lift what she called the "skirts" of the bushes in the lawn while she pushed the old reel mover under them—but from her point of view; he seemed to feel within his mother's head the situation, herself and this small son, this defenseless gurgling hatched creature, and the tentative motions of her mind and instincts as she, as new to mothering as he was to being alive, explored the terrain between them. (128)

His grief springs from his ultimate identification with his mother, his first understanding of what it must have been like to be her. But the image is all that is left of her, and he controls the image: "Trying to do the right thing, the normal thing, running toward her farm, her death. In his vision of her running she was bright and quick and small, like an animal caught in a gunsight. This was the mother Joey had loved, the mother before they moved, before she betrayed him with the farm and its sandstone house" (129). Now that she is dead, she is caught in his own mythic imagination, even as he must still live with hers. Despite Aristi Trendel's claim that this story describes the completion of "Joey's conversion to the mother's gospel,"[21] the conversion is always incomplete, and the story describes a perpetual tension rather than a resolution.

In "The Cats" (1996), the mother's mythic imagination gets a physical manifestation in the form of the clowder of cats that remains on the farm after her death. David Kern—the protagonist of many of the early Olinger stories—cannot help but feed the cats, as doing so keeps some dream of his mother's alive, but he disclaims all responsibility for the farm that her imagination all but brought into being. A woman at the humane society suggests that he trap the cats a few at a time and allow the others to flee into the woods, but he is aghast at the suggestion: "Somehow she had seen me as replacing my mother on the property, its eighty-two acres of milkweed and horseflies and red mud, as if my whole life had been killing time until I could take possession."[22] This is, in fact, exactly what Mrs. Kern had in mind; as the humane-society woman reports, "she always spoke of you as the one who'd take charge. She'd say to me,

'Amy, I know the neighbors think I'm crazy, but I'm just holding the fort for Davey'" (78). Even so, David has his own life in New Jersey and must abandon the land, writing a large check to the humane society to remove the cats so it can be sold. Though he has always hated the farm, his mother's death makes it the object of nostalgia for him: "The last days of owning the farm were strange. It was as if I had a phantom limb; I could feel it move, but not see it" (83). The farm has played such an incredible role in the formation of his own imagination that he feels its absence as a virtual presence. Likewise, despite the claims of a local that the cats will not survive hunting season, a later visit to the land reveals that they, too, have endured: "As I drifted in my inherited coat across the lank grass, a few shadows filtered out of the orchard and flickered toward the house, eagerly loping. Several more materialized from the direction of the woods. These cats had survived. They thought I was my mother and that good times had returned" (84). This story, along with "A Sandstone Farmhouse," demonstrates that genuine escape from the parental imagination is ultimately impossible. We are all held captive, to some extent or another, by our parents' dreams. The best we can hope for is to transport our captivity into another milieu, in which it will be transformed into a barely expressible longing.

Notes

1 Updike, "Introduction to the Czech Edition of *Of the Farm*," 82–83.

2 Ibid., 83.

3 Hunt, *John Updike and the Three Great Secret Things*, 87.

4 Updike, *Of the Farm*, 109. Hereafter cited in-text.

5 Campbell, *Updike's Novels*, 90.

6 Galloway, *The Absurd Hero in American Fiction*, 41.

7 Hamilton and Hamilton, *The Elements of John Updike*, 187.

8 Wordsworth, "The Solitary Reaper," ll. 1–8.

9 Ibid., ll. 27–36.

10 Updike will later describe both Angela Hanema, of *Couples*, and Joan Maple as incorporeal in this same way.

11 Galloway, *Absurd Hero*, 42.

12 Taylor, *Pastoral and Anti-Pastoral Patterns*, 106.

13 Plato, *Meno*, 79d.

14 Ibid., 80b.

15 It is surely telling, too, that Mrs. Robinson has already invoked Plato as a philosophical authority, telling Richard about Aristophanes's soulmate myth from the *Symposium* (69).

16 I am inclined to agree with Mrs. Robinson here—Peggy is the one character in this novel who does not have idealizing tendencies. Edward Vargo suggests that Peggy's mythology is to "appropriate[ ] Joey through her sexuality" (*Rainstorms and Fire*, 113)—but that appropriation seems to me to move from Joey to Peggy instead of the other way around. In other words, Joey treats Peggy as a blank slate onto which to project his sexual idealizations; she is the body for his mind, in a prefiguration of the works I examine in part 3.

17 Newman, *John Updike*, 90.

18 Taylor, *Pastoral and Anti-Pastoral Patterns*, 110.

19 Campbell, *Updike's Novels*, 89.

20 Updike, "A Sandstone Farmhouse," 106. Hereafter cited in-text.

21 Trendel, "The Resurgence of the Repressed," 166.

22 Updike, "The Cats," 78. Hereafter cited in-text.

Part II. Collective Hallucination in the Adulterous Society

5: "Man and Daughter in the Cold," "Giving Blood," "The Taste of Metal," and "Avec la Bébé-Sitter"

AFTER *OF THE FARM*, Updike seems to have lost interest in the ability of the parental imagination to shape the world of the child. More commonly in his 1960s fiction, we find scenes in which a father realizes that his imagination no longer shapes the life of his child, generally a daughter. Near the end of "Man and Daughter in the Cold," for example, the protagonist, Ethan, recognizes that, in her adolescence, his daughter, Becky, is breaking away from his control. The effect is almost nihilistic: "He was looking upon his daughter as a woman but without lust. The music around him was being produced, in the zero air, like a finger on crystal, by this hollowness, this generosity of negation. Without lust, without jealousy. Space seemed love, bestowed to be free in, and coldness the price. He felt joined to the great dead whose words it was his duty to teach."[1] Ethan's lust—frequently an imaginative agent in Updike's work—cannot touch his daughter, and thus she slips out of his grasp. As he does for Mrs. Robinson in *Of the Farm*, Updike connects Ethan's imagination with art (the literature he teaches) and with nature (the coldness that seeps in from the ski slope on which the story takes place)—but where her imagination is a live, vibrant force, his is ineffectual and dead, at least as far as it concerns his daughter. The moment recurs late in *Couples*, when Piet Hanema, his two daughters in tow, runs into his future lover, Bea Guerin, in the supermarket: "Piet was shocked to see that his elder daughter was, though not yet as tall as Bea, of a size that was comparable. While her father had been looking elsewhere she had abandoned the realm of the miniature. In this too strong light he also saw that her heated face, though still a child's, contained the smoky something, the guarded inwardness, of womanhood."[2] He feels, in this moment, his daughters slipping away from him, moving outside the realm of his understanding.

We have, then, two models of parent-child relationships. In *The Centaur*, *Of the Farm*, and several of the Olinger stories, we have parents whose imagination is so powerful that it creates a labyrinth through which their children must wander. In "Man and Daughter in the Cold," *Couples*, and several other important pieces of fiction from the mid-to-late 1960s, we have parents whose imaginative hold over their children is weak almost to the point of disappearance. The difference is largely generational. Parents with powerful imaginations appear in the fiction in which Updike addresses his own childhood; fiction about the childhood of his own children features parents with weak imaginations. Or more accurately, it features parents whose imagination is directed away from their children altogether. As Angela Hanema puts it early in *Couples*, the adults in Tarbox, Massachusetts, give their children "neglect so subtle they don't even notice it. We're not abusive, we're evasive" (10). She speaks for an entire generation of parents—in Updike's fiction if not in real life—who are so lost in the labyrinths of their own sexual exploration that they can barely even register the suffering of their offspring. For Augustine, the essence of sin, and thus the origin of unhappiness, is disordered love;[3] likewise, for Updike, the cause of the suffering of these children is a disordered imagination on the part of their parents.

Besides *Couples*, first published in 1968, the Updike novel that most clearly demonstrates this tendency is *Marry Me: A Romance*. Despite *Marry Me*'s 1976 publication date, however, I will be examining it before *Couples* for two reasons. First, *Couples* is a much more expansive novel than *Marry Me*, which hones down its *dramatis personae* to four. *Couples*, on the other hand, includes intimate portraits of a dozen or so adulterers and attempts to make broader social commentary that is largely lacking from *Marry Me*. Second, *Marry Me* is actually an earlier novel than *Couples*. Because it is intensely autobiographical, giving the lurid details of Updike's affair with Joyce Harrington in barely fictionalized terms, he published *Marry Me* twelve years after he completed it, not until his marriage to Mary Updike had already ended. This means that readers and critics have failed to see it in its proper context, as Adam Begley explains: "In the true chronology of his novels, it follows *The Centaur* and precedes *Of the Farm*; more significantly, he finished it two full years before he began work on *Couples*, the bestselling novel that planted in the public imagination the idea that the adulterous society was territory belonging to him by right of discovery. It's likely that if *Marry Me* and *Couples* had been published in the order in which they were written, the critical reception and popular appeal of each would have been quite different."[4] Indeed, *Couples* is the novel that made Updike's reputation—but it is also, after its first hundred pages, the weakest of his major novels. It sinks beneath the weight of its panoply of characters, its near-pornographic depiction of sexual acts, and its heavy-handed metaphysical structure.[5] *Marry Me* is not a top-tier Updike novel, but in comparison with *Couples* it seems breezy and enjoyable, with moments of real power and beauty. As Begley points out, restoring it to the proper composition order of Updike's novels keeps us from seeing it as a mere retread of *Couples* and allows us to see it as its own phenomenon, albeit one closely associated with the other novel.

Before I get to either of them, however, I will examine several important shorter pieces from the 1960s that share the concerns and themes
of the novels. Updike begins exploring mutual acts of the imagination
as early as 1963's "Giving Blood." Richard Maple—introduced to readers seven years earlier in "Snowing in Greenwich Village"—attempts to
use his imagination to wound his wife Joan, to extract her permission for
him to have an affair, and to keep the marriage together. Appropriately
enough for Richard, who writes advertising copy for a living, the vehicle
by which he attempts this operation is words. But unlike Updike, he cannot quite control his words. "I asked you not to talk," Joan tells him.
"Now you've said things that I'll always remember."[6] And yet he cannot
keep quiet, either; he constantly tries to imaginatively re-create the world
around him: "It would have been strategic and dignified of him to keep
the silence; but he could not resist believing that just one more pinch of
syllables would restore the fine balance which with each wordless mile
slipped increasingly awry" (21). Words themselves also slip away, as Richard's memory of the teletype machines he used at the beginning of his
career demonstrates. The hospital room in which the Maples give blood
"reminded Richard of the days years ago when he had tended a bat-
tery of teletype machines in a room much this size. By now, ten o'clock,
the yards of copy that began pouring through the machines at five and
that lay in great crimped heaps on the floor when he arrived at seven
would have been harvested and sorted and pasted together and turned
in, and there was nothing to do but keep up with the staccato appearance of the later news and to think about simple things like coffee" (25).
Richard is Goethe's sorcerer's apprentice, conjuring up streams of words
that quickly escape his control, threatening to overwhelm him and sink
his marriage. And he discovers, through his encounter with an elderly
employee of the hospital, that he is not the only such apprentice. When
Richard announces loudly, annoyed, that he does not want any coffee,
he "saw himself transposed, another Iris, into the firmament of the old
man's aggrieved gossip" (29). The hospital contains multiple universes
made of words, all of them smashing into each other, none of them ultimately secure. The human imagination becomes a destructive force that
promises to tear asunder all human institutions.

However, an act of the imagination momentarily rejuvenates the
Maples' flagging marriage. As they donate their blood, the two lie at a
right angle, and Richard's mind expands to fill the room: "Here, conscious of a pointed painless pulse in the inner hinge of his arm but incuri-
ous as to what it looked like, he floated and imagined how his soul would
float free when all his blood was underneath the bed. His blood and
Joan's merged on the floor, and together their spirits glided from crack
to crack, from star to star on the ceiling" (27). The vision is Richard's,
but Joan likely shares in it, as the two are joined together in some sort of

quasi-religious revelation: "As in some theologies the proliferant deities are said to exist as ripples upon the featureless ground of Godhead, so these inconstant images lightly overlay his continuous awareness of Joan's blood, like his own, ebbing. Linked to a common loss, they were chastely conjoined; the thesis developed upon him that the hoses attached to them somewhere out of sight met" (28). This shared imaginative vision bestows on the Maples a new faith in their marriage, which had threatened to collapse under the weight of Richard's individualist attempts to control his wife's imagination through language. As David Crowe puts it, "As their individual essences mingle into one conjoined flesh, they grow coincidentally less irritable, mutually more patient and loving."[7] As they exit the hospital together, Richard whispers in Joan's ear, "Hey, I love you. Love love *love* you" (31). The shared experience and the remaking of the world it engendered has allowed them to see each other, and their marriage, in a new light: "Almost always it was dark when they shared a car. The oval of her face was bright in the corner of his eye. She was watching him, alert to take the wheel if he suddenly lost consciousness. He felt tender toward her in the eggshell light, and curious toward himself" (32). But the change is only temporary; by the end of the story, Joan has told her husband that she does not care if he has an affair or not, and he has reacted not with relief but with anger: "That smugness; why didn't she *fight?*" (34). But for a moment, the illusion holds; for a moment, their marriage is full of life again.

Another Maples story, 1967's "The Taste of Metal," takes on many of the same themes as "Giving Blood," but is distinctly darker than the earlier story. It opens with Richard Maple at a party after having his teeth capped. The physical sensation of the dental procedure provokes a spiritual uneasiness in him; he experiences the metal in his mouth "as disciplinary, as a *No* spoken to other tastes."[8] This description parallels the motions of the imagination and the physical world in the story. Richard Maple will construct an ideal world composed of "other tastes," to which the actual world around him will offer a resounding *No*. His dental work thus serves as a metaphor for the boundaries he transgresses over the course of the story—boundaries that, again, will not allow infinite transgressions—and as a reminder of his own guilt. The metal's "regularity masked holes and roughnesses that had been a kind of mirror wherein his tongue had known itself" (235). The process makes him feel not quite himself, and his solution is to drink away this unpleasant consciousness. The alcohol allows him to foster the illusion of security in his budding extramarital relationship with Eleanor Dennis, whom he offers to drive home alongside his wife. The alcohol coursing through his system shields him from all bad feelings as he drives home: "Richard felt resiliently cushioned; Eleanor was beside him, Joan behind him, God above him, the road beneath him" (237). But this security is an illusion, fostered by lust and alcohol, an illusion shattered by the telephone pole on which he wrecks his car. Updike's language in describing the accident suggests an utter refusal of the physical world to yield to the machinations of Richard's imagination: "Richard felt the sudden refusal of motion, the *No*, and knew, though his mind was deeply cushioned in a cottony indifference, that an event had occurred which in another incarnation he would regret" (238). His illusions have melted away, and if he does not quite see a world stripped of his mind, he at least recognizes that such a world exists.

The second half of the story involves guilt's taking over Richard's consciousness. The metal in his mouth, as it were, overpowers the alcohol in his system: "Music and snow poured down upon them, and he imagined that, if only the oboe sonata were played backwards, they would leap backwards from the telephone pole and be on their way home again" (239). Music, as Kierkegaard points out, is the least physical of all art forms, and so is uniquely qualified to express "the most abstract idea conceivable," that is, "the spirit of sensuality."[9] But even music will not bend to Richard's will and imagination here, let alone the world of rocks, trees, and telephone poles. The event becomes completely unmalleable. Richard has committed an action that cannot be undone or explained away, just as he cannot return to his natural teeth. Fearing that Eleanor has been paralyzed, he thinks, "Never again, never again, would his car be new, would he chew on his own enamel, would she kick so high with vivid long legs" (241). The universe of *l'être-en-soi* has proven itself to be indifferent to his life: "Though his system was still adrift in liquor, he could not quite forget the taste of metal in his teeth. That utterly flat *No*: through several dreamlike thicknesses something very hard had touched him" (241). The imaginative world Richard has created in order to sleep with Eleanor Dennis has foundered in the face of *l'être-en-soi*. Eleanor, incidentally, has not quite learned this lesson. After the accident, she remarks that the telephone pole that they have hit is "a nuisance to the neighborhood" (240), suggesting that the physical world ought to reorganize itself around the imaginations and the wishes of its human inhabitants. Alice and Kenneth Hamilton point out that Eleanor "speaks for all who see the permanence of marriage vows (among other fixed rules) as an unnecessary restriction on the individual's freedom to live by his own standards" and argue that hers is a world "where the *No* of reality is ignored by people whose minds, like that of Richard at the time of hitting the pole, are 'deeply cushioned in a cottony indifference.'"[10] Marriage is a cultural rather than a natural phenomenon, of course, but it is a cultural phenomenon so firmly entrenched in the Maples' social set that hardens into something like the permanence of *l'être-en-soi*. For those within a marriage, as the Hamiltons see it, marriage itself belongs to the naysaying physical world, and adultery is a powerful but ultimately doomed act of the imagination.

Doomed acts of the adulterous imagination run through Updike's work of this period, much of which fictionalizes the affair he had with Joyce Harrington in 1962—an affair that very nearly ended his marriage. Their relationship ended in a confrontation between John and Mary Updike and Joyce and Herbert Harrington:

> Herbert sat them down with Joyce in the living room, served them all wine, and insisted that they resolve the situation there and then. His forceful attitude goaded John into taking precisely the step he knew he couldn't take, which was to declare his intention to leave Mary for Joyce. The next day, Herbert persuaded Mary to consult a lawyer—she and John would have to divorce so that John could marry Joyce. When Mary did drive down to Boston to see a lawyer . . . she was sitting in the office, about to set the legal process in motion, when the telephone rang; it was John, asking to speak with his wife. "I took the phone," Mary remembered, "and John was saying that he'd changed his mind, that he wasn't going to leave me, that he didn't want a divorce—so I went home."[11]

In the aftermath of this situation, Herbert drove the Updikes to flee overseas for several months, in one of the darkest periods of Updike's life. And the stories he wrote during this period—among them "Solitaire," "Leaves," "The Stare," and "The Morning"—were largely too autobiographical to be published until several years later. They are also almost uniformly bleak. Like "Giving Blood," "Avec la Bébé-Sitter" is a possible exception, although they are cheerful only in the context of these other stories and the upheavals in Updike's personal life.

The protagonist of "Avec la Bébé-Sitter" is Kenneth, a magazine illustrator whom Updike presents as being able to live only in the imaginative worlds he constructs for himself. He is a man who gets into trouble when he is forced to deal with the world of flesh and blood outside his own mind. In fact, "he was not, despite a certain surface knowingness, an educated person at all. The magazine illustrations, poised somewhere between the ardently detailed earth of Norman Rockwell and the breezy blue clouds of Jon Whitcomb, with which Kenneth earned his living were the outcome of a rather monomaniacal and cloistered youth devoted to art."[12] He learns his art, then, not by looking at the material world but at the world of art; this practice puts him in league with the passengers of "English Train Compartment," who look out the window and see paintings of the world instead of the world itself. Kenneth's art is the water in which he swims like a fish—and like a fish, he flops around helplessly when he is out of his element: "At his drawing board, in the little room spattered and daubed from floor to ceiling, he was a kind of master, inventive and conscientious and mysteriously alert to the oscillations of chic that galvanized the New York market; outside this room he was impulsive and innocent and unduly dependent upon improvisation" (66–67). Updike's clear implication is that it is this reliance on improvisation and immersion in the ideal world of art that has led Kenneth to make such a mess of his life, his marriage, and his family—a theme that will be played out in more detail in *Marry Me*.

The story's emotional turning point, fittingly enough, happens alongside an act of the imagination and the memory. Kenneth, exiled on the French Riviera, attempts to draw for Marie—the titular French baby-sitter—the house in which he and his family normally live:

> And he found himself drawing, in avidly remembered detail, the front of their house on Marlborough Street, the flight of brown steps with the extra-tall top step, the carpet-sized front lawn with its wrought-iron fence and its single prisoner of forsythia like a weeping princess, the coarse old struggling vine that winter never quite killed, the tall windows with their many Colonial panes; he even put the children's faces in the second-story windows. This was the window of Vera's room, these were the ones that Nancy and Charlie watched the traffic jams out of, this was the living-room window that at this time of year should show a brightly burdened Christmas tree, and up here, on the third story, were the little shut-tered windows of the guest bedroom that was inhabited by a ghost with a slender neck and naked moonlit shoulders. Emotion froze his hand. (73)

Forced out of the world of imagination and art, Kenneth realizes for the first time in the story the true magnitude of what he has done. His art has failed to give him the necessary tools to make sense of his life, and the naked reality of his situation appears to him. And here, as in so many other Updike stories about adultery, it is the children who suffer from their parents' extramarital antics. Kenneth tells Marie that he and his wife are staying together "*pour les enfants.*" As he makes this excuse, he ges-tures "toward the outdoors and abruptly follow[s] the direction of his gesture, for Vera had begun to cry in the distance. About once a day she speared herself on one of the cactuses" (74). Despite Kenneth's claims of protecting his children, they suffer anyway. They are doomed to suffer—in part, yes, because Updike's universe is one in which guilt and suffer-ing are universal and unavoidable; as the narrator of "The Music School" famously declares, "The world is the host; it must be chewed."[13] But the particular form of these children's suffering springs from the disordered imaginations and loves of their parents, their misplaced and misdirected affections. If adultery is Richard Maple, drunk and driving, and marriage is the telephone pole that stops him dead in his tracks, children tend to be smashed between the car and the pole—innocent victims of their parents' pleasure-seeking.

Notes

[1] Updike, "Man and Daughter in the Cold," 106.

[2] Updike, *Couples*, 396. Hereafter cited in-text.

[3] For example, Augustine claims that the human race continued to descend after the Fall because they sought after physical, feminine beauty and neglected truth and ethics: "Now physical beauty, to be sure, is a good created by God, but it is a temporal, carnal good, very low in the scale of goods; and if it is loved in preference to God, the eternal, internal, and sempiternal God, that love is as wrong as the miser's love of gold, with the abandonment of justice, though the fault is in the man, not in the gold. This is true of everything created; though it is good, it can be loved in the right way or in the wrong way—in the right way, that is, when the proper order is kept, in the wrong way when the order is upset" (*City of God*, 15.22).

[4] Begley, *Updike*, 250.

[5] Angela Hanema, quoting Freddy Thorne, spells out the metaphysical lesson early on in *Couples*: "He thinks we're a circle. A magic circle of heads to keep the night out. He told me he gets frightened if he doesn't see us over a weekend. He thinks we've made a church of one another" (8–9).

[6] Updike, "Giving Blood," 21. Hereafter cited in-text.

[7] Crowe, *Cosmic Defiance*, 78.

[8] Updike, "The Taste of Metal," 235. Hereafter cited in-text.

[9] Kierkegaard, *Either/Or*, 69.

[10] Hamilton and Hamilton, *The Elements of John Updike*, 73.

[11] Begley, *Updike*, 229. This confrontation is dramatized in both *Marry Me* and *Couples*.

[12] Updike, "Avec la Bébé-Sitter." Hereafter cited in-text.

[13] Updike, "The Music School," 190.

6: *Marry Me*

OF ALL OF UPDIKE'S EARLY NOVELS, *Marry Me* (1976) is most clearly set in the realm of fantasy. It announces its position with its subtitle, "A Romance," and this is an important label. Jeff Campbell delineates two ways that the word *romance* is typically used. In the most common contemporary usage, a romance designates "a story that draws largely on the author's imagination and makes very little effort to re-create details of the active world, in contrast to the more realistic 'novel.'"[1] But *Marry Me* is realistic the way that all of Updike's novels are realistic; it attempts to reproduce the physical world down to its smallest detail. And so Campbell is much more interested in an older usage of the word *romance*, a term that has "for centuries been associated with medieval stories of knights, kings, and damsels in distress. In contrast to the sterner epics which preceded them, medieval romances were full of fantasy and light-hearted, sometimes aimless, adventures. Above all, love, missing or at least of only minor interest in the epics, was supreme in the romances, and reflected the artificial ideals of chivalry" (163). Campbell points to a number of images from medieval romance that appear in the novel—ogres, knights, castles—and argues that "the whole plot of the novel revolves around Jerry's idealized love for Sally, who is portrayed much like the 'Unattainable Lady' of courtly love" (164). In particular, Campbell connects Jerry and Sally's romance to that of Tristan and Iseult—a story dissected by the Swiss theologian Denis de Rougemont in *L'amour et l'Occident* (*Love in the Western World*, 1939), a book much on Updike's mind as he was writing *Marry Me*. Rougemont's influence on the novel has been well established by previous critics; I will therefore focus less on *Marry Me*'s debt to the romantic tradition and more on its connection to Updike's other morality plays about the imagination, though Rougemont and medieval romance will help me to make my case at certain key points.

Marry Me opens with Jerry Conant, our protagonist, on his way to an oceanside assignation with Sally Mathias. Both Jerry and Sally are married to varying degrees of happiness, and so they must build their affair in the cracks of their legal and spiritual commitments. Such a system, as Rougemont points out, allows clandestine lovers like Jerry and Sally to situate their relationship outside the bounds of the world of daily experience: "Actually, then, like all other great lovers, they [Tristan and Iseult] imagine that they have been ravished 'beyond good and evil' into a kind of transcendental state outside ordinary human experience, into an ineffable absolute irreconcilable with the world, but that they feel to be *more real than the world*."[2] But this world exists only in their mutual imaginations. Updike tips us off to this world's nonexistence— and its eventual deleterious effects—by having Jerry listen to a Ray Charles song on his way to the beach: "*Every dream / Has only brought me pain*."[3] Music itself becomes the medium for Jerry's adulterous imagination: "Songs on the radio were rich with new meaning for him, as he drove to one of their trysts. He wanted to share them with her, but they were rarely in the same car together, and as week succeeded week that spring the songs like mayflies died from the air" (4). Thus, even as he attempts to live in this fantasy world he and his lover have constructed, he recognizes, on some level, from the earliest pages of the novel, its unsustainability. He asks Sally,

> "What can we *do*?"
> "I don't know," she said. "Go on like this a little more?"
> "It won't stand still." He gestured upwards and stared as if to blind himself. "The fucking sun won't stand still." (12)

As Donald J. Greiner points out, the beach becomes "a place to hold back mortality, to trick time by indulging the illusion that the joy of adultery, the lure of new love, creates new life."[4] But just as important, it is new life that will never change or evolve; it is a distinctly idealist eternity, almost Platonic in its form. As Samuel C. Rickless notes, "It is a consistent refrain of [Plato's] middle-period dialogues that the forms are changeless,"[5] that is, that what is genuinely eternal is not subject to modification. For example, in Συμπόσιον (Symposium, ca. 385–370 B.C.E.), Diotema tells Socrates that the Beautiful "is always one in form; and all the other beautiful things share in that, in such a way that when those others come to be or pass away, this does not become the least bit smaller or greater nor suffer any change."[6] In Φαίδων (Phaedo), Socrates passes this message on, asking Cebes, "can the Equal itself, the Beautiful itself, each thing in itself, the real, ever be affected by any change whatever?"[7] The answer is clearly *no*, and it is no accident that Socrates claims a few lines later that "those that always remain the same can only be grasped by the reasoning power of the mind."[8] Changelessness demands idealism, and idealism demands changelessness; thus Jerry's longing for the sun to stand still is in effect a longing to access a perfect world through his mind.

Sally, too, longs for the changelessness of a Platonic eternity, and even manages to make herself believe in it from time to time: "She pictured them entering a lifetime of airports, depots, piers, and hotel lobbies, and knew that they would always look like this, tallish, young, bumping together a bit too much" (40). But the scene of her fantasy undermines it: The locations of their supposed changelessness are places of enormous and endless change—eternal motion, not eternal stillness. And so when the temporal world refuses to comply with Sally's wishes, she feels it as a great loss. Before the action of the novel, Sally and Jerry went on a trip to Washington, DC, together, as if they were husband and wife, or at least as if their love were not illicit. In the second chapter of the novel, Sally surprises Jerry by appearing in Washington during another of his business trips there. But she is disappointed to realize that things have changed, that the lovers' fantasy cannot make the sun stand still. She wakes to "a sharp deserted feeling. The room was different from the first one. The walls, though it was the same hotel, were yellow instead of white, and instead of the flowered prints there were two pallid Holbein portraits" (31–32). The world has shifted. Their relationship has shifted with it, and to her disgust, she begins to see it from an outsider's perspective: "It was brightening enough beyond the blinds for her to see the faces, so dim they seemed real presences—small-mouthed, fastidious. How many adulterous and drunken couplings had they been compelled to witness?" (32). The human world is even worse, and "for the rest of the day that unfolded Sally was laid open to a vivid and frightening sense of her existence in other people's eyes. The puffy-lidded news vendor in the perfumed lobby saw her as a spoiled young matron. The waitress who served them breakfast at the counter cheerfully took her for a fucked secretary. When Sally relinquished Jerry to a taxi and became alone, she felt herself reflected in every glance and glass entryway. To the Japanese souvenir-store attendants she was big. To the Negro doorman she was white. To everybody she was nobody" (34). Her pain at this realization comes from recognizing that she and Jerry are not the Archimedean point of the universe, that other people have subjectivities and consciousnesses that are unavailable to her: "Was she unique? That young black girl like a chocolate swan, that dowager in rouge and wool—was each of these also prey to a clawing love that could literally lift her into the sky? Sally could not believe so; yet she did not like to believe either that she was totally unique, eccentric, mad" (34–35). She is being torn between the world she and Jerry have created for themselves and the world as it exists for others.

Sartre describes this pain in *Being and Nothingness*. When I see another person, he says, "there is a total space which is grouped around the Other, and this space is made *with my space*; there is a regrouping in which I take part but which escapes me, a regrouping of all the objects which people my universe."[9] In other words, because *l'être-en-soi* must always be organized by *l'être-pour-soi*, I generally experience myself as the center of the universe, but the presence of other people suggests the existence of other subjectivities, each of which sees itself as the center of the universe. The effect is disconcerting because "suddenly an object has appeared which has stolen the world from me. Everything is in place; everything still exists for me; but everything is traversed by an invisible flight and fixed in the direction of a new object. The appearance of the

Other in the world corresponds therefore to a fixed sliding of the whole universe, to a decentralization of the world which undermines the centralization which I am simultaneously effecting."[10] The existence of the Other turns me into *l'être-en-soi*, into blank material, for a moment. Updike expands this Sartrean observation in that Jerry and Sally at least occasionally share a world-centering consciousness, creating a world in which their love can exist and prosper. But even so, Sally experiences just such a Sartrean "decentralization" on her second day in Washington. On her first day, "She felt airy, free. The federal buildings, fantastically carved and frosted, floated around her walk; their unreality and grandeur permeated her mood. Through the gaps between guards and greenery, she looked in at the White House; it was made of brilliant fake stuff, like meringue" (26). The illusion of her relationship with Jerry holds. But on the second day, the external world becomes oppressive, and the presence of the other residents of and visitors to Washington threatens to crush her: "In walking down Fourteenth Street alone, the pavement pricking her eyes with mica, she began to cry, and realized it didn't matter, for no one was looking at her, no one at all in these multitudes" (40). Not only do these people see her as a member of *l'être-en-soi*, as a mere object, but she is also a forgotten object, real to no one. From being the center of the universe she has become detritus at its margins, and it is no surprise that this takes place when she is alone, for her relationship with Jerry creates the illusory world in which she lives at her happiest.

At the same time, she slowly begins to realize that if her relationship with Jerry is the center of the universe, that means that she as an individual cannot be—thus, even this most intimate connection threatens to undermine her subjectivity, her connection to the world. As she shops for antiques in Washington, its meaning suddenly disappears from the world:

> Once she had cared about these things; once, being in a city alone had fulfilled her and coveting objects and fabrics had been a way of possessing them. Now she sought herself in bronze and silk and porcelain and was not there. When she walked with Jerry, there was something there, but it was no longer her, it was them: her explaining to him, him to her, exchanging their lives, absorbing fractions of the immense lesson that had accumulated in the years before they had loved. She saw each thing only as something to tell him about, and without him there was nothing to tell; he had robbed her of the world. (36)

She has been stripped of her ability to re-create the world by her own lights, and the world becomes pure *l'être-en-soi*, meaningless matter that can offer her neither sustenance nor shelter. And her relationship with Jerry and the mutual act of the imagination that they enact together feeds her anxiety, even though it also assuages it by providing her a world to live in, at least occasionally. The high point of their relationship in the novel is the oceanside tryst that opens it: "As usual, Jerry and Sally walked in and out, down ragged paths between scratching bayberry bushes and up slithering slopes, laughing with exertion, looking for the ideal spot, the spot where they had been the last time. As usual, they failed to find it and finally put the blanket anywhere, in a concavity of clean sand that became, instantly, perfect" (6). The imaginative re-creation is most effective here—effective in a way that we never again see it, though at moments it comes close. Later, as they wait for a flight from the Washington airport, they sit on the sidewalk outside and see a pleasant, if unexceptional, landscape: "There were trees, and some reddish rows of government housing, and a distant plantation manse on a low blue ridge, and an immense soft sky going green above the hushed horizon" (51). Their being together lifts this unremarkable landscape into something approaching perfection: "It was a landscape of unexpected benevolence. Her toes felt cool out of her shoes, and her man regained his reality in the presence of air and grass" (51). Jerry immediately re-creates this landscape for her in the image of their shared dreams: "I see us . . . in Wyoming, with your children, and a horse, and a cold little lake we can swim in, and a garden we can make near the house" (51). The pastoral scene by the beach has returned, albeit at a lower pitch.

Their mutual imaginative projection on the physical world—the projection of their love, spiritual and physical—turns these spots into ideals. And in these ideal spots they are able to turn themselves into ideal beings: "They felt no hurry; this was perhaps the gravest proof that they were, Jerry and Sally, the original man and woman—that they felt no hurry, that they did not so much excite each other as put the man and woman in each other to rest" (7). This peace, a mutual product of their imaginations, echoes back into them individually: "The sense of rest, of having arrived at the long-promised calm center, filled him like a species of sleep even as his insteps tightened upward into the arches of her feet" (7). Thus, despite Judie Newman's claim that "as Jerry casts Sally as his heaven-on-earth, Sally herself ceases to be more than an accessory and adjunct to his personal illusion,"[11] Sally is very much involved in creating the imaginary world they inhabit together—even if she, more than Jerry, feels it as an encroachment on her own subjectivity. After all, when he is not with her, she projects his presence onto the world around her: "Alone in her bathroom, she conjured up Jerry; she gave the air his eyes" (19). And when he goes to Washington, DC, and tells her not to follow him, she turns the entire world into his prohibition:

Under the tranquilizing June sun the Sound was a smooth plane reflecting the command, *Don't go*. . . .
She discovered herself crying again; she didn't notice until her cheeks registered the wetness. *Don't go*. Everything agreed on this—the

grains of sand, the chorus of particles alive on the water, the wary
glances of her sons, the distant splashes and shouts that came to her
when she lay down and closed her eyes, like the smooth clatter of
an ethereal sewing machine. *Don't go, you can't go, you are here.* The
unanimity was wonderful. (20)

Updike is saved from the pathetic fallacy in this passage because both he
and the reader know perfectly well that the world is not really telling Sally
these things, that she is projecting them onto the blank canvas of materi-
ality in a kind of temporary insanity. We are told, in fact, that "she feared
for her sanity" (23), since part of her knows that this is just a projection.
Sally's imagination is just as strong as Jerry's, though it does not always
manifest itself identically.

   In the midst of their re-creation of the physical world as an ideal
world, Jerry and Sally believe themselves to be getting at the essence of
the objects they encounter. For example, the wine they drink together on
the beach becomes a mystical act of communion, and Sally suggests that,
in drinking it straight from the bottle, they are accessing the essence of
the wine: "It doesn't taste of paper this way," she reports. "It just tastes
of itself" (9). Jerry's experience takes things even further and suggests
an access to a kind of super-essence, something more real than reality
itself: "when he tipped his head back, the redness of the sun and of the
wine mixed" (9). He may not be getting the essential wine here, but he
is getting something higher and more spiritual—the liquid going into his
body blends with the center of the solar system, the sun. That this is the
same "fucking sun" that "won't stand still" a few pages later suggests that
his sense of accessing the ideal is illusory—but in the meantime the illusion holds. In fact, for the moment, they are able to replace the sun with
themselves, fixing their relationship at the center of the universe. This is
not an uncommon trope in romantic literature. John Donne's "The Sun
Rising," for example, brags to the titular heavenly body that the narrator
and his mistress are a microcosm of the entire world:

> If her eyes have not blinded thine,
>   Look, and to-morrow late tell me,
> Whether both th'Indias of spice and mine
> Be where thou left'st them, or lie here with me.
> Ask for those kings whom thou saw'st yesterday,
> And thou shalt hear, "All here in one bed lay."[12]

Similarly, Updike tells us that "to [Sally] the past was a dingy pedes-
tal erected so she could be alive in this moment" (26). Not just all
of the material world but all of human history takes her affair with
Jerry as its Cartesian origin. The external world begins to seem insubstantial in comparison, and she and Jerry exist on a higher plane of

reality—Platonic forms for the shadowy stuff of the material world. This is, I think, why *Marry Me* seems so sparsely populated compared with Updike's other novels. As Adam Begley points out, "The two couples are . . . the only citizens of Greenwood, or at least the only ones Updike breathes any life into—their friends and neighbors, babysitters and housekeepers are all minimally sketched. The focus is exclusively, obsessively on the four principals, with their small children (three on each side) occasionally intruding."[13] I suspect this agoraphobia is by design—after all, in the imaginative world of the two sets of affairs, the external world has disappeared.

Jerry's relationship with Sally, then, is marked by its unreality and by its desire to transgress and transcend the roles given to the lovers. Sally notes that Jerry "refused to remain fixed in the role of lover as she imagined it should be played" (15). When she says that he will miss his wife, Ruth, as well as her while he is in Washington, he says that he will not miss Ruth as much. She thanks him for putting it that way when "a real lover would have said, 'Not at all'" (17). His response is telling: "That's what I am. An unreal lover" (17). Instead, as they imagine it, he is an ideal husband:

> Jerry's fault as a lover, his cruel fault, was that he acted like a husband. She had never had a husband before. It seemed to Sally now in the light of Jerry that she had been married ten years to a man who wanted only to be her lover, keeping between them the distance that lovers must cross. Richard was always criticizing her, analyzing her. When she was young it had been flattering; now it just seemed mean. Out of bed he must always try to strip her down to some twisted core, some mistaken motive. Whereas Jerry kept trying to dress her, flinging at her sad little scarves of comfort and advice. He saw her as pathetically exposed. (16)

But this conception, too, is unreal. Jerry cannot be the ideal husband because he is not Sally's husband. He is Ruth's, and he is a long way from being the ideal husband to her. The perfection of Jerry and Sally's relationship exists only in their collective imagination and is possible only as an escape from the dreary reality of their respective marriages. "I wish the world was just you and me" (18), Jerry tells her, as if the wish made it reality. Likewise, as Judie Newman points out, "By going to Washington Sally intends to fix Jerry back in that ideal role,"[14] even though such an attempt is doomed to failure.

Most critics contrast the fantasy and romance of Jerry's relationship with Sally with his marriage to Ruth. Jeff Campbell, for example, suggests that "as the summer wears on, Ruth proves to [Jerry] that in the realm of the real she is a better wife than Sally" (168). And it is true that Ruth presents herself as a hard-headed realist. In her own affair with

Richard, a summer before, "Ruth has not turned Richard into a Tristan; rather, in reflecting on their relationship, she discovers that 'one can sleep with a person, and have him still be a person, no more'" (168–69; *Marry Me*, 92). Donald Greiner agrees, even suggesting that Updike wants "the reader to understand that Ruth may recover her imagination, her artistic vision, only if she frees Jerry from her bedroom to the world."[15] Ruth, in this reading, is the voice of the material world, the wall against which Jerry's dreamy nonreality beats itself.

And certain passages of the novel support this reading. When Ruth learns about Jerry and Sally's affair, for example, she finds herself fading away into oblivion, placed "in the impossible position of needing to will belief; somehow she could not quite believe in Jerry and he, feeling this inability, nurtured it, widened it, for it was the opening by which he would escape. He encouraged her illusion that there was a world into which she had never been born" (147). Here Ruth exists primarily in the imagination of her husband; she is losing her position in the real world. Worse still, he tries to turn her into Sally: "Usually on Sunday nights, stirred up, he would insist on making love, and she would accede, and fail to come, because she was not there: it was Sally under his hands. His touch fluttered over her as if conjuring her body to become another's, and that in her which was his, wifely, would try to obey. In the dark twist of this effort of obedience she would lose all orientation. Finally he would force her as one forces a hopeless piece of machinery and, sighing from the effort, would fall away pleased" (148–49). In passages like these, Ruth really is an emissary from the usual world of things, sent to destroy Jerry's fantasy world or else be destroyed by it.

But Jerry's relationship with Ruth is also built on a kind of artistic idealism, bloodless in its aestheticism: "They were students at an art school in Philadelphia, naïvely immersed in the cult of true color, of vital line. They adored the silent gods of the museum-temple that floated above the city. When they first saw each other naked, it was as if a new object of art had been displayed to each, and their marriage carried forward this quirk of detachment, having more in it of mutual admiration than mutual possession" (76). This is idealism of a different sort than that found between Jerry and Sally, but it is idealism nevertheless. Jerry's relationship with Ruth is delicate, and marriage all but spoils it: "Their merger was perhaps too easy, too aesthetic. As the art school receded, and Jerry became an unsuccessful cartoonist and then a successful animator of television commercials, and Ruth became a housewife and mother, too harassed to unpack the paintbox and load the palette, unexpected shadows deepened, emphasizing differences overlooked in the ideal overhead light they had once painted by" (77). In marriage, the real shatters the ideal—but Ruth creates a world for herself to live in just as much as Jerry and Sally do. For example, when she finds herself in danger of disappearing in the aftermath of her husband's infidelity, she seeks comfort, as we might expect her to, in the physical world: "The medium in which Ruth sank seemed to be something other than space, for the furniture continued to float on the wide pine boards, the inverted blur in the side table silently upheld the empty flower vase, and the books in the bookcase maintained against all her doubts of her own existence the certain fortress of their own, a compacted solidity more sickening than a city's, for each book was a city, if opened" (112–13). She also retreats into her memory, albeit memories of the physical world, thinking "of her parents' house in Vermont, of the pine woods, of the soft lane that was a double path of dirt between blackberry bushes, of the blackberries' scratching, of the hidden pebble that would bite her foot, of the baggy pants her father put on day after day all summer, of the pantry her mother kept there, so impeccably and thriftily stocked she and her sister never hungered, and never overate" (113). And yet she also takes comfort in the least physical of all the arts, music: "Lacking time to paint, she had lately rediscovered satisfaction in her clumsy access to Bach. The gentle liquor and her spreading hands found a green floor from which music rose in chords; her heart moved upward in the arabesque currents, and her ankles ached from pedaling" (113–14). This is an imaginative reconstruction of the world she lives in, one that makes it more hospitable to her. When Jerry returns, she refigures him as an idealized work of art behind the velvet rope of a museum: "She saw him, in this rare moment, as beautiful, a statue out of reach, not a furiously beautiful Renaissance David but a medieval Adam, naked on a tympanum, his head bent to fit the triangular space, the bones of his body expressing innocence and alarm" (114). This vision echoes Jerry and Sally's earlier feeling that they are "the original man and woman" (7) and suggests that Ruth, like her husband and his lover, is more than capable of imposing an idealist vision on the bare world of *l'être-en-soi*. Passages like these, in which Ruth re-creates the world in specifically aesthetic terms, contradict Donald Greiner's assertion that "Ruth's painter's vision, her sense of color and proportion, grants her a wider view of domestic life in America than Jerry's."[16] In fact, both husband and wife have a "painter's vision"—and both use it to create and falsify the world.

Even so, Ruth conceives of herself as the voice of hard reality over and against the voice of the imagination. She comes to this conclusion a few days after Jerry asks her for a divorce:

> She saw that he was determined to punish her if she did not [allow the divorce], and that her dignity lay with the immediate sacrifice of their marriage. Such sacrifice would be simple, bold, pure, aesthetic. . . . But she could not break through to it. In good conscience she could not. An innocent man and a greedy woman had fornicated and Ruth could not endorse the illusions that made it

> seem more than that. They were exaggerators, both of them, and
> though she could see that beauty was a province of exaggeration,
> someone must stand by truth. The truth was that Sally and Jerry
> were probably better married to Richard and her than they would be
> to each other. (143)

But Ruth, supposedly the voice of reason, has her own illusions, as indicated by her belief that Jerry and Sally's affair was between "an innocent man and a greedy woman." Sally, after all, is already rich in both money and lovers, and, as George W. Hunt points out, Jerry is not an innocent but "a moral malingerer."[17] And later, as she is driving, she sees the world through a series of classic painterly canvases: "The so-intensely green trees beside the road—she had seen them before, in a Monet, or was it a Pisarro? The bits of salmon pink along the birch trunks were Cézanne's" (158). The echo of Updike's "English Train Compartment," in which travelers interact with the world of art rather than the world of nature, is unmistakable, and indicts (or praises) Ruth as an imaginer. What is more, although Ruth criticizes Jerry for his idealism, Updike hints that she does not actually object to the ideal in principle, she merely despairs that she will ever reach it. After she gets in a car accident,

> The officer asked her how fast she had been going. She guessed
> about forty, it couldn't have been much faster than that. "Since
> thirty-five," he said, writing slowly, "is the speed limit at that curve,
> let's say you were going thirty-five."
> The elegance of this flat maneuver dazzled her. All summer she
> had been struggling with inequalities like the one between the speed
> limit and her actual speed, and this Polish prince showed her how to
> abolish them, to make the real ideal. (163)

And ultimately, when Jerry stays with her through the summer, Ruth realizes that she has become mired in a fantasy world as much as her husband has: "She had ceased to understand herself; the distinction between what she saw and what she was had ceased to be clear. As September wore thin, the heating man came and reactivated the furnace, and in the cooling nights it switched itself on and off. Lying awake, Ruth was troubled by the unaccustomed murmur, and uncertain if it were real and, if it were, whether it came from the furnace beneath her, an airplane overhead, or the transformers on the pole outside the bedroom window. Somewhere in the spaces of her life an engine was running, but where?" (185–86). Eventually, she comes to see her husband's affair as the product of her own mind, a horrible desire and nightmare nauseatingly made flesh:

> The world is composed of what we think it is; what we expect tends
> to happen; and what we expect is really what we desire. As a nega-
> tive wills a print, she had willed Sally. Why else the impatience with

which she had viewed the imperfections in Sally's beauty—the bitter crimp in one corner of her mouth, the virtual fattiness of her hips? She wanted her to be perfect, as she wanted Jerry to be decisive. Ruth disliked, religiously, the satisfaction he took in being divided, confirming thereby the split between body and soul that alone can save men from extinction. It was all too religious, phantasmal. The beast of his love had been too easily led by the motions of Ruth's mind. (186)

Ruth thus finds herself stuck, "a prisoner; the crack between her mind and the world, bridged by a thousand stitches of perception, had quite closed, leaving her embedded, as the white unicorn is a prisoner in the tapestry" (186). The division between mind and world has been smoothed over, and all is confusion.

At the same time that Ruth is diving deeper and deeper into the well of her imagination, Jerry begins to realize that his affair with Sally has existed in an unreal world. The major blow is struck during the long, unpleasant meeting between the Conants and the Mathiases. Jerry realizes that he may have been creating an image for Sally, "that perhaps only to him did she seem inhumanly kind, her face brimming with kindness, this face he had seen submerged—eyes closed, lips parted—in passion, hovering beneath his face like a reflection submerged in a pool. Having seen too much, he was as good as blind, and possibly it was they, Richard and Ruth, who saw her accurately" (226–27). And once the fantasy becomes reality, it loses much of its luster for Jerry: "Their love, their affair, had become a great awkward shape, jagged, fallen between them. Jerry was ashamed of his desire not to touch her; he wanted to explain that it was not a change in her, but a change in the world. Richard's knowing had swept through things and left them bare; the trees were stripped, the house was polished and sterile like a shop-window, the hills dangled as skeletons of stones, so that lying embraced even in the earth Jerry and Sally would be seen" (257). The gaze of the Other that so troubles Sally in Washington sees through Jerry in these passages, and given this outsider's perspective on their relationship, he can no longer quite believe in it. Once he has determined to leave Ruth, he looks at Sally and wonders, "*Is this the face I want to see?*" (269). His reaction disappoints him: "Asking it was the answer: her face pressed upon his eyes like a shield, he saw no depth of sympathy in Sally's face, no help in making this passage, only an egoistic fear, fear so intense her few faint freckles looked pricked, in her skin pulled taut by the hand clamped at the back of her head" (269). It is Sally's very physicality that threatens Jerry here; together they have invented a fantasy world in which they can be together. Now that they stand on the cusp of being together, he realizes that he cannot make her body something that it is not, at least not permanently. On his way home from the confrontation with the Matthiases, Jerry pulls the car over so he can urinate: "Beyond his awareness of the night he tried to make himself conscious, as if of the rotation of the earth, of the huge and mournful turn his life had taken. But there seemed to be only this grass, and Ruth waiting for him in the car, and his diminishing arc of relief" (231–32). As Jeff Campbell explains, Jerry "would like to feel the high tragic dimensions of his fateful love affair. He is unable to do so, however" (169), and the myth dissolves. As Jerry tells Ruth later, "As an actual wife or whatever, she stopped being an *idea*, and for the first time, I *saw* her" (284). Reality has intruded, crushing the fantasy world the lovers created for themselves—though, given the patterns in this novel and in Updike's other works, the reader should be skeptical of Jerry's claim that he now sees Sally for who and what she is.

It is tempting to suppose that Updike means to blame Jerry, Sally, and Ruth for the worlds they create for themselves, that he means to suggest that imagination is a destructive force that must be curtailed for human beings to live comfortably in the real world. But such a suggestion goes against the very heart of his aesthetic and metaphysical project. Living without imagination, as I argue in my first chapter, means losing oneself in finitude, in the blank world of *l'être-en-soi*. To be a human being is to project one's imagination on the world of mere things, even though such a projection always involves the risk of falsifying that world. *Marry Me* drives this point home in that its only character who lacks the tendency toward idealism is the cynical atheist Richard Matthias, whose missing eye serves as the physical emblem of his spiritual condition.[18] Jerry, trying to see the world through Richard's eyes, "closed one of his and looked at the room—the chairs, the women, the glasses invisibly shed a dimension. Things were just so, flat, with nothing further to be said about them; it was the world, he realized, as seen without the idea of God lending each thing a roundness of significance. It was terrible" (225). We have in *Marry Me* an indictment of Jerry as a hopeless dreamer who will never be able to escape his own idealism—but also an indictment of Richard as a man who, because he cannot bring an imaginative dimension to the world, will forever see the world as an unremarkable mass of *l'être-en-soi*. Both imagination and its lack cause serious problems; we need a synthesis, although such a synthesis never actually arrives in *Marry Me*. What we get instead is a Kierkegaardian dialectical struggle, a shifting from idealism to disenchantment and back again.

Thus, after Jerry's long disillusionment in the novel's third and fourth sections, the imagination strikes back in the strange closing chapter of the novel. Updike presents us with three different visions of Jerry's future: one in which he marries Sally and moves to Wyoming; one in which he stays with Ruth and vacations in France; and one in which he goes alone to the Caribbean. This final dream "satisfied him that there was a dimension in which he did go, as was right, at that party, or the next and stand, timid and exultant, above the downcast eyes of her gracious, sorrowing face, and say to Sally, *Marry me*" (303). The novel thus ends in imagination and idealism, just as it began.[19] Greiner suggests that, in this final illusion, "Jerry finds a visionary place that makes him happy. Here amid the color and the beauty and the light, he may detach himself from everyone, indulge his greatest fancy, and, like a character in a romance, turn to an imaginary Sally and say, 'marry me.'"[20] The failure of the Wyoming and Nice visions suggests that the sort of mutual act of the imagination that Jerry had with Sally and with Ruth necessarily falls apart, but that this man, anyway, cannot help but construct false and imaginary worlds for himself. Further, all three of these visions are vaguely dissatisfying, and the combination of them is disorienting. Judie Newman points out that the novel, and its ending, become "a hall of mirrors, flashing illusions and illusions,"[21] so that reality and imagination become hopeless blurred. All three of these endings ring false—and yet Updike privileges them all simultaneously: The first vision gives the chapter its title ("Wyoming"), the second is what actually happened when Joyce Harrington's husband forced the Updikes to go to France for a few months, and the third ends with the title of the novel. Readers are forced to choose, and when they cannot do so, they are in the same position as Jerry, the hopeless dreamer. We are grounded in fantasy, not reality, and the novel eats its own tail. Because the movement of the novel is from idealism to disenchantment to idealism, we can only assume that, whichever of these scenarios is true, the ideal world it offers will satisfy Jerry only until the material world again intrudes, and the cycle will continue unabated. The book, in refusing to allow Jerry and Sally (or Jerry and Ruth, or Jerry by himself) to live happily ever after, leaves romance behind and becomes a novel after all.

Notes

[1] Campbell, *Updike's Novels*, 163. Hereafter cited in-text.

[2] de Rougemont, *Love in the Western World*, 39.

[3] Updike, *Marry Me*, 3. Hereafter cited in-text.

[4] Greiner, *John Updike's Novels*, 190.

[5] Rickless, *Plato's Forms in Transition*, 42.

[6] Plato, *Symposium*, 211b.

[7] Plato, *Phaedo*, 78d.

[8] Ibid., 79a.

[9] Sartre, *Being and Nothingness*, 343.

[10] Ibid.

[11] Newman, *John Updike*, 96.

[12] Donne, "The Sun Rising," ll. 15–20.

[13] Begley, *Updike*, 252.

[14] Newman, *John Updike*, 98.

[15] Greiner, *John Updike's Novels*, 195.

[16] Ibid., 193.

[17] Hunt, *John Updike and the Three Great Secret Things*, 143.

[18] Perhaps not coincidentally, Richard is the character in *Marry Me* who feels the least "real," the most stylized. When he enters the novel, it suffers aesthetically.

[19] Updike himself, it must be admitted, meant for Wyoming section to be a dream, "But then the next two I meant to be real, that they really did go to France and really did go to St. Croix" (Iwamoto and Updike, "A Visit to Mr. Updike," 118). But this is not clear in the novel itself, where all three locations feel somewhat dreamlike and insubstantial.

[20] Greiner, *John Updike's Novels*, 198.

[21] Newman, *John Updike*, 108.

7: *Couples* and "The Hillies"

As I suggested several chapters ago, *Couples* in some ways rewrites and expands *Marry Me*, replicating the imaginary universe created by Jerry and Sally as an incredible act of collective imagination on the part of five suburban Boston couples. A writer's most commercially successful novel is rarely his most artistically successful, however, and Updike is no exception. *Couples* made him a household name, but it is the weakest of his novels of the 1960s and 1970s. Its moments of genuine power tend to come from smaller relationships within the larger panoply of marriages and affairs that make up the fabric of the novel. That the whole adds up to less than the sum of its parts, however, does not make those parts any less interesting, and that the novel as a whole does not succeed does not mean it is not worth the pages of ink that have been spilled over it. But I do think that *Couples* makes the most aesthetic and thematic sense when considered as a rewriting of *Marry Me*, a necessary repression of the novel that Updike wanted to write (and had already written) for the good of his marriage and family. Spreading his infidelities out over the whole of Tarbox, Massachusetts, allows him to conceal the real-world analogues of the events that inspired the novel, to the point where he could claim, incredibly, in *Time*'s famous 1968 cover story on him, that he was a mere observer of this milieu instead of an active participant in it—that he was "personally Puritan."[1]

Even so, *Couples* has clear connections to Updike's earlier fiction, and its central husband and wife—Piet and Angela Hanema—are instantly recognizable as stand-ins for John and Mary Updike. Something in Angela calls Piet to a higher lifestyle. Nine years into their marriage, "Piet still felt, with Angela, a superior power seeking through her to employ him."[2] But he resents this call to a better life. His resentment will be familiar to readers who know "Marching through Boston," published a few years before *Couples*. There, returning from a civil-rights demonstration, Joan Maple "removed underwear she had worn for seventy hours and stood there shining; to the sleepy man in the bed it seemed a visitation, and he felt as people of old must have felt when greeted by an angel—adoring yet resentful, at this flamboyant proof of better things."[3] Richard Maple is drawn to and repulsed by this call, just as Piet is drawn to and repulsed by Angela. And Piet's complaint about Angela is the same as Richard's complaint about Joan: Her goodness elevates her out of the world of mere mortals, making her essentially nonsexual, verging on noncorporeal: "His wife's languid unexpectedness, a diffident freshness born of aristocratic self-possession, still fascinated him. He thought of himself as coarse and saw her as fine, so fair and fine her every gesture seemed transparently informed by a graciousness and honesty beyond him" (4). She is indeed an angel—and is thus frigid, at least as he sees her. It is no accident that he first meets her in Nun's Bay, in view of "the great chocolate-dark rock that suggested, from a slightly other angle, a female profile and the folds of a wimple" (4). He does not immediately see this cloistered side of her, but nine years of marriage have revealed it. Angela, in Piet's view, cannot (or, probably more accurately, does not want to) accept sexuality as a method of transcendence: "Her throat, wrists, and triangular bush appeared the pivots for some undeniable effort of flight, but like Eve on a portal she crouched in shame, stone. She held rigid. Her blue irises cupped light catlike, shallowly. Her skin breathed hate" (9–10). This is an important unwillingness, because the essence of Tarbox's imaginative world is sexual. Angela is thus cut off from its wellspring, which is why she is the one to voice her concerns about the children of Tarbox—she belongs to this community, but only barely. She does not even sleep with another man until her husband essentially forces her to do so. Updike thus codes Angela's weak sex drive as a lack of imagination— this despite her noncorporeality. The proof Piet finds is that "she claimed she never dreamed. Pityingly he put his hand beneath the cotton nightie transparent to his touch and massaged the massive blandness of her warm back, hoping to stir in the depths of her sleep an eddy, a fluid fable she could tell herself and in the morning remember. She would be a valley and he a sandstorm. He would be a gentle lion bathing in her river. He could not believe she never dreamed. How could one not dream? He always dreamed" (10). Angela approaches both sex and dreams clinically rather than existentially; later in the novel, we find her reading Freud's *The Interpretation of Dreams*, approaching imagination from the outside rather than as an active participant.

Piet, on the other hand, is a man with a powerful imagination, sexual and otherwise; Donald Greiner argues, in fact, that Piet has this imagination instead of the religious faith toward which he occasionally gestures.[4] His imagination, as befits a builder, is simultaneously mathematical and artistic, as we see when he builds a hamster cage for his daughter: "The cage, completed, seemed beautiful to him, a transparent hangar shaped by laws discovered within itself, minimal, invented, Piet's own" (106). And yet Angela sees the cage as a misshapen wreck, suggesting either that his view of reality is not as accurate as he believes it to be or that she has no appreciation for the work of the imagination. He thinks back to when they first moved to Tarbox:

> They had not felt much in need of friends then. Piet, not yet consciously unhappy with Angela, had dimly dreamed of making love to

other women, to Janet or to stately gypsy-haired Terry Gallagher, as one conjures up fantasies to induce sleep. But two summers ago the Ongs built their tennis court and they saw more of Georgene; and when, a summer ago, Piet's dreams without his volition began to transpose themselves into reality, and unbeknownst to himself he had turned from Angela and become an open question, it was Georgene, in a passing touch at a party, in the apparently unplanned sharing of a car to and from tennis, who attempted an answer, who was there. She said she had been waiting for him for years. (60)

His imagination, at least in this passage, is an incredible creative force—one that seems to operate without his consent or even his knowledge. And yet it· is also an incredible destructive force because the things it brings into being undermine and eventually destroy his marriage. It is also worth noting that it is a collaborative force, that Georgene is somehow involved in turning his dreams into reality, and that she is aware that this process is taking place before he is. The same will be true of the other women he sleeps with, and of the other men they sleep with, until the imaginative fabric of Tarbox is a thatched roof, complex and criss-crossing.

Piet builds his adultery, then, on acts of the imagination, and it slides into idealism when he is with Georgene Thorne: "Suddenly she felt to be all circles, circles that could be parted to yield more circles. Birds chirped beyond the rainbow rim of the circular wet tangency holding him secure. Her hand, feathery, established another tangency, located his core" (62). Despite Updike's claim that "Piet was an Aristotelian" (114), this sexual description is consummately Platonic. Plato, after all, describes the circle as the metaphysically perfect shape, the shape of the universe.[5] When Piet sleeps with Georgene, he begins to access the higher world of Platonic metaphysics, the world of ideas, not material things. That he does so through the world of material things suggests the same sort of paradox, albeit reversed, as Angela's simultaneous lack of imagination and idealist existence. Later in the same scene, Piet sees "all things double. Without duality, entropy. The universe God's mirror" (63). In fact, Piet is much more of a Platonist than he imagines himself to be: "Piet, hammer in hand, liked to feel the bite taken into gravity. The upright weight-bearing was a thing his eye would see, and a house never looked as pretty again to him as it did in the framing, before bastard materials and bastard crafts eclipsed honest carpentry, and work was replaced by delays and finagling with subcontractors—electricians like weasels, grubby plumbers, obdurate motionless masons" (235–36). The essence of the house is in its skeleton, its blueprint—just as for Plato, the essence of a material object is its invisible form. The essence of sexuality, likewise, is in the spiritual heights it transports a person to. The burgeoning sexual revolution of 1963 thus represents an incredible breaking-free, a ticket to an ideal world. As the novel's most famous line puts it, "*Welcome . . . to the post-pill paradise*"

(63). In separating sex from its physical consequences, the couples have created a fantasy world for themselves—one that will be shattered, in part, when physical consequences reintrude on their lives.

Piet's sexual Platonism pushes him through a series of affairs, progressively idealized. His marriage to Angela dissatisfies him because she lacks both sexual imagination and physical reality. Updike explicitly compares Angela to Georgene on this front; Piet's first mistress offers him a corporeality that his wife cannot match: "Her flesh gentle in her underthings possessed a boyish boniness not like Angela's elusive abundance. Touch Angela, she vanished. Touch Georgene, she was there. This simplicity at times made their love feel incestuous to Piet, a connection too direct" (58). The meeting of their bodies allows for the meetings of their souls, an essential connection. Jeff Campbell argues that this idealization does not take place with Foxy, that Piet "simply enjoys her—and finally marries her, in direct contradiction to the [Tristan and Iseult] myth."[6] This may be true at the end of the novel, but Piet certainly idealizes Foxy in the early days of their relationship; he turns her, in fact, into even more of an ideal than Georgene. Their affair begins just before a solar eclipse, and so there is something surreal, something almost unreal, about it. Foxy's pregnancy adds to this strange quality, making "their lovemaking lunar, revolving frictionless around the planet of her womb" (289). Updike tells us that Piet's "life with Angela suffered under a languor, a numbness that Georgene had never imposed. His blood brooded on Foxy; he dwelled endlessly upon the bits of her revealed to him—her delicate pubic fleece, her high-pitched coital cries, the prolonged and tender and unhoped-for meditations of her mouth upon his phallus. He became an obsessed inward housekeeper, a secret gardener" (243). Foxy, in other words, is even more idealized than Georgene, even as Piet dwells on her physical features. He finds himself disappearing into her: "He lived dimly, groping, between those brilliant glimpses when they quickly slipped each other from their clothes and she lay down beside him, her stretched belly shining, and like a lens he opened, and like a blinded skier lost himself on the slopes of her presence" (244). The presence of this ideal makes the reality of his wife even more difficult to bear because "compared to these shifting and luminous transparencies, Angela was a lump, a barrier, a boarded door" (247). Once again his adulterous imagination threatens his marriage. Foxy—or, more accurately, the world they are creating for themselves—makes him want out: "He was so full of Foxy, so pregnant with her body and body scents and her cries and remorses and retreats and fragrant returnings, so full of their love, that his mind felt like thin ice" (247). Angela becomes less and less real to him: "She seemed to Piet to be growing ever more beautiful, to be receding from him into abstract realms of beauty" (260). His idealization of his mistress makes the rest of the world unreal by comparison, and in the flashes where Piet recognizes this transference, the tone of Updike's prose becomes nearly apocalyptic: "Stepping outdoors onto treeless Hope Street, Piet was struck by the summer light so hard that his eyes winced and the world looked liquid. It was all, he saw, television aerials and curbstone grits, abortive—friendships, marriages, conversations, all aborted, all blasted by seeking the light too soon" (267–68). The sun, as in the opening chapter of *Marry Me*, simultaneously symbolizes the beauty of the imagination and its destructive force. The community destroys itself by inventing a world to live in, a world in which marriage is thin and airy and sexuality has no consequences other than pleasure.

And, as I have suggested, the fantasy world of Tarbox is a group effort. Although not every member of the community shares Piet's idealizing tendencies and adulterous imagination, many of them do. The Smiths and the Applebys, for example, are the first couple to swap partners—the rest of the town half-mockingly calls them the Applesmiths—and Updike describes their various couplings using the language of idealism. From Harold Smith, for example, we get a pretty clear picture of the role of the imagination in bridging the subject/object divide: "Harold believed that beauty was what happened between people, was in a sense the trace of what had happened, so he in truth found [Janet Appleby], though minutely creased and puckered and sagging, more beautiful than the unused girl whose ruins she thought of herself as inhabiting" (167). Harold recognizes, in other words, that *l'être-pour-soi* plays a major role in constructing the world that it encounters; he sees that Janet's beauty is a mutual projection of their two imaginations. In Frank Appleby, on the other hand, we see an idealism through which the subject negates the object. While Harold Smith makes love to Janet, "for Frank, a space away, Marcia was transparent, gliding, elusive, one with the shadows of the room; he enlarged, enlarged until she vanished quite and the darkness was solid with himself, then receded, admitting her silvery breathless voice saying lightly, 'How lovely. Oh. Fuck. How lovely. Fuck. Fuck" (184). Updike's language here suggests his essay on "Whitman's Egotheism," examined more fully in chapter 3. Frank, like Peter and Joey before him, projects a world for himself to inhabit; at first, it seems that the act will destroy or at least minimize his lover, but at the last second she is admitted into this world, too, and perhaps even helps him to create it. Janet Appleby is less fortunate. Her imagination has been tempered and controlled by the media to which she has been exposed since childhood: "All her informal education, from Disney's *Snow White* to last week's *Life*, had taught her to place the highest value on love. Nothing but a kiss undid the wicked apple. We move from birth to death amid a crowd of others and the name of the parade is love. However unideal it was, she dreaded being left behind. Hence she could not stop flirting, could not stop reaching out, though something distrustful within her, a bitterness like a residue from her father's medicinal factory, had to be circumvented by each motion of her heart" (190). Janet is thus akin to Don Quixote—except that Quixote creates himself in the model of the romance books he reads, whereas Janet is created by the movies and magazines with which she fills her time. Blinded by them, she cannot help but follow deeper into the fantasy world inhabited by her husband and their lovers.

Other residents of Tarbox resemble Angela in lacking imagination. For example, Foxy Whitman's complaints about her husband, Ken, double Piet's about Angela. As they drive home from a party one night, "She saw that moonlight lived on the water, silver, steady, sliding with the motion of their car, yet holding furious myriad oscillations, like, she supposed, matter itself" (38). Ken is a biochemist, and so he "worked down there, where the protons swung from molecule to molecule and elements interlocked in long spiral ladders" (38). He tells her a moment later that "that's what we all are. Chemicals" (39). In his steadfast materialism, he is the novel's corollary to Richard Matthias—in a narrative as well as a philosophical sense, since he, like Richard, is the husband of the protagonist's lover—and he is ultimately a creature of logic, not imagination. When Foxy's parents demanded that she end her relationship with the Jewish painter to whom she lost her virginity before the action of the novel, she clings to Ken for the contrast: "Ken appeared, was taller than she, wanted her, was acceptable and was accepted on all sides; similarly, nagging mathematical problems abruptly crack open" (40). He is more a mechanical being than an imaginative human being: "From Farmington, he was the only son of a Hartford lawyer who never lost a case. Foxy came to imagine his birth as cool and painless, without a tear or outcry. Nothing puzzled him. There were unknowns but no mysteries" (40). This includes her; as she explains to her mother, "It's just so devastating, to have a husband whose job is to probe the secrets of life, and to feel yourself dying beside him, and he doesn't know it or seem to care. . . . He cares about his equipment and I'm part of it" (341). Ken cannot understand the world of passion and imagination that his wife and neighbors live in—and we are not supposed to admire him for it any more than we are supposed to admire Richard Matthias. His materialism, as it turns out, cannot explain a number of important human concepts. He thinks, for example, about an elderly colleague of his: "The old man was unmarried. In his youth there had been a scandal, a wife who had left him; Ken doubted the story, for how could any woman leave so good a man? . . . Prichard's virtues might be a product of being left, a metabolic reduction necessary to growth, a fruitful fractionation. Inspiration died: he looked within himself and encountered a surface bafflingly smooth" (118). Materialism has no satisfactory answer for the question of virtue, nor for the question of suffering. It cannot even really provide Ken with an answer for the question of who he is. In this, he resembles Kierkegaard's systematic philosopher

whose system explains everything but himself.[7] On the other hand, Piet
and Foxy are able to understand both virtue (the guilt they feel over their
affair is part of what appeals to them about it) and suffering (which drives
them to the Christian faith they both profess)—even if their understanding is an imaginative projection onto the world of *l'être-en-soi*.

Ken and Angela notwithstanding, the clouds of imagination rest
pretty strongly on the entire community. In the novel's first scene, Angela
reports a conversation she's just had with Freddy Thorne, the couples'
ringleader and Georgene's husband. "He thinks we're a circle," she
explains. "A magic circle of heads to keep the night out. He told me he
gets frightened if he doesn't see us over a weekend. He thinks we've made
a church of each other" (7). This is one of the first things Foxy notices
about the Tarbox couples:

> She was to experience this sadness many times, this chronic sadness
> of late Sunday afternoon, when the couples had exhausted their
> game, basketball or beachgoing or tennis or touch football, and saw
> an evening weighing upon them, an evening without a game, an eve-
> ning spent among flickering lamps and cranky children and leftover
> food and the nagging half-read newspaper with its weary portents
> and atrocities, an evening when marriages closed in upon themselves
> like flowers from which the sun is withdrawn, an evening giving like
> a smeared window on Monday and the long week when they must
> perform again their impersonations of working men, of stockbrokers
> and dentists and engineers, of mothers and housekeepers, of adults
> who are not the world's guests but its hosts. (89)

This passage describes the intrusion of reality on the world of the imagination that the couples have created for themselves and for one another.
The intruding reality described here is, in fact, the real world, the world
of children and marriage and news, and it threatens to destroy the world
of games, irresponsibility, and consequence-free sex in which the couples
attempt to live.

Updike makes this point more strongly through the novel's frequent references to world events, events that seem a universe away
from the cloistered actions of the couples. For example, when describing the *ménage à quatre* of the Applesmiths, Updike writes: "This pattern, of quarrel and reunion, of revulsion and surrender, was repeated
three or four times that winter, while airplanes collided in Turkey, and
coups transpired in Iraq and Togo, and earthquakes in Libya, and a
stampede in the Canary Islands, and in Ecuador a chapel collapsed,
killing a hundred twenty girls and nuns. Janet had taken to reading
the newspaper, as if this smudgy peek into other lives might show her
the way out of her own" (195). The image recurs when Piet begins
his affair with Foxy: "Television brought them the outer world. The

little screen's icy brilliance implied a universe of profound cold beyond the warm encirclement of Tarbox, friends, and family. Mirrors established in New York and Los Angeles observed the uninhabited surface between them and beamed reports that bathed the children's faces in a poisonous, flickering blue. This poison was their national life. Not since Korea had Piet cared about news. News happened to other people" (259). For much of the novel, however, the collective imagination of the community is too strong, and the affairs and games continue unabated. The tragedy is that the couples' children belong to the world of outside reality, which they steadily tune out: "Desultory parties, hardly organized, social weeds, sprang up to fill the pale nights bloated by Daylight Saving, parties mixed of tennis leftovers and sunburned half-couples and cold salami and fetched pizza and Bitter Lemon and sandy stray forgotten children lulled asleep by television's blue flicker" (207). Earlier in the novel, Piet's older daughter, Ruth, calls him from dream to reality: "Ruth, standing beside the bed with almost a woman's bulk, was crying and by speaking woke him from a dream in which a tall averted woman in white was waiting for him at the end of a curved corridor" (91). Here she—and in particular her suffering, because the children's hamster has been killed—belongs to the outside world that interrupts his ideal world of chivalry and mystery. We do not get much clue as to how this affects the children of Tarbox, at least not in *Couples* itself. Updike shows the chickens coming home to roost in "The Hillies," which I analyze below.

As the novel continues, cracks begin to undermine the foundation of the couples' world. Updike tells us that "one of their unspoken rules was that professions were not criticized; one's job was a pact with the meaningless world beyond the ring of couples" (282). And yet when Ben Saltz loses his job, we discover that this unreal connection to the outside world is absolutely necessary to maintain one's position within the ring. Angela notes the change in his wife's appearance: "She looked ghastly. Ravished. All of a sudden, you know how pretty she's been looking this summer, she was a weighed-down Jewish middle-aged woman" (296). The outside world is making itself known in Irene Saltz's countenance, and the result is that the Saltzes are cut off from the incestuous and solipsistic world of the couples: "Piet wanted to approach Ben, to express fellow-feeling, but he dreaded the man as he dreaded the mortally diseased. His own life felt too precarious to be drawn into proximity with a life that had truly broken through" (308). And he is not alone in this feeling; the Saltzes are quietly cast out of the community. Even so, Ben seems to have been set free by his "breaking through"; Piet gets the impression that he "had touched bottom and found himself at rest, safe" (309). He has dropped out of the fantasy world of Tarbox and into the more sturdy outside world. The Saltzes end up moving out of Tarbox.

But the ultimate intrusion of the outside world is the assassination of John F. Kennedy, which Foxy learns about as she is anesthetized while Freddy Thorne is filling her cavities. The moment before the announcement comes across the radio, she is deep in numbness. The announcement sends Freddy's nurse into hysterical grief, and though Foxy's response is more measured, it reveals the gulf between life as the Tarbox couples live it and the life outside the community: "She tried to picture the dead man, this young man almost of her generation, with whom she could have slept. A distant husband had died and his death left less an emptiness than revealed one already there. Where grief should have dwelt there was a reflex tenderness, a personal cringing" (356). For his part, Freddy can only think that this enormous national tragedy "fucks up our party" (355). When Foxy tells him to cancel, he whines, "But I've bought all the *booze*" (355). He resists the intrusion of the outside world, and so do the rest of the couples, for the party goes on as scheduled. The assassination drives the couples even further together, though this time their ideal circle admits the news and the children, the novel's dual representatives of a world beyond their imaginations: "The three days of omnipresent mourning had passed for these couples of Tarbox as three tranced holidays each alike in pattern. The men each afternoon had played touch football on the field behind the Applebys', by Joy Creek, while the women and children stayed indoors watching television in the library. During dull stretches of the Washington ceremonies or the Dallas postmortems . . . some of the women would come outdoors and arrange themselves in Frank's hay and watch their men race red-faced up and down the hummocky field, shouting for the ball" (386–87). These days, too, have the aura of a dream: "The space in the cars as they drove home was stuffy with unasked questions, with the unsayable trouble of a king's murder, a queasy earthquake for little children, a funny stomach-gnawing only sleep eased" (387). The end of the holidays is not a return to the "real world," though—instead, it is a leave-taking from the children and their constant questions about the assassination. Hence, "school and Tuesday came as a relief" (387); the adults are once more free to take neither their children nor national affairs particularly seriously.

When Piet visits Foxy at home that day, "he embraced and held her as if there were no baby, as if there were no one alive in this sunken barren world but themselves" (388). They create a fantasy within a fantasy. As Foxy puts it, "You're the only thing real I have. Ken is unreal. This marsh is unreal. I'm unreal to myself" (391). Even so, Piet feels the fantasy fading away: "They had been let into God's playroom, and been happy together on the floor all afternoon, but the time had come to return the toys to their boxes, and put the chairs back against the wall" (391). Piet, as Updike's stand-in, feels more strongly than the other men in the novel the fantasy world of the couples slipping away and the outside world making itself known. As his affair with Foxy begins to wind down, "The summer seemed dreamlike and distant. She had vanished—the slam of a car door after church. He missed the thrift of a double life, the defiant conversation. Faithful, he was going to waste. Attenuated hours spread lifeless around him" (343). As the outside world beckons, his imagination recedes—and since it has nowhere to go other than adultery, it threatens to disappear altogether. It is with this sense of desperation that he begins an affair with Bea Guerin, and his idealizing tendency turns ugly. This woman, already pathetic to her friends and neighbors, brings out something horrible in Piet, who hits her midcoitus:

> She had been above him on all fours, a nursing mammal, her breasts pendulous, with a tulip sheen, and as if to mark an exclamatory limit to happiness he had cuffed her buttocks, her flaccid sides, and, rolling her beneath him, had slapped her face hard enough to leave a blotch. Seeing her eyes incredulous, he had slapped her again, to banish all doubt and establish them firmly on this new frontier. Already he had exploited her passivity in all positions; the slap distracted his penis and he felt he had found a method to prolong the length of time, never long enough, that he could inhabit a woman. (406)

When she tells him that her husband also hits her, he is casually cruel in his response: "You invite it. You're a lovely white hole to pour everything into. Jizz, fists, spit" (406–7). This is the ugliest side of the creative male lust that we see throughout Updike's fiction—if the woman exists as a lump of clay to be formed by the male imagination, then violence may be just the thing to do it. Piet is aroused, finding that "in abusing her he had strengthened the basis of his love, given his heart leverage to leap. He loved any woman he lay with, that was his strength, his appeal; but with each woman his heart was more intimidated by the counterthrust of time. Now, with Bea, he had made a ledge of guilt and hurled himself secure into the tranquil pool of her body and bed" (407). He still manages to rise above the material world; his orgasm is "an ebbing of light above the snow-shrouded roofs" (407). But Updike has shown that idealism can be violent and dehumanizing. Before, the imagination was something misleading and potentially destructive; here the potential has become reality.

Updike's ultimate point in *Couples* is that the fantasy world inhabited by the couples is in reality a failure of their imagination—a misdirection of a beneficial human faculty rather than a surplus of it. The only genuine artistic product any of them can produce is the community itself. Their other attempts at imaginative work resemble Carol Constantine's paintings, "humorless mediocre canvases, coarse in their coloring, modishly broad in their brushwork, showing her children on chairs, the Tarbox wharf and boatyard, Eddie in a turtleneck shirt, the graceless back view of the Congregational Church, houses, and trees seen from her studio windows and made garish, unreal, petulant. Cézanne and John Marin, Utrillo, and Ben Shahn—her styles muddled theirs, and Piet thought how provincial, how mediocre and lost we all are" (281–82). Their imaginations, as the subjects of these paintings suggest, are too stuck on one another to create anything genuinely beautiful or meaningful. Piet, too, lacks a genuine artistic faculty, as Carol points out: "Why do you build such ugly houses? You're clever enough, you wouldn't have to" (282). Even Freddy Thorne's erotic drama can't get beyond a juvenile *dramatis personae*. Art and architecture and literature are perhaps the natural channels for the human imagination, but the Tarbox couples cannot actually create anything. Instead, they create one another. Terry Gallagher, who does not participate in their mass infidelities, is a talented musician, as if her talent and her chastity were one and the same.

The failure of the "post-pill paradise," Piet's impregnation of Foxy Whitman, ultimately breaks the community apart, ending Tarbox's alternate reality once and for all. Though Freddy Thorne procures an illegal abortion for Foxy, Ken is furious when he finds out and convenes a late-night meeting between the Whitmans and the Hanemas. He announces that he will divorce Foxy and points out the destructive power of the Tarbox imagination: "In less than a year you, you and this sick town, have torn apart everything my wife and I had put together in seven years. Behind all this playfulness you *like* to destroy. You love it" (488). As his relationship with Angela collapses, Piet has a moment of clarity akin to Jerry Conant's near the end of *Marry Me*. Jerry recognizes that he has been wrong about Sally—but in *Marry Me* the imaginative world is the product of these two lovers. In *Couples* it is the product of the community itself, and so Piet's disenchantment is with the ringleader of that community. He has "been redeemed from Freddy Thorne's spell; the old loathing and fascination were gone. Freddy's atheism, his evangelical humanism, no longer threatened Piet; the dentist materialized in the drizzle as a plump fuzzy-minded man with a squint and an old woman's sly mouth" (494–95). When Angela leaves him, he loses imagination entirely—"Perhaps because each night he dosed himself with much gin, his dreams now were rarely memorable—clouded repetitive images of confusion and ill-fittingness, of building something that would not stay joined or erect" (522)—even as Angela, set free from her husband, develops her own: "The strangest nicest thing. I've begun to have dreams. Dreams I can remember. It hasn't happened to me for years" (515). When Foxy visits him in his sad bachelor's apartment, their lovemaking lacks the idealist quality that once typified it: "As he felt himself under the balm of love grow boyish and wanton, she aged; his first impression of her smoothness and translucence was replaced by the goosebumped roughness of her buttocks, the gray unpleasantness of her shaved armpits, the backs of her knees, the thickness of her waist since she had had the baby" (527). As Jeff Campbell points out, whereas "Jerry [Conant] maintains something of his idealism, . . . Piet loses his as he actually gets the woman he sought."[8] I would add that part of his loss springs from his moving beyond the set of couples: Because he has been ejected from the Tarbox community, he is no longer capable of the powerful acts of the imagination that he once was. The novel ends with his marrying Foxy and moving closer to Boston, where he works "as a construction inspector for federal jobs, mostly military barracks . . . Piet likes the official order and the regular hours" (557). This seems to be the opposite of his former degenerate life in Tarbox—and yet Updike concludes by telling us that "the Hanemas live in Lexington, where, gradually, among people like themselves, they have been accepted, as another couple" (557). The ending of *Couples*, then, is, like that of *Marry Me*, cyclical. The novel begins with Ken and Foxy's moving to Tarbox and becoming integrated in the community, and it ends with Piet and Foxy's moving to Lexington and becoming integrated.[9] Updike provides us with no information about this community other than that it is composed of "people like themselves"— but what does this mean? David Heddendorf suggests that the last sentence of the novel "brings to a close the Tarbox era of adulterous fun. As 'another couple' Piet and Foxy can circulate among new friends, no longer a problem and potential scandal,"[10] and this is certainly a valid reading of the phrase. But Updike's phrasing is ambiguous, and may also suggest that Piet and Foxy's new friends are, like them, inveterate idealists, in which case the events of the novel will broadly repeat themselves. That this possibility is open, perhaps even likely, suggests, like the ending of *Marry Me*, that the human imagination is in some sense unkillable— life-giving, but always dangerous.

I argued at the beginning of this section that the misdirected imaginations of the adults in Updike's fiction of this period cause real havoc in the lives of their children. Take Sally Matthias's son Peter: "in the last few months he had learned to dress himself, all except for the buttons, and she had hardly found it in her scattered wits to praise him. Poor child, he had been standing there fore ten minutes waiting for his mother to get through talking [on the phone to Jerry]; waiting and listening, waiting and watching with that wary simmering expression on his face" (*Marry Me*, 14). The source of her neglect is not a mystery; Updike tells us that Jerry "had robbed her of all joy in her children" (15). Instead, Jerry presents himself and Sally as each other's replacement children. "*Do you remember*," he thinks, "*how, in our first room, on the second night, I gave you a bath and scrubbed your face and hands and long arms with the same methodical motions I used on my children?*" (33). Their affair is thus an Augustinian misdirection of affection that reverses their development and turns them back into infants: "*I became your child. With a drenched blinding cloth that searched out even the hollows of my ears, you, my mother, my slave, dissolved me in tender abrasions"* (34). The sort of imaginative affair embarked on by Jerry and Sally makes adulthood nearly impossible. And if adulthood becomes impossible, the children who are entrusted to adults will suffer. As such, abandoned and abused children show up at a few key places in the novel. As she calls Jerry from the Washington airport, Sally "saw a Puerto Rican child Peter's age standing apparently abandoned on the waxed floor outside the phone booth" (25). Likewise, Jerry's son Geoffrey breaks his collarbone while Jerry and Sally are in Washington, and when Jerry returns, he hits his son on the head for saying grace at the wrong time. And yet it is his children that keep Jerry from leaving his family; when Ruth tells Charlie that Jerry wants to live with Sally instead of them, Charlie loses control of his emotions, and Jerry calls it off. As such, children belong to the outside world that crushes the fantasies of the lovers—after they have already been damaged by those fantasies.

Couples, too, is full of examples of the suffering of children. It is generally not dramatic, but it is insistent. For example, Georgene tells her lover, Piet, that her son "had a fever yesterday but I sent him off to school in case you decided to come" (60). And Piet's attempts at comforting his daughters after the death of Ruth's hamster backfire spectacularly: "Nancy at nursery school had burst out crying because of the hamster. The child suddenly saw with visionary certainty that its death had been her fault. *Daddy said*, she said. Her hysterics had been uncontrollable" (113). Piet is unnervingly cold in his response: "The kid sure knows how to get herself sympathy" (113). He has no genuine interest in her suffering, no real compassion. Later, when the Smiths and the Applebys prepare to swap spouses, they have "to rearrange the children. Catharine Appleby, her heavy flushed head lolling, was moved into bed with dainty six-year-old Julia Smith; and the door to Jonathan's room . . . was closed, so no noise from the master bedroom would wake him" (194). The children are little more than an impediment to their parents' desires. More often than not, they are not even mentioned in the novel because their parents do not think of them terribly often; when we do hear about them, they tend to be at home with a faceless babysitter. The misdirected imaginations of their parents have left them abandoned in a world of assassinations and war.

But there is no direct judgment of the adults in *Marry Me* or *Couples* for their neglect and abuse of their children. Updike's rebuke comes in the short story "The Hillies" (1969), a sequel of sorts to *Couples*. The town of Tarbox, the narrator explains, "was founded, in 1634, on the way north from Plymouth, by men fearful of attack. They build their fortified meetinghouse on a rock outcropping commanding a defensive view of the river valley, where a flotilla of canoes might materialize and where commerce and industry, when they peaceably came, settled of their own gravity."[11] It has thus always been an insular community, and in *Couples* we have seen that insularity as an act of collective delusion. The community, which begins to fall at the end of *Couples*, has fully collapsed by the time of "The Hillies"—but not as a result of an invasion from outside, "For lately these leaden, eerily veined rocks and triangular patches of parched grass *have* been settled, by flocks of young people; they sit and lie here overlooking downtown Tarbox as if the spectacle is as fascinating as Dante's rose. Dawn finds them already in position, and midnight merely intensifies the murmur of their conversation, marred by screams and smashed bottles" (19). The invasion, then, comes from within. The "hillies," as they are called by the adult residents of Tarbox, "are less exotic than hippies. Many are the offspring of prominent citizens; the son of the bank president is one, and the daughter of the meatmarket man is another" (19). The presence of the hillies has made Tarbox feel alien and threatening to its adult residents because "even children one recognizes from the sidewalk days when they peddled lemonade or pedalled a tricycle stare now from the rocks with the hostile strangeness of marauders" (19–20). Updike notes, however, that "some of these effects—of intense embarrassment, of menace—may be 'read into' the faces of the hillies" (20) by their parents, who are guilty of the original sin of insularity.

In some ways, the hillies are true representatives of the town. After all, "they claim they want only to be left alone" (20), which is certainly in keeping with the founding spirit of Tarbox. In the story's final paragraph, Updike suggests that "the hillies are slowly withdrawing upward, and clustering around the beeries, and accepting them as leaders. They are getting ready for our attack" (25)—but the attack is the adults', not the teenagers'. And because the invasion is not an invasion, because it is closer to a *coup de ville*, the adults cannot quite figure out what to do about it. One resident suggests that they be sent back to where they come from, "but this ancient formula, so often invoked in our history, no longer applies. They came from our own homes. And in honesty do we want them back? How much a rural myth is parental love? The Prodigal Son no doubt became a useful overseer; they needed his hands. We need our self-respect. That is what is eroding on the hill—the foundations of our lives, the identities our industry and acquisitiveness have heaped up beneath the flag's blessing" (24). What is more, the adults do not understand the cause of this peaceful revolution: "The town discovers itself scorned by a mystery beyond drugs, by an implacable 'no' spoken between its two traditional centers" (21). We have encountered this "implacable 'no'" before, in the taste of metal that keeps Richard Maple from living purely in his own fantasy world. What has happened in "The Hillies" is that the children who were neglected in 1963 have become young adults and are forcibly putting an end to their parents' insular imaginative universe. The final irony, however, is that the hillies are also metaphysical idealists—particularly the hillies who take hard drugs: "It is these pillies, stretching bemused between the Spanish-American War memorial urns, who could tell us, if we wished to know, how the trashy façades of Poirier's Liquor Mart and Leonard's Pharmaceutical Store appear when deep-dyed by LSD and ballooned by the Eternal" (22). Like Joey Robinson, in attempting to break away from the mythical world created by their parents, the hillies have merely reproduced that world in another form. The cycle continues.

Notes

[1] Reston, "John Updike Works Three Hours," 20.

[2] Updike, *Couples*, 4. Hereafter cited in-text.

[3] Updike, "Marching through Boston," 223.

[4] Greiner, *John Updike's Novels*, 147.

[5] Plato, *Timaeus*, 33c–34c.

[6] Campbell, *Updike's Novels*, 182.

[7] Kierkegaard, *Concluding Unscientific Postscript*, 122.

[8] Campbell, *Updike's Novels*, 177.

[9] Greiner points out another cycle: "Politically active younger couples move into the void caused by the collapse of the post-pill Eden, and the tenor of Tarbox takes another turn" (*John Updike's Novels*, 159).

[10] Heddendorf, "The Modesty of John Updike," 329.

[11] Updike, "The Hillies," 18. Hereafter cited in-text.

Part III. Imaginative Lust in the *Scarlet Letter* Trilogy

8: "The Football Factory," "Toward Evening," "Incest," "Still Life," "Lifeguard," "Bech Swings?" and "Three Illuminations in the Life of an American Author"

IN HIS INTRODUCTION TO Bruno Schulz's *Sanitorium under the Sign of the Hourglass*, Updike muses: "From the mother, perhaps, men derive their sense of their bodies; from the father, their sense of the world."[1] His language here places him in a masculine idealist tradition dating back to Descartes, who famously splits the human experience into body and mind. In Descartes, as Susan Bordo notes, "The spiritual and the corporeal are now two distinct substances which share no qualities (other than being created), permit of interaction but no merging, and are each defined precisely in opposition to the other."[2] The body becomes *res extensa*, and the mind *res cogitans*; thus Descartes is able to formulate "complete intellectual independence from the body, *res extensa* of the human being and chief impediment to human objectivity" (355). And at the same time, he separates the intellectual world from the natural world, privileging the former over the latter. Bordo argues that Descartes implicitly and explicitly codes the marginal terms in his dichotomy—body, nature, subjectivity—as feminine, and thus his metaphysical project "appears, not merely as the articulation of a positive new epistemological ideal, but as a reaction-formation to the loss of 'being-one-with-the-world' brought about by the disintegration of the organic, centered, female cosmos of the Middle Ages and Renaissance. The Cartesian reconstruction of the world is a 'fort-da' game—a defiant gesture of independence from the female cosmos, a gesture which is at the same time compensation for a profound loss" (359). Updike, it must be said, does not go as far as Descartes on this front; his existentialist orientation prevents him from praising Cartesian objectivity as an ideal, let alone as an attainable position—and, after all, in his introduction to Schulz he associates masculinity not with the intellect but with the world. And yet he still continues Descartes's project, both in this essay and in much of his fiction, in which male lust is presented as a powerful imaginative force, *l'être-pour-soi* that performs its operations upon the inert *l'être-en-soi* of the female body.

This process is clearly at play in the somewhat obscure short story "The Football Factory" (1989), in which an unnamed upper-class dignitary visits the titular factory. He is lost in its machinations, realizing only after being told "that the hopeless-looking assemblages of leather were inside-out footballs. Amid the many, impressive, implacable machines he had lost sight of basic objectives."[3] The problem is that he has devoted himself to the life of the mind and lost sight of the physical world: "His whole adult life had been spent in the realm of the immaterial—speaking, thinking, performing, conferring, making impression on men's minds. His childhood acquaintance with matter and its earthly principles had been perfunctory and not pleasant enough to prolong. He had yearned for a life free of dirt and calluses, and his success was measured by how much time he now spent in airplanes. Only in airplanes, above the clouds, going somewhere at someone else's expense, did he feel fully himself—impervious, clean, transient, a lord of thin air" (19). His freedom comes in an utter separation from the material world and the blue-collar labor that immerses itself in it.

He attempts to bridge the gap by imagining a relationship with a beautiful female factory worker: "In his mind he bent down and asked her to marry him. She looked up, her blue eyes a bit faded and dull and cautious, and, with less surprise and gratitude than he had expected, consented" (21). What follows is a lengthy imagining of their life together, one in which she provides him with a connection to the material world that he feels he has lost sight of: "She returned to the factory after their honeymoon on a charter flight to Las Vegas, and he loved the way she would bring home on her body every evening the smells not only of sweat and cigarettes and coffee and machine oil but raw leather" (22). In this marriage, the woman provides the material body, the man provides the immaterial mind.

"The Football Factory," however, immerses itself much less in lust than Updike's other explorations of the topic. The early story "Toward Evening" (1956), in this sense, sets the terms for much of the later fiction. Its protagonist, Rafe,[4] is an inordinately lusty man traveling home through New York City to his young wife and infant child. Updike gives his lust the force of an artist's imagination. It creates the world he finds himself in, or at least it gives that world its essence. Over the course of the story, he lusts after a series of women on a city bus, and in so doing, he seems to create them, to give them their existence. It begins with a woman with, as he sees it, "a fine face, lucid brow. The kind of mouth you felt spoke French. . . . The indentation in the center of the upper lip—the romantic dimple, Rafe's mother had called it, claiming, in the joking, sentimental way she had assumed to raise a child, that in its depth the extent of sexual vigor could be read—was narrow and incisive."[5] As it turns out, at least one of these imaginings is true; she is reading from a French-language copy of

Proust. The dreamlike tone of the story suggests that Rafe's imaginative work may have actually made this happen; certainly the reader does not get the feeling that Rafe, Sherlock Holmes-style, has observed details carefully and then induced a conclusion. However, his lustful imagination turns sinister in the next section, in which Rafe turns his gaze toward a young black woman, whom he gazes at even more intently: "because his imaginings concerning himself and the girl were so plainly fantastic, he could indulge them without limit" (65). Alas, however, the limit asserts itself, and by the time Rafe's gaze strays from this woman, he has become a cold consumer. By the time he gets off the bus, "the Negress had dwindled to the thought that he had never seen gloves like that before" (65). His lustful imagination has nearly winked this young woman out of existence, and so a pattern emerges: He will amuse himself by creating an ideal sexual object out of a flesh-and-blood woman—then, when the amusement wears off, he will allow her to recede into nonexistence.

In fact, Rafe never really leaves his mind for the rest of the story. After dinner, "A curious illusion was unexpectedly created: his wife, irritated because he had failed to answer some question of hers . . . dropped a triangular piece of bread from her fingers, and the bread, falling to her lap through a width of light, twirled and made a star" (67). These intrusions from his wife are not only utterly uninteresting to him but they also disenchant his imaginary world, which must be re-created with the bread and the light. The story ends with Alice's having faded out of existence, like the two women on the bus, while Rafe invents an elaborate back story for a neon sign outside their window. In the final paragraph, the nihilism of Rafe's imagination is revealed: "The black of the river was as wide as that of the sky. Reflections sunk in it existed dimly, minutely wrinkled, below the surface. The Spry sign occupied the night with no company beyond the also uncreated but illegible stars" (68). We have ended with the limits of the human imagination, and though Adam Begley suggests that this nihilism "conjures . . . the possibility of divine knowledge" because a religious writer like Updike "is bound to read in the 'illegible' stars the possibility of a divine plan,"[6] such an epiphany never arrives in the story, and Rafe's lustful imagination is figured as a force that nihilates everything it attempts to re-create, ending with itself.

In "Incest" (1957), the male imagination becomes surreal, and vaguely threatening. Its protagonist, Lee, has had an erotic dream about a woman other than his wife, and the dream—the product of his imagination—becomes more powerful, more real, than the flesh-and-blood woman standing before him. As he tells her about the dream, he leaves out the incriminating details, feeling that in doing so he is protecting his wife. But the details he omits are "sensations momentarily more vivid in the nerves of his fingers than the immediate texture of the bamboo chair he occupied."[7] Dream thus becomes, in some sense, reality; in imagining these things, and in struggling not to recount them, Lee gives them physical being. This sort of imagination is always irresponsible; as Lee puts it, "I can't be held accountable for the people I meet in dreams. I don't invite them" (146). But there is another, more conscious, form of imagination in the story. Lee creates, or re-creates, his wife using his mind: "As she sat there, studious, he circumscribed her, every detail, with the tidal thought *Mine, mine*" (160). Eventually, in the strange logic of his waking dream-world, his infant daughter—his co-creation—becomes an object for his lust: "His sense of her sullenness may have been nothing but his anxiety to win her approval, reflected; though her features were hard to make out, the emotion he bore her was precise: the coppery, gratified, somewhat adrift feeling he would get when physically near girls he admired in high school" (162). Lee is vaguely sexually excited by his daughter because his imagination can, at least in the context of the story, express itself only through lust, only through the creation or re-creation of a female body. So accustomed is he to the connection between lust, vision, and imagination that he can scarcely conceive of one without the others.

"Still Life" (1959) furthers this relationship, adding to it both the aesthetic world Updike encountered in his year at the Ruskin School of Painting and a refutation and simultaneous reification of philosophical idealism. Leonard studies at the Constable School, in Oxford, and he is forced there to create mimetic art—copies from real life. This brings Updike to a certain sniffing Platonism early in the story: "For freshman at the Constable School were to start off banished from the school itself, with its bright chatter and gay smocks, and sent into these sad galleries to 'draw from the antique.'"[8] The echo is of Plato's famous condemnation of art, in Book 10 of *The Republic*. In Plato's metaphysics, the highest form of reality belongs to the ideal forms of the objects we encounter in the material world. These objects are thus mere copies from a higher reality. Art is a further step removed from reality; it is "far removed from the truth, for it touches only a small part of each thing and a part that is itself only an image."[9] Art, in other words, is a copy of a copy, and each time reality is copied, some of its reality is lost. Updike extends the metaphor; the students at the Constable School are mere copiers—but they are copying copies of earlier, more famous statues (which are, in the Platonic view, already copies of a copy). Updike has thrown us into a mimetic *mise-en-abîme*. And yet the process still has a certain power. When Seabright, his professor, tells Leonard to join Robin—the story's female protagonist—in drawing Venus, he says that "at least there you do get some echoes of the Greek grace" (32–33). The mimetic practice has thus at least the potential to impart grace, however much Plato would have denied it. After all, Plato suggests that our focusing on the material world (and mimetic images of it) strands us in a lower level of reality, where we are encouraged to mistake shadows for the truth. This is the point of the famous allegory of the cave:

> Imagine human beings living in an underground, cavelike dwelling, with an entrance a long way up, which is both open to the light and as wide as the cave itself. They've been there since childhood, fixed in the same place, with their legs and necks fettered, able to see only in front of them, because their bonds prevent them from turning their heads around. Light is provided by a fire burning far above and behind them. Also behind them, but on higher ground, there is a path stretching between them and the fire. Imagine that along this path a low wall has been built, like the screen in front of puppeteers above which they show their puppets.[10]

This is the ordinary human condition, as Plato sees it. Because our only experience has been of a material world that merely copies a higher reality, we cannot imagine a reality beyond that material world. We live in a cave that blocks our view of what is most real. Updike invokes this cave in his description of the room in which the Constable students paint their still lifes: "The Constable School could not afford to waste its precious space on still lifes, and imposed upon the museum's good nature by setting them up in the Well, a kind of basement with a skylight" (40). But this, too, Updike affirms: "As he followed his friend's blond hair down the reverberating iron of the spiral stairs, Leonard felt he had at last arrived at the radiant heart of the school" (40). Not the higher forms but the artistic reproduction of the material world is what is really real. This is still a form of idealism, however—it's just that the copy of a copy (of a copy of a copy) becomes the ideal that we must seek; the higher form is meaningless until it has been reproduced by the human imagination. As Updike puts it in an autobiographical essay much later in his career, "art should body forth the idyllic."[11] The world of the imagination is the highest reality available.

Not surprisingly, Leonard's idealist imagination eventually focuses itself on his British love interest, Robin Cox, whom he transforms into a sort of national essence: "Across Robin's incongruities—between her name and body, her experiences and innocence—was braced a certain official austerity, a determined erectness of carriage, as if she were Britannia in the cartoons, and her contours contained nothing erotic but limned a necessarily female symbol of ancient militance" (36). His way into understanding the foreign land in which he finds himself, in other words, is an idealized version of the female form. Their relationship is heavily aestheticized, as we might expect from two painters; when they paint side by side, they are given a unity through idealized art: "To have her, some distance from his side, echoing his task, and to know that her eyes concentrated into the same set of shapes, which after a little concentration took on an unnatural intensity, like fruit in Paradise, curiously enlarged his sense of his physical size; he seemed to tower above the flagstones, and his voice, in responding to her erratic exclamations and complaints, struck into his ears with grave finality, as if his words were being incised into the air" (40–41). Leonard, like Peter Caldwell, is undergoing an egotheistic transformation—but whereas the agent of Peter's transformation is his idea of the city, the agent of Leonard's was his idea of the female body near him. Thus his relationship with Robin takes on a Platonic quality: "He much preferred the days, full of light and time, when their proximity had the grace of the accidental and before their eyes a constant topic of intercourse was poised" (42). Next to this ideal world of art and light, the material world can intrude only dimly: "The sounds of museum traffic drifted in from a comparatively dark and cluttered world" (41). The material world is the world of shadow; the idealized world of art is the highest reality.

Eventually, however, Leonard's imagination becomes unhinged in its lust, and, in a process that we will see again in *Roger's Version*, he begins to create a sexual world for Robin to inhabit with his old rival, Jack. His imagination runs wild when he tours the continent without her: "In Paris the idea that she even toyed with such a proposition excited him; it suggested an area of willingness, of loneliness, that Leonard could feasibly invade. In Frankfurt he wondered if actually she would turn [Jack] down—he knew she was staying around the university during vacation—and by Hamburg he was certain that she had not; she had consented. He grew accustomed to this conviction as he and his companion slowly circled back through the Lowlands. By the time he disembarked at Dover he was quite indifferent to her nakedness" (46). Set free from Robin's material body, Leonard's imagination exhausts even the possibility of its lust, and his absence from the school crumbles the ideal world of art they had created together:

> In the Well, the arrangements of fruit had decayed; with the hope that some of the students would continue to work despite the vacation, the things had not been disturbed. Their own still life was least affected by time. The onions were as immutable as the statues; but the cabbage, peeled by Robin to its solid pale heart, had relaxed in wilting, and its outer leaves, gray and almost transparent, rested on the gold cloth. His painting, still standing in its easel, preserved the original appearance of the cabbage, but the pigments had dulled, sinking into the canvas; their hardness made the painting seem finished, though there were several uncovered corners and numerous contrasts his fresh eye saw the need of adjusting. (46)

Like the cabbage, their burgeoning relationship has wilted—not because of any physical relationship between Robin and Jack, but because, as she tells Leonard, "you refuse to take me *seriously*" (47). And he cannot take her seriously because fundamentally he is dealing not with her but with his idea of her. Once too much pressure is placed on this idea, the world created by his imagination falls to pieces, and he is left in despair.

Museums and women recur, naturally enough, in the title story (1967) of *Museums and Women*. The story opens with an aesthetic analysis of the two key words: "Set together, the two words seem to be mutually transparent; the E's, the M's blend—the M's framing and squaring the structure lend resonance and a curious formal weight to the M central in the creature, which it dominates like a dark core winged with flitting syllables. Both words hum. Both suggest radiance, antiquity, mystery, and beauty."[12] Our narrator moves from an ideal aesthetic form—the shape and contours of the printed words themselves—outward to specific museums and women, who will be imaginatively shaped by these typographical ruminations. And he is further drawn into the ideal world by the artwork that he views with his mother when he is a child:

> I think it was the smallness of these figures that carried them so penetratingly into my mind. Each, if it could have been released into life, would have stood about twenty inches high and weighed in my arms perhaps as much as a cat. I itched to finger them, to interact with them, to insert myself into their mysterious world of strenuous contention—their bulged tendons burnished, their hushed violence detailed down to the fingernails. They were in their smallness like secret thoughts of mine projected into dimension and permanence, and they returned to me as a response that carried strangely into parts of my body. (4–5)

This description suggests a two-way street between the artistic work and the narrator's imagination. It is clear that this encounter has changed the way he figures the world (and its female residents)—but at the same time, he clearly believes that his own imagination has in some sense created these works that chronologically pre-date him. When he imaginatively enters them, he becomes a different person, but they also become different works for his presence in them. Later, he will describe a museum as a home for everything insubstantial in him—as a home for him when he becomes, in a sense, imaginary. This seems to have been true for Updike, as well, who reports elsewhere that in the early stages of his career, "the Museum of Modern Art was a temple where I might refresh my own sense of artistic purpose."[13] In "Museums and Women," the narrator and his mistress visit a New York museum: "We had come from love-making, and were to return to it, and the museum, visited between the evaporation and the recondensation of desire, was like a bridge whose either end is dissolved in mist—its suspension miraculous, its purpose remembered only by the murmuring stream running in the invisible ravine below. Homeless, we had found a home worthy of us" (13–14). The process begun when he was a child continues when he is an adult; he lives, at least for the moment, in the ideal aesthetic world offered to him by the museum. In this space, he is able to create his mistress through the enhanced power of his own imagination: "The woman's sensibility was more an interior decorator than an art student's, and through her I felt furnishings unfold into a world of gilded scrolls, rubbed stuffs, cherished surfaces, painstakingly inlaid veneers, varnished cadenzas of line and curve lovingly carved by men whose hands were haunted by the memory of women. Rustling beside me, her body, which I had seen asleep on a mattress, seemed to wear clothes as a needless luxuriance, an ultra-extravagance heaped upon what was already, like the museum, both priceless and free" (14). His lover has become a work of art, crafted not by God but by his own museum-fueled imagination.

But perhaps the fullest expression of lust-as-imagination in Updike's short stories comes from "Lifeguard" (1961), which I have already examined in chapter 1. The story largely takes the form of a mock sermon from the divinity-student-cum-lifeguard narrator. The sermon abruptly turns to the subject of his lust for the women whose lives he protects, and he interrogates the reader/parishioner directly: "You are offended that a divinity student lusts? What prigs the unchurched are. Are not our assaults on the supernatural lascivious, a kind of indecency? If only you knew what de Sadian degradations, what frightful psychological spelunking, our gentle transcendentalist professors set us to, as preparation for our work, which is to shine in the darkness."[14] Lust becomes for the narrator a theological act, a means for God's grace to enter the eyes of the lustful man. He assures us that "a woman's beauty lies, not in any exaggeration of the specialized zones, nor in any general harmony that could be worked out by means of the *section aurea* or a similar aesthetic superstition; but in the arabesque of the spine. The curve by which the back modulates into the buttocks. It is here that grace sits and rides a woman's body" (216). In this idealized physical womanhood, sex becomes infused with deep spiritual significance. "To love a woman," the narrator proclaims, "is to desire to save her. Anyone who has endured intercourse that was neither predatory nor hurried knows how through it we descend, with a partner, into the grotesque and delicate shadows that until then have remained locked in the most guarded recess of our soul: into this harbor we bring her" (216–17). Sex becomes a sacrament—a descent of the ideal into the shadowy realm of material reality. The narrator presents it as a kind of confession, a fundamentally religious act: "We are all Solomons lusting for Sheba's salvation. The God-filled man is filled with a wilderness that cries to be populated. The stony chambers need jewels, furs, tints of cloth and flesh, even though, as in Samson's case, the temple comes tumbling. Women are an alien race of pagans set down among us.

Every seduction is a conversion" (217). But real sex, perhaps inevitably, is disappointing compared to this idealist vision: "As if we are an island upon which a woman, tossed by her laboring vanity and blind self-seeking, is blown, and there finds security, until, an instant before the anticlimax, Nature with a smile thumps down her trump, and the island sinks beneath the sea" (217). The ideal world crumbles before the bleak reality. But the lifeguard returns again and again to the ideal world, and thus his lust is the product of a profoundly theological and artistic imagination. He wishes to save the women he seduces by raising them into idealist immortality. His mission, then, is akin to Updike's own aesthetic project: "My chief exercise, as I sit above the crowds, is to lift the whole mass into immortality" (217). Lust becomes the agent of this immortality—but he imposes it on women without their consent, and quite possibly without their knowledge.

That this process of lustful creation can be dangerous to men as well as to women is demonstrated by a pair of stories about Henry Bech, Updike's Jewish American alter ego. In "Bech Swings?" (1970), Updike gives the aging novelist a familiar lustful gaze that transforms its objects:

> It was his charm and delusion to see women as deities—idols whose jewel was set not in the center of their foreheads but between their legs, with another between their lips, and pairs more sprinkled up and down, from ankles to eyes, the length of their adorable, alien forms. His transactions with these supernatural creatures imbued him, more keenly each time, with his own mortality. His life seemed increasingly like that sinister fairy story in which each granted wish diminishes a magic pelt that is in fact the wisher's life. But perhaps, Bech though, one more woman, one more leap would bring him safe into high calm pool of immortality where Proust and Hawthorne and Catullus float, glassy-eyed and belly up. One more wasting love would release his genius from the bondage of his sagging flesh.[15]

Bech thus hopes that his idealization of the women he encounters will allow for a kind of nonreligious transcendence of his own—if he can only transform a woman of flesh and blood into the perfect woman, he will be lifted out of the disappointment of his long literary silence. Eventually he will set this imagination loose on Merissa, a British woman whom he wants to transform into an American woman for his next novel: "Bech was sure he could fill in her gaps with bits of American women, could indeed re-create her from almost nothing, needing less than a rib, needing only a living germ of his infatuation, of his love" (172). There is something Frankensteinian in this desire; he wishes to patch together the scraps of every woman he knows, using his imagination as the sutures, and thus create something perfect. A similar process is at play in the mind of Franz Budendorf, the loathsome antihero of Vladimir Nabokov's *King, Queen,*

Knave. As Franz rides a train to Berlin, he begins to cut apart and piece together the women around him:

> He bared the shoulders of the woman that had just been sitting by the window, made a quick mental test (did blind Eros react? clumsy Eros did, unsticking its folds in the dark); then, keeping the splendid shoulders, changed the head, substituting it for the face of that seventeen-year-old maid who had vanished with a silver soup ladle almost as big as she before he had had time to declare his love; but that head too he erased and, in its place, attached the face of one of those bold-eyed, humid-lipped Berlin beauties that one encounters mainly in liquor and cigarette advertisements.[16]

Nabokov's description makes clear the spiritual violence inherent in such fantasies—violence that is not substantially lessened by Bech's using them for aesthetic rather than auto-erotic purposes. Besides, Bech's aesthetic project fails. One morning, "He awoke and found that *Think Big* had died. It had become a ghost of a book, an empty space beside the four faded spines that he had already brought to exist. *Think Big* had no content but wonder, which was a blankness" (174). The violence of the male imagination has turned inward and brought about not creation but annihilation.

In a further irony, Bech realizes that he has swapped the world of the imagination—paradoxically, for the artist, the world of real things—for the shadowy world of social success. "In the beginning," he sees, "the fresh flame of his spirit had burned everything clean—the entire gray city, stone and soot and stoops" (174). But eventually "unreality had swept in. It was his fault; he had wanted to be noticed, to be praised. He had wanted to be a man in the world, a 'writer.' For his punishment they had made from the sticks and mud of his words a coarse large doll to question and torment, which would not have mattered except that he was trapped inside the doll, shared a name and bank account with it" (175). An irony is at play: This is exactly what he has attempted to do with Merissa and the other women in his life; as he has taken on their essences and shaped them to his will, he has allowed his own essence to be shaped by the diabolic imagination of the publicists and journalists who feed on him.

Bech literally creates a woman in "Three Illuminations in the Life of an American Author" (1970). At the outset of this story, Updike presents the life of a novelist as one in which the line between imagination and reality constantly blurs. Bech's writer's block continues unabated, and the effect is that his selfhood begins to slide into the books he has already written: "Though Henry Bech, the author, in his middle years had all but ceased to write, his books continued, as if ironically, to live, to cast shuddering shadows toward the center of his life, where that thing called his reputation cowered. To have once imagined and composed fiction, it seemed, laid him under an indelible curse of unreality."[17] The only way to stop from being fictional himself, ironically enough, is to create new fiction. Thus, while trying to write his next novel, *Think Big*, he imagines a woman named Lenore. He cannot figure out which of his characters to pair her with because "no man was good enough for this woman, unless it were Bech himself" (12–13). His imagination brings her to life, and "she became as real to him as the nightglow on his ceiling during insomnia" (13). But then Lenore actually appears, more or less, in the physical world: "Was this truly Lenore? Though he had failed to imagine some details (the little gold hoop earrings, and the tidy yet full-bodied and somewhat sensually casual way in which she had bundled her hair at the back of her head), her physical presence flooded the transcendent, changeable skin of his invention with a numbing concreteness" (14–15). Such is her reality that "he revised what he had written" (15), having been corrected by the genuine article.

But as time goes by and he enters into a sexual relationship with this flesh-and-blood woman, he realizes that his imagination has not, in fact, created her, that he has been attempting to force a round peg into a square hole: "He had been slightly wrong in a hundred details, the months revealed. Their affair did not last until her students were in the fifth grade. It was his literary side, it turned out, his textbook presence, that she loved" (18). Once again the tables are turned on Bech; in trying to re-create this woman in his imagination, he finds that she has re-created him, loving him for "his textbook presence," the myth created for him by the press and his own silence rather than for himself. And even worse, she destroys his ability to write the fictional Lenore: "Still, she gave him enough of herself to eclipse, to crush, 'the rare and radiant maiden whom the angels name Lenore,' and once again *Think Big* ground to a grateful halt" (18). By the end of the story, Bech's imagination is utterly exhausted; signing thousands of autographs, he freezes, gazing "deep into the negative perfection to which his career had been brought. He could not even write his own name" (27). Not just his imagination but his very selfhood slips away. These are the dangers of the imaginative male gaze, as Updike presents it—it does spiritual violence to the women on whom it is focused, but it also endangers the selfhood of the gazer himself, since it unmoors him from the physical world around him.

Notes

1 Updike, "Polish Metamorphoses," 493.

2 Bordo, "The Cartesian Masculinization of Thought," 355. Hereafter cited in-text.

3 Updike, "The Football Factory," 19. Hereafter cited in-text.

4 The similarity of Rafe's name to the word *rape* further underlines his devouring sexual vision.

[5] Updike, "Toward Evening," 63. Hereafter cited in-text.

[6] Begley, *Updike*, 127–28.

[7] Updike, "Incest," 145. Hereafter cited in-text.

[8] Updike, "Still Life," 28. Hereafter cited in-text.

[9] Plato, *Republic*, 598b.

[10] Ibid., 514a–b.

[11] Updike, "What MoMA Done Tole Me," 13.

[12] Updike, "Museums and Women," 3. Hereafter cited in-text.

[13] Updike, "What MoMA Done Tole Me," 7.

[14] Updike, "Lifeguard," 216. Hereafter cited in-text.

[15] Updike, "Bech Swings?" 149. Hereafter cited in-text.

[16] Nabokov, *King, Queen, Knave*, 13–14.

[17] Updike, "Three Illuminations," 3. Hereafter cited in-text.

9: *A Month of Sundays*

UPDIKE'S INTEREST IN IMAGINATIVE male lust—and the harm it does to both men and women—continues in his so-called *Scarlet Letter* trilogy, three novels that reproduce the love triangle at the center of Nathaniel Hawthorne's *The Scarlet Letter*: a woman is torn between a man of science and a man of faith.[1] Each novel is told, via first-person narration, from the perspective of one corner of the triangle. *A Month of Sundays* (1975), which pre-dates its two sequels by more than a decade, is narrated by the Dimmesdale figure, a disgraced Midwestern minister named Tom Marshfield. Marshfield writes to the deceptively named Ms. Prynne,[2] the matron of a specialized establishment in the American Southwest where ministers with serious ethical failures are sent. His lust, predictably enough, has temporarily banished him from his congregation, as he has had a torrid affair with his church's (unbelieving) organist, Alicia Crick. This affair incites an almost psychotic jealousy in him when she moves on to Marshfield's effeminate, liberal assistant pastor, Ned Bork (presumably the Roger Chillingsworth figure, though his interest in science is rather limited).[3] Lust is therefore at the center of this novel—almost literally, since in the opening paragraph, Marshfield describes the shape of the motel in which he sits as "an O, or more exactly, an omega."[4] The narrative is also an O, or more exactly, an omega, and the space in the middle of it is devoted to Marshfield's lust, which is combined in this rather unattractive character with a Christian existentialist fideism. Every single one of Marshfield's actions is motivated by one of these two noetic forces—such that it may make more sense to call them a single force.[5]

From the beginning of the novel, Marshfield presents the male imagination as a defiling force, initially expressed not in sexual but in literary terms. "Though the yielding is mine," he writes, "the temptation belongs to others: my keepers have set before me a sheaf of blank sheets—a month's worth, in their estimation. Sullying them is to be my sole therapy" (3). In this sense, the blank sheets of the paper represent the female body and soul, onto which the desires and caprices of the male imagination will be transferred. Masculine lust, thus connected with the literary act, becomes a potent creative, or perhaps re-creative, force. As Marshfield admits near the end of the novel, "before we love something we must make a kind of replica of it, a memory-body of glimpses and moments, which then replaces its external, rather drab existence with a constellatory internalization, phosphorescent and highly portable and in the end impervious to reality's crude strip-mining" (181). As he sees it, then, we do not love things or people as they exist in reality; instead, we love the images of them that we create in our minds. But once again, this is not a pretty process. Marshfield's imagination, so bound up in lust, is almost always ugly and destructive. He remembers lying in bed with his sleeping wife, Jane, where "he masturbated again, imagining for spite some woman remote, a redhead from the attic of his youth, her pubic hair as nicely packed around its treasure as excelsior around an ancestral locket" (11). The creative act is thus infused with antisocial mood—his sexless wife, who fails to satisfy him sexually, must be spited with this illusory figure from the past.

It was not always so, however. Marshfield says of his wife, "My impulse, to *eat* her, to taste, devour, and assimilate, which continues into even this our misery, though my bite has become murderous, began with the first glimpse" (49). But even Marshfield's predatory imagination is shocked by Jane's corporeality: "This was not my first naked female. You will remember the redhead deftly evoked pages ago, and there was a bony fellow-counsellor one summer we may never find the space for. But Jane was as to these as the cut marble is to the melted wax of the preliminary models. No formula, utilitarian or idealist, could quite do justice to the living absoluteness of it. Here was a fact, five foot seven inches long, and of circumferences varying with infinite subtlety from ankles to hips, from waist to skull" (52). Jane's realness—her ability to transcend his imagination, or more accurately, his imagination's inability to get all the way around her—eventually sours him on her. Male lust needs something insubstantial, something that can be easily molded and transformed to fit the needs of the moment. The redhead, vaguely remembered from adolescence, does the trick nicely—as does Alicia Crick, since he is able to speak of their lovemaking in mythological terms: "The lover as viaduct. The lover as sky-god, cycling moisture from earth to cloud to earth" (35). Alicia's transparency makes Jane, who cannot be mythologized, even more opaque. Marshfield imagines that his soul is a circle, half-black and half-white, with one side labeled *good* and the other side labeled *depressing*: "Alicia, by reclaiming a wedge of mankind for the Good and Beautiful, shifted the axis of the divider 10° (rough estimate) and caused a relabeling of the now-titled halves: the white was the Live, the black was the dead. . . . There was one casualty: in the wedge of the circle directly across from Alicia and her peachy cries and floating nipples was an innocuous sector, labeled "*ux.*," inhabited by my wife Jane, née Chillingworth. This wedge went as dark as an attic window" (40–41). When his affair with Alicia goes sour, he moves on to a parishioner, Frankie Harlow. If his sexual relationship with Alicia was mythologized, his relationship with Frankie might be called *demythologizing*, as the pastor attempts to mold the faithful Frankie into the image of Alicia, an unbeliever: "You dumb cunt, . . . how can you be so dumb as to believe in God the Father, God the Son, and God the Holy Ghost? Tell me you really don't. Tell me, so I can fuck you" (156–57). Clearly Marshfield's sexuality only functions when he can mold his partner into an image of his choosing, be it divine (Alicia) or blasphemous (Frankie).

He also tells us that "one cannot know and not love" (191), implicating knowledge itself in this same imaginative morass. (Obviously the traditional Christian distinction between love and lust holds little sway over Marshfield.) Knowledge thus becomes involved in the same destruction that marks the imagination: "By knowing, we dissolve the world enough to move through it freely. We dispel claustrophobia. . . . By knowing, we dissolve the veneer our animal murk puts upon things, and empathize with God's workmanship" (191). Knowledge, imagination, love, lust—these things allow us to transcend the physical world around us. They become a kind of faith, albeit a sinister one. Marshfield wonders, "Isn't there something demonic in such dissolution; can it be the devil urging us into wider and wider transparency, where we no longer see to marvel, and feel nothing but the sticky filaments of our analysis, and have a Void where once there had been a Creation?" (191–92). We see, then, the degree to which the male imagination teeters on the edge of nihilism in this novel—in re-creating and re-presenting the world, it threatens to dissolve the very meaning it attempts to impart or discover.

The pull in the opposite direction comes from Marshfield's pet theologian (and Updike's), Karl Barth, who posits God as an unimaginable entity, Something Wholly Other from human understanding and conception. God, Barth suggests, occupies an entirely different plane of existence from us, and "we who stand in this concrete world know nothing, and are incapable of knowing anything, of that other world."[6] This means that we cannot imagine God; we are in fact the imaginings of God: "Men are related to God as the thing formed is related to him that formed it, as clay to the potter. Who now dares to speak of partners or of links in a chain of causality? On the one side stands the purpose-full master, on the other side the material which serves his purpose and becomes his work. No bridge, no continuity, links the potter and the clay, the master and his work. They are incommensurable. The distinction between them is infinite and qualitative; the link which connects them is altogether indirect and unobservable."[7] No human action or thought is capable of approaching God in any way. As Barth says in a passage that Updike quotes in *Roger's Version*, "There is no way from us to God—not even a *via negative*—not even a *via dialectica* nor *paradoxa*. The god who stood at the end of some human way—even of this way—would not be God."[8] When we attempt to conceive of God, be it through our imagination or our reason, "we come to our own rescue and built the tower of Babel."[9] Our only knowledge of God must proceed from the opposite direction, from up to down, from God to man. And thus our knowledge of God comes from the divine incarnation, word being made flesh in Jesus Christ: "The point on the line of intersection at which the relation becomes observable and observed is Jesus, Jesus of Nazareth, the historical Jesus—**born of the seed of David according to the flesh**."[10] An appropriate relation- ship with God, then, does not spring from the human imagination but from a relationship with a flesh-and-blood person, a person who, like Jane Marshfield, resists the imposition of our imaginations.

Oddly enough, this is what Marshfield admires about Barth; transparency, he tells us, belongs to the lecherous Paul Tillich, and Barth gives us a reality that bites back: "Better Barth, who gives us opacity triumphant, and bids us adore; we do adore, what we also love in the world is its resistance—these motel walls that hold us to this solitude, this woman who resists being rolled over, who is *herself*" (192). But despite this declaration, Marshfield clearly prefers women whom he can re-create with his lust. He is not as good a Barthian as he imagines himself to be. He tells us early on that "I have never knowingly failed to honor the supreme, the hidden commandment, which is, Take the Natural World, O Creature Fashioned in Parody of My Own, and Reconvert its Stuff to Spirit" (8). Despite his admonishment, later in the paragraph, to "Despise all Precepts which Take their Measure from Man" (8), what he proposes here is a Barthian tower of Babel, a move upward from flesh to spirit, from the human world to the divine world, an attempt to break by force into the domain of the Wholly Other God. And his imposition of his imagination on the women in his life—which he conceives of as an analogue to his faith—is in fact a miniature version of that idolatry. His lust makes him the Cartesian origin of the universe. For example, in his jealousy he imagines Alicia having sex with Ned Bork: "Then the image of her car under its streetlight returned, and the thought of her cries under caresses, and of her skin under clothes, and of her voice under silence—for there was no doubting, this act of hers addressed itself to *him*" (11). His language here suggests not so much a spurned lover as a jealous God, a refusal to have any of the beloved's attention focused anywhere but on himself.

Sex becomes not only a product of his imagination, as it is in this scene, but also something to be hoarded and locked into his head: "I feared such depth of pleasure was not enough of my creation, was too much hers, and could too easily be shifted to the agency of another" (36). Male lust is, Updike suggests, an attempt to control the female other.[11] As he puts it, imagination "is fun! First you whittle the puppets, then you move them around" (12). The image recurs toward the end of the novel: "Gerry, Frankie, Julie, Barry—how small remoteness has whittled them. They seem dolls I can play with, putting them now in this, now in that obscene position. I put the Frankie doll in a nightie, and lie her in bed, and spread her jointed legs, and set the Gerry doll on top, while the Julie and Barry dolls sleep the dreamless sleep of the safe and the ignorant. I look down upon the copulating dolls by removing a section of the roof no bigger than a chessboard" (178). Such is the power of Marshfield's imaginative lust that even watching his lover copulate with his archrival brings him a certain amount of pleasure. There is disgust, yes, "but, twinned with horror and bedded snugly beside it, a warm body of satisfaction lay detectable within myself. This pleasure, though alloyed, was deep, deeper than the half-believed masochism, deeper than my truffler's hunger for secrets, of which the bare foot was now one" (16). He explains further in the next chapter: "So my pleasure in verifying that Ned and Alicia were screwing might be, deeply, pleasure in discovering that my parents in their silence were not dead but alive, that my birth had not chilled all love, that the bower of their union continued to flourish above me" (19). Lust again becomes a kind of faith in the afterlife, but the afterlife in turn becomes an endless chain of sexualities.

We are a long way from the elevated religious discourse that Marshfield earlier employed; Marshfield is not "Tak[ing] the Natural World, O Creature Fashioned in Parody of My Own, and Reconvert[ing] its Stuff to Spirit." The imaginer has instead become a god of his own, a half-benevolent god whose imagination forcibly re-creates the world around him. The book we are reading is a second re-creation, and an unreliable one at that; Marshfield freely fills in the gaps in his memory with his imagination, as he admits while disclosing the conversations that led to his infidelity: "Perhaps the conversation as I have set it down is a medley of several, scattered through a number of post- or pre-rehearsal interludes, in drafty ecclesiastic nooks haunted by whiffs of liquid wax and spilled cider, or on awkward frozen lawns while our gloved hands groped for the handles of differing automobiles (mine a coffee-brown 1971 Dodge Dart, hers a 1963, if memory serves, Bel Air)" (33). Or even worse, he makes up details to amuse himself and confuse his readers: "Or perhaps these words were never spoken, I made them up, to relieve and rebuke the silence of this officiously chaste room" (33). We are thus at a double remove from the events of Marshfield's life.

Eventually, his enforced practice of daily writing sucks him toward solipsism: "Then, grain by grain, this place stopped moving, it became a *place*, and now the danger is it has become the *only* place. And this accounting the only accounting and you my reader my only love" (181). The world itself exists only in Marshfield's imagination—an extreme version of the heresy he has been committing the whole time. The reader is the only possible channel out of his solipsism, and indeed, Jeff Campbell points to Marshfield's frequent addresses to the reader as proof that he is "acknowledging the reality of and the need for a self outside his own ego."[12] But this reader hardly exists. Elsewhere, Marshfield calls her the "Ideal" reader, and the sense is that he speaks to another product of his imagination. The fact that these passages are clearly allegorical, suggesting "the writer's seduction and penetration of the reader,"[13] does not change their imaginative nature. Ms. Prynne, in other words, is another Alicia Crick, and so are we, the public readers of his confessions. That he figures these addresses as a kind of sexual expression should not be surprising. For example, he reports his daily schedule: "Mornings: write, *ab libidum*" (6). The pun is on *ad libitum*, "at one's pleasure," with an added sexual ring to it. Later his own writing will lead him to nauseous masturbation: "I jerked off, lying on the wall-to-wall carpet of goose-turd green, rather than sully my bachelor cot where the Navajo chambermaid might sardonically note the spoor of a wounded paleface. My seed sank into polyester lint and the microscopic desert grits of a hundred transient shoes. I shouldn't have done it, for now my hymn to my mistress will be limp and piecemeal, tapped out half by a hand still tremulous and smelling of venerable slime" (34). Marshfield is so libidinous that any exercise of his imagination becomes, de facto, an exercise of his lust.

This is true even of his pastoral vocation. Marshfield uses his sermons as an opportunity to mentally undress his female parishioners, bragging that, as he preached, "my collection of interior pornography improved in technical quality" (27). His functioning in the world requires the imposition of his imagination on the female body. And so his forced confinement in the desert among overwhelmingly male companions blocks his lustful imagination to some extent. (At the very least, it forces it onto the page.) Marshfield admits that "imperceptibly these errant and bankrupt clergymen have replaced the phantoms that chased me here, phantoms it now seems my heart had conjured from its own fevers, had bred like fungi in an unlit dank of self-absorption. This desert sun has baked them away" (198). With no women to focus his imagination on, Marshfield must live in the world of men, the world of other minds that cannot be shaped by his own. But the motel is not entirely free of women; after all, the mysterious Ms. Prynne is there. And toward the end of the novel, Marshfield focuses his imagination on her: "A common fall, mine, into the abysmal perplexity of the American female. I feel, however, not merely fallen, but possessed, and such is demonology that the case needs for cure another woman; and the only woman here, on this frontier, is, Ms., you" (201). Because *A Month of Sundays* is narrated in the first-person, we meet all its characters filtered through Marshfield's imagination and interpretation. Even in this milieu, however, Ms. Prynne is a special case. We encounter her only through Marshfield's direct address. She scarcely even has a physical body, and so, even more than Alicia Crick, she seems wholly the product of his imagination—and this is true even though she has a physical presence in his life at the time of the novel's action that the other women do not, since they exist primary in his memory.

When Ms. Prynne does appear in the flesh, it is to annotate the "sermon" that represents Marshfield's twenty-seventh entry. The next day, he is enraptured: "You spoke. You exist. The palm of my left hand tingles like that of a man with an hour to the electric chair" (212). Her intrusion into his diary is a confirmation of faith: "The handwriting was yours as I have always imagined it—hurried yet legible, pragmatic yet a shade self-congratulatory in the formation of the capitals" (213). His imagination has again triumphed over the physical world; Ms. Prynne's real presence does not correct it but instead proves it as powerful as Marshfield has always believed it to be. He can thus quickly turn this female authority figure into yet another object for his lust: "Once, emerging at dusk from the pool, I saw, my eyeballs chlorinated to match the sunset, you pushily passing through a double glass door from having chastened a jeaned and rebellious chambermaid, and I thought, of your ass, which had always before loomed as much beyond me as a mesa, that it was manageable. That indeed it was, for all its authoritarian majesty and apparent imperviousness, grabbable, huggable, caressable, kissable. And knew itself as such. And knew itself as such in my sunset eyes" (215). Marshfield's language here is, as always, calculated and telling. He has reduced Ms. Prynne's being to her physical form—in fact, to a specific section of her physical form. To the degree he grants her consciousness and selfhood (her ass "knew itself as such"), it is only through his gaze and his imagination (it "knew itself as such in my sunset eyes"). She has been assimilated, like Alicia Crick before her.

Ms. Prynne does not appear for a few days after this performance, and as such she becomes another object of Marshfield's faith. He believes with childlike certainty that she will return and submit herself to him: "Still, I have this mustard seed. And you have this gap in your armor" (220). In his objectifying of her body, Marshfield converts Ms. Prynne into a being that exists for his benefit alone: "You are a gossamer ephemerid treading my edges. You are yet the end, the *intelligens entis*, of my being, insofar as I exist on paper. Give me a body. Otherwise I shall fall through space forever. Stop me" (220). We have returned to the idea that the man is a soul and the woman a body to be animated by that soul; Marshfield is guilty of the sort of masculinist idealism that Susan Bordo condemns in the Western metaphysical tradition. And indeed, when his faith fails, when Ms. Prynne resists his re-creation, he turns to more blatant misogyny: "Then don't come, you bitch. You sashaying cunt. I hardly slept a dream's worth, for listening for your step, your fingers on the latch, the rustle of your silk, the little tearful twinned *suck* as you remove the contact lenses it is your vanity to wear when you go out with one of your dreadful square-state 'dates.' You didn't know I knew that about you, did you?" (224). Stripped of his ability to control her, he has resorted to name-calling, to accusations of female vanity and promiscuity (as if he himself were not dreadfully vain and promiscuous).

But Ms. Prynne does eventually come to him, interrupting him mid-sentence ("I cannot cope. I cannot" [227]) to have sex with him:

> What remains, at this moment, a moment of this my last hour, was the brave way in which you undressed without comment, disclosing with not the flicker of a plea that you were, not fat, but thick, certainly thick, so that my startled arms, embracing, felt to be encircling the trunk of a solid but warm tree. And the tranquility of you upon your back! Permitting your breasts to be molded again and again—amazing breasts, so firm they seemed small, the nipples erect upon little mounds of further erectile tissue, so that a cupola upon a dome was evoked, an ascent in several stages, an architectural successiveness. Difficult, from your profile, to guess your pleasure. You seemed lost in thought, only your hand speaking to me, lightly drawing my penis up into its ideal shape, so it could once again lose its ache in the almost—nay, veritably—alarmingly liquid volume of the passage to your womb. (228)

This is, at first glance, a strange way for Marshfield's story to end. He has been sent to Ms. Prynne's establishment, after all, specifically because he cannot control himself sexually, cannot keep from imposing his lustful imagination on other women. How could Ms. Prynne's sleeping with him cure him of this problem? But his lovemaking with her is of strikingly different character than the book's earlier incidents. Before, his partners either resisted his ability to re-create them (Jane Chillingworth Marshfield) or were utterly transformed by him (Alicia Crick, Frankie Harlow). Ms. Prynne is something different entirely. He does re-create her; he describes, after all, his "molding" her breasts. But he also submits himself to being re-created by her, since she draws his penis "into its ideal shape." The act has a mutuality that we have not seen before in Marshfield—the two work on each other, and yet Ms. Prynne remains somewhat opaque to him; her soul is hidden inside her body in a way Alicia's and Frankie's are not. The novel's concluding paragraph acknowledges this fact: "What is it, this human contact, this blank-browed thing we do for one another? There was a moment, when I entered you, and was big, and you were already wet, when you could not have seen yourself, when your eyes were all for another, looking up into mine, with an expression without a name, of entry and alarm, and of salutation. I pray my own face, a stranger to me, saluted in turn" (228). Here we see the sexual imagination appropriately fulfilled. There is not an active partner and a passive partner. Instead, both partners are simultaneously active and passive, simultaneously seeing and seen, simultaneously re-creating and re-created. The novel does not restore Marshfield to a traditionally ethical position—it ends, after all, with yet another act of adultery, and we get no indication that he plans on being faithful to his wife when he returns to the Midwest—but it does bring him, for the first time we have seen, to a sexual mutuality. Allegorically, James Schiff argues, the ending of *A Month of Sundays* "is a first step in repairing the split found in American life between body and soul."[14] But this repair takes place on a personal scale as well as a mythic scale— Marshfield goes beyond man-as-intellect and woman-as-body and grants both body and soul to both man and woman.

Notes

[1] *A Month of Sundays* marks a turn in Updike's fiction from the collective imagination found in *Marry Me, Couples*, and their related short stories toward a more individualistic imagination. There is a biographical reason for this shift: When Updike married the former Martha Ruggles Bernhard in 1975, he left Ipswich and its convivial, orgiastic parties behind for good, moving to the more isolated town of Georgetown, Massachusetts. As Adam Begley relates, "the town suited him nicely. He and Martha made little or no effort to find new friends. A manically crammed social calendar had once seemed to him essential; now he preferred it blank. Though he occasionally drove over to see his children when they gathered at Labor-in-Vain Road, his contact with his gang of Ipswich friends was virtually nil. Sunday sports were a thing of the past, so, too, the weekly parties—all that frantic commingling had ground to a halt when he left Mary" (*Updike*, 385). His fiction, accordingly, turns from the social scene to the individual imagination, and, at least in the three novels covered in these chapters, he moves from biographical fiction to fiction about fiction, appropriate for a man married to a woman who "held the world at bay, gradually assuming the management of his time, doing her best to make sure that nothing and no one encroached on the hours devoted to his work" (383).

[2] Although Marshfield propositions Ms. Prynne near the end of the novel, the book's real analogue for Hester Prynne is Alicia Crick, the organist with whom Marshfield conducts an affair. Or perhaps we should say that both stand in for Hester, or that neither of them fully does. In his groundbreaking study of the three *Scarlet Letter* novels, James A. Schiff cautions us against the temptation to place Updike's novels neatly over the top of Hawthorne's. Schiff identifies Updike's major retelling techniques as condensation and fragmentation. Condensation takes place when "more than one prefiguration is related to a single contemporary character or event" (*Updike's Version*, 14). Schiff's example is Marshfield, who generally stands in for Dimmesdale but resembles Chillingworth when he spies on Ned Bork and Alicia Crick, and for Hester when he speaks of his contamination. Fragmentation is the opposite effect, wherein a single character is spread out into multiple characters. Hester, it seems, has been fragmented and implanted into both Ms. Prynne and Alicia.

[3] Here again we are dealing with fragmentation—Marshfield's father-in-law is named Wesley Chillingworth, and this passionless professor of Christian ethics, as Schiff argues, prefigures Roger Lambert, the Chillingworth of *Roger's Version*

(40). But the central love triangle of the novel is not between Marshfield and Chillingworth.

4 Updike, *A Month of Sundays*, 4. Hereafter cited in-text.

5 In fact, both lust and faith are frequently figured as imaginative acts in Updike's fiction; Richard Matthias, for example—the character with the least faith in *Marry Me*—is also the character with the least imagination, his bad eye turning the world flat and ugly.

6 Barth, *Epistle*, 30.

7 Ibid., 356–57.

8 Barth, "The Problem of Ethics Today," 177.

9 Barth, "The Righteousness of God," 14.

10 Barth, *Epistle*, 29.

11 Writing is another method of controlling people by re-creating them, of course, and for Marshfield if not for Updike, lust and writing belong to the same category of re-creative human action. See Schiff, *Updike's Version* and Tanner, *Adultery in the Novel* for further analysis of this connection.

12 Campbell, *Updike's Novels*, 218.

13 Schiff, *Updike's Version*, 22.

14 Ibid., 53.

10: *Roger's Version*

UPDIKE WOULD NOT RETURN TO *The Scarlet Letter* for more than a decade. *Roger's Version*, as the title suggests, comes from the perspective of the Roger Chillingworth character, the man of science who is cuckholded by the man of faith. But the categories are confused, because Updike's Chillingworth is not a scientist but a professor at a divinity school, a former minister whose career was ended by an affair. Roger Lambert still identifies as a Christian believer, but his faith lacks the passion that Søren Kierkegaard demands from genuinely religious people. "I have," Roger tells us in the novel's opening paragraph, "been happy at the Divinity School. The hours are bearable, the surroundings handsome, my colleagues harmless and witty, habituated as they are to the shadows. To master a few dead languages, to parade sequential moments of the obdurately enigmatic early history of Christianity before classrooms of the hopeful, the deluded, and the docile—there are more fraudulent ways to earn a living."[1] He has transferred personal faith into the academic realm, becoming the sort of loathsome character that Kierkegaard lampoons as the "assistant professor." Assistant professors, he tells us in the *Afsluttende Uvidenskabelig Efterskrift til de Philosophie Smuler* (Concluding Unscientific Postscript to the Philosophical Fragments, 1846), lack not only faith but even humor; they are "so devoid of comic power that it is shocking; even Hegel, according to the assurance of a zealous Hegelian, is utterly devoid of a sense for the comic. A ludicrous sullenness and paragraph-pomposity that give an assistant professor a remarkable likeness to a Holberg bookkeeper are called earnestness by assistant professors."[2] In his journals, Kierkegaard takes the attack further:

> How ludicrous an assistant professor is! We all laugh when a Mad Meyer tugs at a huge boulder which he believes is money—but the assistant professor goes around proudly, proud of his knowledge, and no one laughs. And yet that is just as ludicrous—to be proud of the knowledge by which a man dupes himself eternally.
>
> Yes, you assistant professor, of all the loathsome inhumans the most loathsome, you may very well manage to say the same thing as the religious person has said, perhaps in even more beautiful language, you also may manage to reap worldly advantages with your shrewdness, yes, even honor and esteem such as the authentically religious person never won in this life—but you are duped eternally.[3]

This blistering critique fits Roger Lambert so closely that it is tempting to believe that Kierkegaard had him in mind when he wrote it. He has no passion for the faith that it is his job to profess and teach, and what is worse, he has contempt for those who do. There is no element of risk to his supposed faith. Certainly his life as a theology professor risks less than his former life as a minister, which he considers, "if not exactly wasted, as a kind of pre-existence, the thought of which depresses me" (3). In fact, he uses that depression as an excuse for not fully examining anything, least of all faith: "I am a depressive. It is very important for my mental well-being that I keep my thoughts directed away from areas of contemplation that might entangle me and pull me down" (4). He is a long way from the "fear and trembling" with which Kierkegaard demands his readers approach these eternal matters. Roger is cold and calculating, and in this stands in for Hawthorne's Chillingworth.

His corresponding Dimmesdale is, in the paradoxes of the novel, a scientist of sorts—a young, evangelical computer scientist named Dale Kohler who thinks he can prove the existence of God through modern science. He criticizes Roger and his divinity-school colleagues for their lack of passion about the things of God; their version of Christianity, he argues, "is what other people call sociology. That's how you teach it, right? Everything from the Gospels to *The Golden Bough*, Martin Luther to Martin Luther King, it all happened, it's historical fact, it's anthropology, it's ancient texts, it's humanly *interesting*, right? But that's so safe. How can you go wrong? Not even the worst atheist in the world denies that people have been religious" (19). He wants to reveal God as "a fact about to burst upon us, right up out of Nature" (19), and when Roger resists, Dale accuses him—not without some justification—of cultivating unbelief: "You don't *want* God to break through. People in general don't want that. They just want to grub along being human, and dirty, and sly, and amusing, and having their weekends with Michelob, and God to stay put in the churches if they ever decide to drop by, and maybe to pull them out in the end" (21). From Dale's perspective, his quarrel with Roger is a matter of passion over and against complacency.

Faith, then, is at the center of *Roger's Version*. But I am less interested in the theological implications of Roger's apathetic fideism and Dale's passionate scientism than in the relationship between the two men themselves. Roger, after all, tells us multiple times that he wishes to remain detached from what Dale sees as pressing theological concerns. He wishes, in fact, to remain detached from almost everything. As James A. Schiff points out, Roger "is resistant to any type of passionate engagement with others."[4] So intense is his detachment that the physical world occasionally disappears in the machinations of his mind: "Amid these books and their prayerful frayed markers, in this tall office riddled with gray autumnal light, while the skies beyond the lancet windows roiled,

Dale and I seemed souls as understood by the Gnostics, shards of shattered Godhead captive in the darks of matter, bewildered amid these shelves as if newly released among the ladders of angels, the impalpable hierarchies, with which popular Gnosticism unaccountably cluttered its common-sense dualism twenty centuries ago. . . . We seemed to float, Dale and I, in lightly etched immensities of space" (26–27). In this spiritual atmosphere, Roger can surrender his passions along with his body. But Dale eventually gets a rise out of him; the theologian finds himself defending his *deus absconditus*, and realizes that "Dale too had hit home; he had aroused passion in me. I cared about this. Free Him, even though He die" (80). And Roger's reaction disturbs him: "I do not like myself when I become engaged. Passion of an argumentative sort makes me feel sticky and hot, caught in a web of exaggeration and untruth. We owe the precision of things, at least, a courtesy of silence, of silent measurement" (88). His relationship with Dale frequently denies him the "silent measurement" he seeks, however, and in his interactions with Dale he finds himself being driven by a passionate imagination in a way that he has not been for years. In the Kierkegaardian sense, then, in which faith is the discoverer of the highest truth and in which truth is *"an objective uncertainty, held fast through appropriation with the most passionate inwardness,"*[5] Roger puts his faith not in God but in Dale—and more specifically in his wife's infidelity with Dale. This faith expresses itself through Roger's extraordinarily vivid imagination, which, in a way that ought to be familiar by now, idealistically creates the world that he lives in.

As Roger sees it, Dale's theological and scientific project is an act of the imagination, the unreliable workings of the human mind on the blank slate of nature. And in fact, when, near the end of the novel, Dale is on the receiving end of a lecture from the cheerful atheist Myron Kriegman, he finds his fantasies revealed as fantasies. Myron talks about the numbers 3 and 24, and Dale finds it "odd that the man would mention these almost-magic, almost-revelatory numbers that Dale used to circle painstakingly in red; he now sees them to have been illusions, ripples in nothingness such as Kriegman is rhapsodizing about" (301–2). His entire project falls down at his feet: "All that has preoccupied Dale through this winter and early spring, inflating his brain tenderly, has proved illusory" (308). But this conversation is itself at least partially the product of Roger's own imagination. Verna does reveals that Dale has "lost his faith. Some guy he met at that party you didn't invite me to made him see how silly it was" (314). But the details of the actual conversation are hidden from us; Roger reports them, but he is not privy to the conversation itself. He presents us with an ideal version of it, a version in which Myron says exactly what he wants him to and in which Dale feels exactly the way he wants him to.

Ironically enough, one of the many things that Roger rails against in his conversations with Dale is idealism, which "makes me intellectually indignant" (168). His major encounters with idealism come when "calf-eyed students" discourse "on quantum mechanics and the Heisenberg principle as proof of that hoary old philosophical monstrosity Idealism" (168). He goes so far as to argue against the very notion of the mind:

> The reason people don't make too much of their minds is that they see how totally at the mercy of the material world the mind is—a brick drops on your head, your mind is extinguished no matter how indeterminate are the motions of the individual atoms composing the clay in the brick. Life, thought—these are no match for the planets, the tides, the physical laws. Every minute of every day, all the prayers and ardent wishing in the world can't budge a little blob of cancer, or the AIDS virus, or the bars of a prison, or the latch of a refrigerator a child accidentally locked himself into. (169–70)

Again familiarly, Roger is expressing the despair of finitude: human hopelessness in the face of the seemingly meaningless material world, a world of *l'être-en-soi* that threatens to wipe out *l'être-pour-soi* altogether. But despite these disavowals, Roger is a man of powerful imagination. James Schiff points out the major role that vision plays in the novel; its narrator, after all, "delights in seeing into and through the eyes of others, and in the process, manipulating those lives."[6] But Roger's imagination goes beyond mere manipulation of other people; he frequently, perhaps constantly, reads meaning, and its absence, into the physical world. "Clouds," he tells us early on, "are strange: at times they seem gigantic sculptures, bulging with three-dimensional form like those musclebound marble Berninis gesturing halfway up Saint Peter's walls, and at other times, the exact copies of those same clouds, mere smudges of vapor, virtually nonexistent" (11). He cannot help turning the merely physical into something transcendent. Fittingly, he later tells Dale that, for early Christians, "Writing was sympathetic magic," and thus "writing something down was to an extent making it so, it was a creative rather than mimetic act" (83). The same holds for Roger's own imagination, which is a method of creating rather than comprehending the world. It is his mind—despite his protests about its weakness—that turns the clouds into Renaissance sculptures. And more sinisterly, it is his mind that, in Updike's words, "encloses the other [characters] and modulates, with his arcane potions and malign remedies, their story."[7] He will note later, when his niece, Verna, predicts that her toddler will be taken away from her, that "like many visions, this was a wish fulfillment" (273). His many visions, his many imaginative flights of fancy, are also wishes. He wants the clouds to be sculptures because that would suggest a cosmic Sculptor. And when he begins to have visions of Dale's affair with Roger's wife, Esther, it is at least in part because he wants such an affair to exist, because Esther's infidelity would justify his own with his niece.

Predictably, then, from adolescence on, Roger's imagination is often focused on the female body. He tells us that, when his half-sister Edna (Verna's mother) "began to menstruate, I had the powerful impression that the days of her 'period' flooded the house with her sticky, triumphantly wounded animal aroma, even to the corners of my room with its boyish stink of athletic socks and airplane glue" (9). The male imagination is at work here—but female sexual power dominates it, at least for a time. Roger's lust for his niece figures as an attempt to wrest control back from her mother. When he visits her apartment, he looks down the front of her shirt, a view that "evoked confused echoes of a day or days with Edna in Ohio, summer days, when I was spending my obligatory month with my father, and we children sought shelter from the sun and insects and boredom in attic games" (134). In the daughter, he sees the mother—a long-ago object of frustrated sexual desire—to the point where the reader cannot immediately tell at whom he is gazing. He remembers Edna winning a wrestling match and leaving him on the ground, from which vantage point he "looked up her legs as now I looked down the front of Verna's low bodice and saw into Edna's shorts up to her underpants" (135). The grammatical confusion of this sentence demonstrates Roger's confusion, spurred on by lust and imagination. He tries to turn Verna into her mother—or, more accurately, into a vision of her mother that he can re-create, control, and position as he likes.

But the joke is on him. Verna, experienced in sex to the point of boredom at the age of nineteen, is onto him from the beginning: "I know you have the hots for me . . . but is it the hots for me really or for my mom?" (139). In this mutual seduction, Roger "felt like women must often feel: the irritating constraint of being inside someone else's sexual fantasy" (142). Even so, his lust reigns. At Thanksgiving dinner, "I was conscious not only of Verna, whose sallow flesh with such confident insolence pressed against the bulging wool of her red dress, . . . but of Esther as seen through the eyes of Dale Kohler: an older woman, petite and wearily wise, yet with a maternal depth of tolerance and nurture beneath her crisp, taut-pulled manner" (114). Both women, then, have their essences in male vision—and in Esther's case, it is male vision as filtered through male imagination, with Roger's attempting to enter Dale's head. Roger's imagination is, in fact, especially drawn to Dale, for whom he feels "an odd and sinister empathy: he kept inviting my mind out of its tracks to follow him on his own paths through the city" (90). The power, however, remains with Roger; we have no indication that the paths down which he "follows" Dale actually belong to the younger man at all.

Even so, the visions recur. When Dale leaves his office for the first time, Roger imagines himself teaching class in a few minutes, and "thus foreseeing my future, I was disconcerted by a strange unwilled vision: I foresaw Dale's as well" (28). Later, as he walks home, he assumes—without any legitimate reason—that Dale has walked the same way and "knew that he, that tall waxy-pale intruder, had noticed this same strange emblematic leaf three hours earlier, on his way through my neighborhood to his dismal, distant own" (30–31). He takes special notice of how his upper-class neighborhood might have affected Dale: "There is a shady narcotic gentility to these blocks that becalms lives, instilling the notion that there is nowhere better to go, and my young man would be attracted and lulled by this quality, trying to imagine, as he walks along, from the glimpses of books and lamps and knick-knacks that the curtained windows allow, the shape and taste of our lives, coveting our possessions before he passes out of the neighborhood" (31). In fact, in none of Roger's interactions with Dale does the reader get the sense that the young man is particularly covetous of his material comforts; Dale is focused on faith, mathematics, and the well-being of Roger's niece Verna. The fact that Roger refers to him, in this vision, as "my young man" suggests that he knows on some level that the vision he receives is a product of his imagination rather than of some mystical connection to Dale—but if he knows this, it does not stop the visions from coming.

Roger's obsession with Dale is important because his imagination takes on a homosexual, or at least a homosocial,[8] attitude that is not as evident in any earlier Updike protagonist's. He tells us, for example, that "Esther, spied upon unawares, looked like prey—someone to sneak up on and rape, another man's precious wife to defile, as a kind of message to him, scrawled in semen" (34). This is not sex as a religious experience; it's not even sex for the sake of the man's pleasure. It's sex as a territorial action aimed at other men. After all, Esther is no longer exciting to her husband: "She came to me, a hundred pounds of well-known woman, and all sense of her being another man's precious wife instantly dissipated. Boredom wafted from her like the scent of stale sweat, boredom so intense as to be the cause of boredom in others" (35). Their marriage interests him only because of the presence of another man: "it was clear to me that without the boy [their son] Esther and I would have almost nothing to talk about, and the coldness between us would increase" (39). It is not surprising, then, that Roger is particularly fond of thinking about Dale in sexual terms. He notes: "The shape and mucilaginous infolded structure of our wrinkly human genitals did not, evidently, amid phenomena that did, strike him as an argument for God's existence. I pictured his waxy face, breaking out in a masturbator's pimples. I felt superior to him, being sexually healthy ever since Esther took over from ungainly, barren Lillian" (57). He feels both "physical repugnance, at his waxiness, and the unreachable luminescence in his eyes," and "a certain attraction, reciprocating what seemed to be his sticky adherence to me" (90). His imagination fixates on Dale, and the novel's purest expression of that imagination is his nauseatingly detailed descriptions of Esther's performing oral sex on Dale—a description that he presents as the gospel truth, though again Updike gives no credible evidence that the two are having an affair at all, let alone an affair that progresses the way he imagines. These visions are attempts on Roger's part to control Dale, just as his lust for his niece is an attempt to re-create her in a more pleasing image. And indeed, Updike hints that Roger's imagination is not as reliable as he believes it to be. When he visits Verna in her terrible neighborhood for the first time, he sees a man standing on the corner, a man who "could have been an aging divinity student, or a TV repairman waiting for his partner to park the van or a madman about to strangle me in order to silence the voices in his head" (52). The certainty with which he imagines the absent Dale is nowhere to be found when confronted with flesh-and-blood presence. We do learn from Verna toward the end of the novel that Dale has "been having an affair with some older woman, somebody married who I guess is a pretty hot ticket. . . . She lives in this really big expensive house, Dale said. Somewhere in your neighborhood, I got the impression" (318–19). But this hardly confirms his visions. For one thing, as Roger says, "It's a big neighborhood" (319); for another, Verna is not the most reliable reporter, and it is perfectly within the realm of possibility that she is play-ing on a fear that she knows her uncle has.[9] The truth about Dale's rela-tionship with Esther is, in other words, fundamentally unknowable; it is an object of faith, perhaps the only one left in Roger's life.

A Month of Sundays ends with female resistance to the re-creating male imagination, and Roger's Version follows its predecessor's lead. Throughout the novel, Roger has shown a distinct lack of interest in his wife, at least in part because she has become boring—because she no lon-ger fires his imagination (and with it, his lust). With Dale out of the pic-ture and Verna sent back to her mother in Ohio, Roger's imagination is blocked; he will, presumably, fall into the morass of boredom offered him by his wife. And yet, as the novel closes, he shows us that she still has some surprises in her: "She has been irritable and abstracted these recent days, and eats late at night, and sleeps more than usual. More strangely, she has stopped watching her weight; I am sure she weighs more now than a hundred pounds" (328). And yet these surprises do not signify that Esther is submitting to Roger's imagination; instead, she asserts her-self in the novel's closing exchange:

> She came into the kitchen dressed in a crisp dark suit, with lace at her throat. Her hair was done up in a somehow triumphant sweep.
> "Where on earth are you going?" I asked her.
> "Obviously," she said, "to church."
> "Why would you do a ridiculous thing like that?"
> "Oh—" She appraised me with her pale green eyes. Whatever emotions had washed through her had left an amused glint, a hint or

seed. In her gorgeous rounded woman's voice she pronounced smilingly, "To annoy you." (328–29)

Esther is interesting to her husband again—but not because he can control her and reshape her. Instead, she is going to church to annoy him; she has never been devout, and Roger himself is not a regular churchgoer. Her real motivations are hidden from her husband just as they are hidden from the reader. Furthermore, the novel ends not with the male vision that has dominated its narration. Instead, it ends with the view through Esther's eyes, or at least the nearest approximation we can get of that view from a first-person narrator who is not her. The limits of Roger's imaginative powers have been revealed to him, and though the novel ends before we can get a good idea of how he will respond to that revelation, it is at least clear that his marriage will not broken in the same way it was at the beginning of the novel. Power has been taken from him, ultimately for his own salvation.

Notes

[1] Updike, *Roger's Version*, 3. Hereafter cited in-text.

[2] Kierkegaard, *Concluding Unscientific Postscript*, 281.

[3] Kierkegaard, *Søren Kierkegaard's Papers and Journals*, XI A 412.

[4] Schiff, "Updike's *Scarlet Letter* Trilogy," 267.

[5] Kierkegaard, *Concluding Unscientific Postscript*, 203.

[6] Schiff, "Updike's *Scarlet Letter* Trilogy," 269. Schiff is, to my eyes, a little too ready to accept Roger's visions as being genuine rather than the product of his own imagination: "In sharing Dale's 'field of vision,' Roger temporarily sheds his gray skin and is able to see anew" (269). Certainly Roger is excited by his visions, but they are, like Verna's, primarily wish fulfillment; he is not sharing but creating a field of vision for Dale, and this gives his world meaning, at least for a time.

[7] Updike, "A 'Special Message,'" 858.

[8] The distinction belongs to Eve Kosofsky Sedgwick, who plots male sexuality on a triangle in her book *Between Men*. The supposed love triangle wherein two men pursue a single woman, she suggests, may in fact conceal amorous attraction between the two men themselves. Updike likely did not have *Between Men* in mind when he wrote *Roger's Version*—the treatise was published the year before the novel—but the parallels are strong, and James A. Schiff notes in *Updike's Version* that between Roger and Dale "there exists an intense degree of attachment, which borders on the homoerotic. However, it is only through the configuration of the adulterous triangle, in which a woman (Hester, Esther, Verna) stands as the supposed object of affection, that these heterosexual male characters are able to express their homoerotic tendencies" (63). Updike has never been known for his positive treatment of homosexuality. In "Scenes from the Fifties" (1995), for example, the narrator recoils from the gay advances of a friend. The

protagonist of "The Rumor" (1991) feels his potential homosexuality as an existential threat. And sexual conversions feature as an O. Henry-esque twist ending in "The Women Who Got Away" (1998), not to mention in *The Witches of Eastwick* (1984). In a twisted way, *Roger's Version* may have the clearest and most serious treatment of male-male sexuality, although no one is going to suggest that Updike is particularly progressive here either.

[9] Other critics seem not to have taken Verna's unreliability into account. Jeff Campbell, for example, says that "Verna gives objective confirmation to Roger's intuitions when she tells him (and the reader) at their concluding luncheon interview that Dale has been having an affair with an older, married woman in Roger's neighborhood" (*Updike's Novels*, 261). But Verna has shown a remarkable ability to see Roger's deepest fears, as when she asks him whether he has the hots for her or for her mother; she also clearly enjoys making him sweat. Do we really have an "objective confirmation" here? Perhaps—but certainly not certainly.

11: S.

A Month of Sundays is presented as a diary; *Roger's Version* is a traditional first-person narration, albeit one that imagines itself to be omniscient. *S.* (1988), the conclusion of the *Scarlet Letter* trilogy, is Updike's only contribution to the venerable genre of the epistolary novel. And whereas *A Month of Sundays* is narrated by the Dimmesdale stand-in and *Roger's Version* by Roger Chillingworth, *S.* comes to us from the point of view of a twentieth-century Hester Prynne—Sarah Price Worth, who abandons her upper-class doctor husband to live on an Arizona ashram with the Arthat, a Hindu spiritual leader. *S.* thus gives us what its two predecessors did not: a woman's point of view. Even so, the movement of the novel remains largely the same as the earlier novels: a woman is forced into the imagination of a powerful man, only ultimately to resist that imagination by the force of her own material existence. Here, however, Updike is much more blatantly concerned with female power, although that power largely fades in the face of the male imagination.[1]

The opening sentences of the novel announce Updike's interest in female power. In *A Month of Sundays*, let us remember, Tom Marshfield expresses his power through his writing, which is figured as an instrument of the male imagination. Fittingly, then, *S.* figures the female imagination as a form of silence. As she flies west to the ashram, Sarah writes to her husband: "The distance between us grows, even as my pen hesitates. The engines drone in the spaces between words, eating up the miles, the acres of the flat farms in big brown and green squares below the wing as it inches along."[2] Women, as Sarah sees it, tend to exist in absence and in silence. This is why she argues that the word *daughter*, "with those mysterious silent letters in the middle," is "a much more satisfying word" than *son* (16). Words—both spoken and written—are the tools of men. And so when Sarah writes, it is necessarily a transgressive act. Female power begins in silence but grows by co-opting male language. Her lawyer, she tells Charles, "sent me these forms requiring both our signatures and I rummaged through your desk for one of those big black felt-tips you always use" (6). She forges her husband's signature on the forms: "I know it so well, that signature, it's been branded into me, I wouldn't be surprised to see it burned into my flank if I looked down, char for Charles, it felt wonderful writing it—being *you* for a second, with all your dark unheeding illegible male authority" (6). This is remarkably similar to the argument made by Hélène Cixous in "Le rire de la Méduse" (The Laugh of the Medusa, 1975). Women, Cixous argues, are largely ashamed to express themselves through the written word "because writing is at once too high, too great for you, it's reserved for the great—that is, for 'great men.'"[3] Heretofore, "far more extensively and repressively than is ever suspected or admitted, writing has been run by a libidinal and cultural—hence political, typically masculine—economy; . . . this is a locus where the repression of women has been perpetuated, over and over, more or less consciously" (1945). And since the metaphysical binaries of Western culture have assigned the soul to men and the body to women, women must write from their bodies— which is to say they must write from the bodies that have been co-opted by the sort of re-creative male lust that informs so much of Updike's fiction. Doing so will result in a new female liberation:

> To write. An act which will not only "realize" the decensored relation of woman to her sexuality, to her womanly being, giving her access to her native strength; it will give her back her goods, her pleasures, her organs, her immense bodily territories which have been kept under seal; it will tear her away from the superegoized structure in which she has always occupied the place reserved for the guilty (guilty of everything, guilty at every turn: for having desires, for not having any; for being frigid, for being "too hot"; for not being both at once; for being too motherly and not enough; for having children and for not having any; for nursing and for not nursing . . .)—tear her away by means of this research, this job of analysis and illumination, this emancipation of the marvelous text of her self that she must urgent learn to speak. (1947, ellipses in the original)

Sarah has distinctly Cixousian goals in putting the text of S. to paper. And we must remember, too, that we are not reading a private diary; we are reading letters, public documents that express Sarah's desired liberation openly, even defiantly at times.

As such, she attacks social institutions that have been used to oppress women. Foremost among these is marriage. Sarah tells Charles that

> one of the things I suppose I've always resented without admitting it to myself is how you tended to call money "yours" that we really earned together since not only was I keeping up our lovely home to enhance your image with your patients and fellow-doctors and raising our daughter virtually unassisted since you were always at the office for reasons that didn't dawn on poor innocent me for years, not to mention how while you so heroically (everybody kept telling me) slogged through medical school and internship I was the one who gave up two years of college and any chance of going on to graduate school. (5)

Female contributions to this marriage are all silent, all behind the scenes and below the surface, and an imperious man like Charles likely misses them altogether. Unsurprisingly, much of Sarah's first letter consists of instructions on how to keep the household together. Her fleeing such a marriage corresponds, in her mind, to her taking pen in hand: it is a rebellion and a liberation.

In her marriage to Charles, Sarah felt her essential self sliding into him, so that eventually—and thrillingly, at least at first—she no longer had anything that wasn't part of him. The effect is painful, and pathetic. Sarah reminiscences to her daughter, Pearl:

> You remember how conscientiously I used to tell him, at dinner-time, of my day?—the little tail-wagging housewife-puppy, whimpering and drooling, offering up her pathetic worried bones and chewing sticks, her shopping trips to Boston and her excursions to the plant nursery in Wenham, her tennis games and her yoga lessons and her boozy little lunches at the club with the same women she played tennis with yesterday, as if to say to this big silent he-doctor, this gray eminence, "Look, dear, how hard I've been working to enhance your lovely estate!" or "See, I'm not wasting your money, I couldn't find a thing I wanted to buy at Bonwit's!" or "Every hour accounted for—not a minute of idleness or daydreaming or sleeping with all those dark handsome strangers that came today to pump out the fat trap!" (15)

In seeking her husband's approval, Sarah now feels, she was seeking an identity, an essence, for herself in the only place one could be grounded in her social milieu. This would be one thing if it were a mutual condition, but Charles hardly seems to notice his wife. His numerous infidelities teach Sarah that she is not the center of his world in the same way that he is the center of hers, and so the relationship is wildly unequal, all the re-creative power existing on Charles's side: "though in some sense you were just another Boston bred preppy brat not much older than I in another you were my creator, you had put me here, in this rocky grassy sparkling seaside landscape, amid the afternoon silence and the furniture" (10). Her spiritual awakening thus demands that she create herself instead. The first step is absence and silence: "Let me become truly nothing to you, at last," she writes her husband. "I will change my name. I will change my being" (12). Thus freed from her husband's imagination she will be able to exercise her own: "This woman you 'knew' and 'possessed' is no more. I am destroying her. I am sinking into the great and beautiful blankness which is our European/Christian/Western avoidance maneuver to clutter and mask with material things and personal 'achievements.' Ego is the enemy. Love is the goal" (12). Set free from her husband—and the "European/Christian/

Western" patriarchy that he represents—she is able to find herself, or to create herself, using Eastern religion and the Arizona ashram. Part and parcel with her setting herself free from her husband is her rejection of her therapist, another man who has perhaps had undue influence on her life. "I feel I *should* render an accounting of what I've been up to," she writes him, "as if the pseudo-daughterly guilty feelings that you led me to override in regard to Charles remain undischarged in regard to *you*. Looking back at my years of therapy, I confess that it all now seems much more patriarchal and Judeo-Christian than it did at the time. Far from being my ally against Charles as I fantasized, you were *his* ally against my liberation" (102–3). In receiving psychoanalysis, Sarah has merely swapped one male imagination for another, and to be free, she must reject it, even though it might offer her wise counsel.

She figures her escape to Arizona, then, as an act of her own imagination, a breaking free. She reports to her mother, as she prepares to enter the ashram, that

> I did feel my entire flight out here the day before yesterday taking place in an upholding atmosphere of love—love streaming against my face and chest like the sunset light in that clipper ship we had framed above the big carved mantel in Dedham. I used to look at the picture as a little girl until I felt myself to be a mermaid in the waves, looking up at this artifact of men from another world—the masts, the riggings, the portholes, the wooden woman on the prow. All the details of that picture—the froth, the clouds, their little dabbed-on crests of sunset red—seemed magical to me, a piece of a Heaven I would some day enter. Think of me as still that little girl. (23)

Sarah clearly means for this description to serve as proof that she is following faith into something that will be beneficial for her, but there are at least three reasons to suspect that she is wrong about this. First, her description of the painting is very similar to the description Joey Robinson gives of the landscape in his mother's house in *Of the Farm*:

> The pentagonal side of a barn was diagonally bisected by a purple shadow cast by nothing visible, and a leafless tree of uncertain species stood rooted in lush grass impossibly green. Beyond, I revisited, bending deeper into the picture, a marvelous sky of lateral stripes of pastel color where as a child I had imagined myself treading, upside-down, a terrain of crayons. The tiny black V of one flying bird was planted in this sky, between two furrows of color, so that I had imagined that if my fingers could get through the glass they could pluck it up, like a carrot sprout. This quaint picture, windowing a fabulous rural world, had hung, after we had moved to the farmhouse, in the room at the head of the stairs, where I had slept as an adolescent.[4]

This landscape is for Joey a physical symbol of his mother's myth-making imagination; it is the agent by which she keeps her son locked into the "fabulous rural world" in which she herself lives. That Sarah's memory of the ship painting reads so similarly—an idealized painting encountered when the narrator was a child and that promised some sort of magical other world—suggests that the feeling of "love" she feels on the airplane is more likely than not the product of her own mind.

Likewise, on the page after she gives us her memory of the painting, she talks about the dangers of driving through the desert, where she has experienced a hallucination: "There *is* this shimmer, you *do* see mirages, they become very common—lakes with not just water but what look like beachfront cottages and I could have sworn sailboats and (this is the point) at one point a big rambling Victorian brown-shingled structure being reflected in the water just like that lodge in Maine we went to once or twice" (24). This report demonstrates the degree to which Sarah imposes her childhood memories on the physical world of her adult life. Finally, she asks her mother, after reporting her memory and the experience on the plane, to "think of me still as that little girl" (24). She obviously means this as a positive thing, means to suggest that she is approaching the spiritual experience she hopes to have with a maximum of wonderment and a minimum of cynicism. And yet, just a few paragraphs later, she is snarling, "How stupid children are" (24). This vision she believes herself to be having, this divine approval of her choices, proceeds from her own mind—and consequently proof of her own stupidity.

Another irony is that, in fleeing the masculine forces that she feels have ruined her imagination, Sarah puts herself under the sway of another: the Arhat. In him, she sees nothingness, an analogue of the silence that takes her further and further away from Charles. This nothingness is figured as a kind of feminine power, hiding between the noisy presences of male power. At the ashram, after all, society's values are reversed. The Arhat is marked by absence rather than presence: "he must conserve himself and needs all these women to hide behind, living so withdrawn you hardly ever see him except at darshan and when he drives by in his limo" (48). And as he explains it, "pursha, motionless inactive spirit, is male, and prakriti—active nature, you could say—is female, so that in the ideal maithuna, that's what they call fucking in Sanskrit, the woman does all the work! The men always sit and she is always on top, the way Shiva and Shakti do it!" (51). The ashram's version of Buddhism thus seems to grant a power to women in a way that Western Christianity does not. One of the Arhat's sermons even presents woman as the path to male transcendence: "For Buddha and his followers, woman is the portal of release. She is that within the world which takes us out of the world. She is that being through whom is made manifest the karuna, the compassion, of nirvana, of non-being. . . . 'Buddhatvam yoshidyonisamsritam.' That is a very important saying. . . . It means, 'Buddahood is in the female organ.' The yoni. The cunt. Buddahood is in the cunt" (106). This language appears to be granting women a power denied to them by Western metaphysics—but, as Kathleen Verduin points out, in the Arhat's anthropology, the female sex organ "comprises also a 'nothingness' reminiscent of Karl Barth's *das Nichtige*, Satanic nonbeing: Buddhist nirvana joins vaginal vacuum as . . . the terror at the core of Updike's psychic plot."[5] What is more, his language, far from giving women power, makes them a mere instrument for male enlightenment, even though the Arhat claims that "woman is in the man and man is in the woman" (109). It is a false power, one that maintains the superior male position. The Arhat's spiritual authority, likewise, manipulates a bevy of women to serve him while he sits in an air-conditioned limousine.

Whatever new creation Sarah receives at the ashram does not come from within her, as she herself admits: "My happiness is deeper than I've ever felt happiness before. It's as if there is a level the sun has never reached before. *He* makes it possible, the Arhat, he *permits* it—his voice, his glow" (42–43). Despite having escaped her husband and her therapist, she is still the product of a man's imagination; as she puts it, "Whatever we do is within the Master's love" (70), as if she and everyone else exist in his mind. And though it is hard to tell exactly what the Arhat is thinking, since we have access only to Sarah's thoughts, he clearly looks at her with the sort of imaginative lustful gaze that we have come to expect from Updike's men: "he has this marvelous gift of taking you in with these enormous sad bulging bottomless eyes, of seeming to be letting you in on some huge unspoken deeply philosophical secret" (71). The Arhat's gaze, unlike that of other lustful men in Updike's fiction, appears to reveal himself rather than the woman at whom he is looking—but this is an illusion, given that the Arhat's entire existence is an illusion, a screen to cover up his being Art Steinmetz, from Watertown, Massachusetts.[6] In fact, despite his high-minded spiritualist rhetoric, the Arhat is as possessive and devouring as his counterparts in *Roger's Version* and *A Month of Sundays*. When Sarah tells him that she is recording a cassette tape for her friends, he asks, jealously, "*They are still real to you?*" (177).[7] Her response is that "only you are truly real" (177), suggesting that he has crowded out everything else from her imagination. They have sex for the first time after this exchange, and his foreplay involves transforming her into an ideal goddess: "*First is concentration, sadhana. We concentrate upon the beloved. It is best if she is parakiya rati—the wife of another. That is why I so much like your Charles. We need him. Otherwise you are apakva, unripe. Otherwise you are samanya, ordinary woman. We must mentally conceive you into vishesha rati—woman extraordinary, divine essence of woman*" (180). He openly admits in this passage that it is his imagination, his gaze, that turns her into the divine essence. And, as with Charles, the movement goes only in one direction. When Sarah asks if she should concentrate on him, too, he replies, "*It is not so necessary, what the woman does*" (180). The woman is body, whereas the man is mind; he is always in control. Accordingly, the Arhat focuses Sarah's imagination until it is identical with his own: "*Think with me of your body cell by cell, as something greater than galaxies, greater than all the jewel trees. You are like a Bodhisattva standing in the Land of Bliss, in Sukhavati. You are infinitely tall, infinitely splendid. You are immeasurably radiant, amitabha. You are amitayus, forever enduring*" (184). He transforms her from body into spirit, from actual existing person into ideal—and yet, because it is his imagination that makes this transformation, she remains body in the sense that she is inert and passive in the face of his re-creation. In the meantime, he hides from her. When she discovers his secret, that the Arhat is a false identity, she tells her mother that "he kept up this pretense and said everything to me in this funny highpitched singsong accent. While I was responding with my whole heart, with my honest voice" (212). He is, in other words, an unseen seer, and she is the matter on which he stamps the meaning of the world. But, as she eventually points out, "In your philosophy, one woman is as good as another. We're all lotus to your linga" (224). The dark side of idealization is that the actual form of the idealized being does not matter very much; as such, idealizing a person is an act of spiritual violence against her.

It is tempting to call Sarah naïve, or even stupid—certainly the reader recognizes that something is amiss with the Arhat long before she is willing to admit it. And yet Updike hints throughout the novel that Sarah knows, or suspects, that the Arhat is not everything he claims to be, that she is living in a fantasy world. She periodically leaves the ashram, for example, to receive and send her mail at a nearby motel. At one point, she returns a long-overdue rental car to the Phoenix Hertz agency, and reports that "The real world hit me like a big hot fist" (99), her language suggesting that deep down she knows that the world of the ashram is a fantasy world, a world of the Arhat's imagining. Her treatment of the consumerist world she is ostensibly leaving behind, too, suggests that she may know more than she lets on. She tells her husband in her initial letter that she "was never really satirical about our material advantages, the socio-economic side of it all. Our comfort did not embarrass me" (8). And this is clearly true; as noted above, her first instructions for her abandoned husband are practical and distinctly nonspiritual. The irony is that it is her consumerist lifestyle that first led her to her spiritual awakening. Her husband, she reports, in "leaving me alone so much amid our piled-up treasures, . . . gave me time to sense that my life was illusion, *maya*" (11). The material goods she surrounds herself with have failed to satisfy her deepest longings: "My spirit, a little motionless fleck of eternal unchanging *purusha*, was invited to grow patient with *prakriti*—all that brightness, all that flow. I would look at the rim of the saucer of my fourth decaf for the day and feel myself sinking—drawn around and around and down like a bug caught on the surface of bathwater when the plug is pulled" (11–12). Eastern mysticism enters this landscape and offers her a way out; yoga gives her the vocabulary to see that she has been "living in a paper house, among miniature trees and gardens raked to represent nothingness. And into this papery world broke love" (12). Her call to higher things, as she conceives it, is a call to desert her husband and the life he has created for her. She will write to him from the ashram, sneeringly: "For you as well as for us here at the ashram, work is worship—but you worship a stupid god, a stodgy pudgy god of respectability and out-shoes and country clubs, of acceptable street addresses and of acquisitions that dissolve downwards into démodé junk rather than, as for those who take the path of yoga and non-ego, dissolve upwards, into Samadhi and the blissful void of Mahabindu" (62). This is all very high-minded talk; she even tells Charles, "I pity you, darling" (62). And it is language that she clearly learned from the tapes of the Arhat that she and her vapid friend Midge listened to. It suggests the unreality of the material world—material both in the sense of physicality and in the sense of consumerism—and the dominance and superiority of a higher spiritual world that can be accessed through the mind, the soul, and the imagination.

The problem is that Sarah often looks like a hypocrite because she hangs onto the material world that she decries, even while trying to grasp the spiritual. "If you decide to sell the house or any part of our joint holdings," she writes to Charles, "I of course expect my legal half" (13). At the end of the letter in which she castigates her husband for his materialism, she instructs him on how to take care of their lawn and says that if he rents out their summer home, "Be sure to send me half the proceeds" (65). She writes to her husband's lawyer that

> Equal division of blame and assets does not seem to me a very radical principle. In fact, as of course all males know, and male lawyers doubly know, the division can never be truly equal, since the man retains the professional skills and status to whose acquisition and consolidation the subservient wife sacrificed her prime years; he can rapidly earn his way out of any momentary financial setback, whereas the wife is forever financially maimed, and unless she leaves the marriage with enough capital to support her—which is rare and growing rarer in this day and age of misogynistic judges and shameless lawyers—will be thrown back upon the job market like a load of old laundry, fit for nothing but the rags and odd buttons of employment. (139)

These are not the words of a person who has transcended the material world. And we cannot reduce Sarah's hypocrisy by saying that she wants her half of the estate in order to give the money to the ashram and thus to extend the reach of the Arhat's imagination. When she first arrives at the ashram, she is asked "how much money was I bringing to the Treasury of Enlightment" (38). She tells her interlocutor that "I had left my success-ful doctor husband on a more or less sudden inspiration and all I could bring away was eleven thousand dollars. I had thought of saying ten, but eleven sounded more like it really *was* all I had" (38). In fact, she has almost $200,000, which she gradually deposits into a secret bank account in the Caymans as the novel progresses—suggesting that she recognizes that the ashram is not all it seems to be long before she learns the truth about Art Steinmetz.

The reader's first instinct is to condemn Sarah for her hypocrisy, and many critics have done just that.[8] But we must always remember that Sarah's hypocrisy is what allows her genuinely to escape the orbit of the Arhat's imagination, and Charles's. She resists being made wholly into the product of either man's imagination by keeping a foot squarely planted in the material world. But her own ingenuity keeps her from being made into the blank matter on which the male imagination stamps itself. She is an imaginative agent in her own right, just as Ms. Prynne and Esther Lambert are at the ends of their respective novels. The reader feels Sarah's triumph more strongly than either of her predecessors, however, partly because we have received the events of the novel through her conscious-ness and partly because we have frequently felt ourselves to be smarter than her (how could she not recognize the Arhat as a fraud?) and more virtuous than her (how could she maintain such a consumerist attitude in the face of spiritual enlightenment?). Sarah, in other words, slips away from our attempts to control and define her, just as she slips away from Charles's and Art's. Hester Prynne triumphs and lives to bury Dimmes-dale and Chillingworth alike.

Notes

[1] I have chosen to examine *S.* in this section because of its connections with *A Month of Sundays* and *Roger's Version*. It probably would have been legitimate to read it in the context of the *female* imagination in *The Witches of Eastwick*— but Updike clearly gives the Arhat the imaginative power for most of the length of the novel, and so I think it belongs more neatly in my examination of male imagination.

[2] Updike, *S.*, 3. Hereafter cited in-text.

[3] Cixous, "The Laugh of the Medusa," 1943. Hereafter cited in-text.

[4] Updike, *Of the Farm*, 18–19.

[5] Verduin, "Updike, Women, and Mythologized Sexuality," 69.

[6] James A. Schiff argues, quite rightly, that Steinmetz "is a prime example of that uniquely American mode of thinking in which one believes that one can transform oneself into anything one chooses. Steinmetz is the Jay Gatsby of religion" ("Updike's *Scarlet Letter* Trilogy," 272). In this sense, the Arhat's re-creation of Sarah is a side effect of his attempt to re-create himself.

[7] The Arhat's words appear in italics in the sections of the novel that represent Sarah's cassette recordings for her friends in Massachusetts.

[8] Schiff, for example, argues that Sarah's lingering materialism causes her to fail "to become the 'destined prophetess' for womankind. Her quest for a new identity, intimately associated with the dream of America, fails largely as she discovers that her old self cannot be fully shed" ("Updike's *Scarlet Letter* Trilogy," 273). Charles Berryman, pointing out that Sarah "is the Updike character whom feminist critics most love to hate," suggests that Updike is mocking her quest for enlightenment: "she is often the last person to understand how her life is a sad comedy of deceit and betrayal" ("Faith or Fiction," 199). Judie Newman recognizes that Sarah's materialism saves her, but suggests that "By looting . . . the fortunes of the cult Sarah reenacts her ancestors' predations and casts contemporary American materialism into sharp relief" ("Guru Industries," 230–31). Very few critics seem to find Sarah loveable.

Part IV. Female Power and the Female Imagination

12: "Marching through Boston," "The Stare," "Report of Health," "Living with a Wife," and "Slippage"

Late in *Couples*, when Georgene Thorne discovers that Piet Hanema has rekindled his affair with Foxy Whitman, she muses on the enthrallment of men to women: "Of Piet she expected nothing except that he continue to exist and unwittingly illumine her life. She had willed herself open to him and knew that the chemistry of love was all within her, her doing. Even his power to wound her with neglect was a power she had created and granted; whatever he did he could not escape the province of her freedom, her free decision to love."[1] Updike's fiction is undeniably male-centered, especially in the 1960s, and yet it does grant to women a particular kind of power: the power to enthrall and to ensnare the male mind. This is the peculiar tenor of the feminine imagination, as Updike sees it: it can control and redirect the male imagination, which must either resist or be overthrown. In "Marching through Boston" (1966), for example, we find the power dynamic in the Maples' marriage shifting from Richard toward Joan, who has reimagined herself as a protestor for African-American civil rights—as, in fact, a leader in that movement: "She spoke on the radio; she addressed local groups. In garages and supermarkets he heard himself being pointed out as her husband."[2] He has lost his ability to define himself and is now defined negatively. Simone de Beauvoir laments in *La deuxième sexe* (The Second Sex, 1949) that every woman "finds herself living in a world where men compel her to assume the status of the Other. They propose to stabilize her as an object and to doom her to immanence since her transcendence is to be overshadowed and forever transcended by another ego which is essential and sovereign."[3] In effect, Joan's virtue has temporarily transformed her into the "essential and sovereign" member of their marriage; Richard is thus subordinated and made into the Other, defined by her actions. What is more, he begins to discover that he exists primarily in the imagination of his wife, and that her imagination does not allow him to be the hero he imagines himself to be. When he meets Joan's former psychiatrist, for example, he "felt himself as a putrid heap of anecdotes, of detailed lusts and abuses" (226). The world has shifted around him because the power dynamic has shifted; Richard no doubt has heretofore felt himself as the mind and Joan as the body, but her involvement in the

civil rights movement demonstrates an imaginative force of her own. She
has changed: "Her shyness stayed with her, but it had become a kind of
weapon, as if the doctrine of non-violence had given it point. Her voice,
as she phoned evasive local realtors in the campaign for fair housing, grew
curiously firm and rather obstinately melodious—a note her husband had
never heard in her voice before" (224). But, as John Donne illustrates in
"A Valediction: Forbidding Mourning," the two members of a marriage
are like the two legs of a compass. If the souls of the two spouses can be
said to be separate at all,

> they are two so
> As stiff twin compasses are two;
> Thy soul, the fixed foot, makes no show
> To move, but doth, if the other do.[4]

In a healthy marriage, the two legs of the compass balance each other out
and allow for a perfect circle to be drawn; as the speaker of Donne's poem
puts it, "Thy firmness makes my circle just, / And makes me end where
I begun."[5] But, though Joan's political imagination is certainly focused
on justice, there is no justness in the circle their marriage draws. As she
changes, Richard, attached to her, changes, too: "He grew jealous and irritable" (224). Ideally, her noble politics would call him to a higher life—and
in fact, Richard knows that she is better than him, and even recognizes that
he could be improved by submitting to her political imagination. When she
returns from a march in the Southeast, she "removed underwear she had
worn for seventy hours and stood there shining; to the sleepy man in the
bed it seemed a visitation, and he felt as people of old must have felt when
greeted by an angel—adoring yet resentful, at this flamboyant proof of better things" (223). But he refuses to accept the call, refuses to be an object
to be re-imagined. Instead, as Alice and Kenneth Hamilton argue, he abdi-
cates his responsibilities as a husband and father:

> Richard realizes that he is incapable temperamentally of sharing his
> wife's enthusiasm. But, because he insists upon punishing her for
> the differences between them . . . , what might be creative tensions
> become destructive divisions. While this situation continues, Joan's
> health means Richard's sickness. Freedom marches for the wife spell
> slavery for the husband. Having warned him of the seriousness of
> his condition, Joan can only leave him alone. For his sickness is self-
> induced; and the way to health lies in his having the courage to face
> the truth about his marriage and the determination to conduct him-
> self as a king instead of a slave.[6]

The problem is not really Joan's—she is merely exercising her own imagination, which, as we have seen elsewhere in Updike's work, is the only

way to avoid despair in the face of a world that seems to be meaningless. The problem is Richard's because he refuses to allow her the imaginative space to assert herself, the sort of space he, like Updike's other men, demands for himself.

Another avenue for female power in Updike's work appears in the hold that a woman maintains over a man after their relationship has ended—her ability, in other words, to engender obsession. "The Stare" (1965), clearly written in the aftermath of Updike's disastrous affair with Joyce Harrington, illustrates this sort of power very well. The titular stare belongs to a former lover of the unnamed protagonist and represents her power over him. That power is engendered at their very first meeting, at a party in which the woman defends a remark her husband makes, earning the narrator's scorn, which "she must have felt, across, the room . . . for she gave him her stare. It was, as a look, both blunt and elusive: somewhat cold, certainly hard, yet curiously wide, and even open—its essential ingredient shied away from being named."[7] She is something of a sorceress here, able to read his thoughts and able to force him into particular frames of mind using nothing more than her eyes. She is also, not insignificantly, able to avoid his classifications of her, suggesting that it is her imagination and not his that is dominant in this relationship from the beginning. Her stare thus serves as a metaphor for her ability utterly to confound him; when he kisses her for the first time, he pulls back, and "expecting to find in her face the moist, formless warmth that had taken his lips, he encountered her stare instead" (59). Her resistance to his understanding spurs him to attempt to re-create her into something more comprehensible to him; his lust is the agent of this attempted re-creation, just as it is for the men whose stories I analyzed in the previous chapters: "In the months that unfolded from this, it had been his pleasure to see her stare relax. Her body gathered softness under his . . . Her laugh no longer flashed out so hungrily, and her eyes, brimming with the secret he and she had made, deepened and seemed to rejoin the girlishness that had lingered in the other features of her face" (60). His seduction of her, in other words, domesticates her, and as long as the affair continues, he is able to imagine their relationship in the terms that are the most beneficial to him. But the end of the relationship restores the power to her; when he refuses to tell her that he loves her, he loses his imaginative hold over her: "she took it as a death blow, and in a face whitened and drawn by the shocks of recent days, from beneath dark wings of tensely parted hair, her stare revived into a life so coldly controlled and adamantly hostile that for weeks he could not close his eyes without confronting it—much as a victim of torture must continue to see the burning iron with which he was blinded" (61). The woman is uncontrollable by anything other than love, and, having broken free from the strictures of a relationship that did not progress on her terms, she becomes a powerful foe for her former lover.

By the time of the action of the story, the relationship has been over for some time, and the former lover essentially exists only in the protagonist's imagination, which projects her everywhere in the city he is visiting. The process begins at a restaurant lunch, when he believes that he has seen her. He hopes, of course, for a rekindling of the affair, but also, perhaps, for something more noble: "And everything would be understood, and the need of forgiveness once again magically put behind them, like a wall of paper flames they had passed through" (57). He wants to make the real pain of their parting less real, but he can do so only in his imagination, only in preferring the unreal restoration to the real separation. After all, he does not actually see his former lover in the restaurant or anywhere else, and reality jerks him back to itself embarrassingly: "He felt the eyes of his companions at lunch question him, and he returned his attention to them, his own eyes smarting from the effort of trying to press this unknown woman's appearance into the appearance of another" (58). But the process is repeated multiple times throughout the story; his imagination hardens into obsession, and he becomes absolutely convinced that he will see this woman and that all will be made right again. What has happened to the protagonist is that his imagination—his male power and dominance over this woman—has been superceded by her imagination, in the form of her stare (more powerful in its absence than even in its presence). She has seen through him and now controls what he sees, which of course is *her*, everywhere, at all times: "The pale disc of every face, as it slipped from the edge of his vision, seemed to cup the possibility of being hers (61). He cannot think of anything but her. Presumably this obsession is only temporary; presumably when he leaves the city and returns home to his wife, his imagination will be restored to him. But the story does not allow us to see that ultimate disenchantment, and when we leave the protagonist, he is more fixated than ever, ready at last to give this absent woman what she demanded of him: "a face cut into the side of his vision at such an angle that his head snapped around and he almost said aloud, 'Don't be frightened. Of course I love you'" (65). Male obsession is female victory—and at least in this case, the female imagination is figured as a rudder for the male imagination.

"The Stare" has much in common with the poem "Report of Health," from *Midpoint and Other Poems* (1969). In the title poem of that collection, Updike presents sex and lust as ways of staving off anxiety and the fear of meaninglessness. In a famous pronouncement, he writes that

$$ASS = \frac{1}{ANGST}[8]$$

As Frederick Crews explains, "sex—the more of it the better—had become Updike's answer to Kierkegaard, his preferred means of validating his existence through immersion in the tangible."[9] This image becomes reversed in "Report of Health," in which Updike addresses a former lover (again, presumably Joyce Harrington):

> There is, within, a ghostly maze
> of phantom tubes and nodules where
> those citizens, our passions, flit; and here,
> like sunlight passing from a pattern of streets,
> I feel your bright love leaving.[10]

And when love vanishes, angst reappears, albeit in a more controllable form than death-anxiety: "As for me, you are still the eyes of the air. / I travel from point to point in your presence. / Each unattended gesture hopes to catch your eye."[11] The speaker's personal imagination scarcely exists anymore; it has been ceded to his former lover's, who fixes it on herself.

Female power controls the male imagination in a different way in another poem, "Living with a Wife" (1977), dedicated to Updike's first wife, Mary. Like so many of Updike's men, the speaker attempts to idealize his wife; as she sits in the bathtub, he says,

> You are a pond mirroring
> pink clouds there is moss
> where your white roots meet
> where you lift your arm to shave
> you are a younger kind of tree.[12]

But this idealization fails because his wife is too powerful to be transformed. Her menstrual cycle reconfigures the world around her emotions, her own imagination:

> My house is on fire red
> pain flickers on the walls wet
> flame runs downstairs
> eggs are hurled unripe from the furnace
> and a frown hurts like smoke[13]

This imagination dismantles the speaker's own—the sexual imagery of the earlier, idealizing stanza has disappeared, replaced by the wife's augmented feelings, painting the narrator's entire world and controlling what he is capable of seeing.

In the short story "Slippage" (1984), Updike uses the shift from male to female imagination as an indicator of advancing age.[14] As he enters his sixties, Morison's once-active libido has slowed to a crawl: "Sex was what had slid away. Not the fact of it—his young wife, though she needed her sleep, was less fussily obliging than any woman of Morison's generation would have been—but the hope, the expectancy that used to draw all days and hours to a point."[15] Morison once possessed one of Updike's great imaginative lusts, and he used it, as so many other protagonists do, to give meaning to the world around him: "The air then was full of signs, of meanings, of flashing immaterial knives" (175). But those days have passed, and his imagination has cooled, perhaps forever. Morison, an academic historian, goes to faculty parties at which he is "amazed that there was not one woman at the table he wanted to sleep with. It was a kind of deafness, a turning down of the sound on a television set" (175). He has become all but blind to the female form; the co-eds he sees every day "in their provoking undress were to Morison like foliage, blandly thronging the sides of his vision" (175). His imagination has been transferred from women he wants to sleep with to his daughters, whom he has guiltily abandoned. He exercises his imagination on their lives instead of on his students' bodies: "When he thought of a daughter, he pictured a pea suspended in the corner of an empty cube, waiting to be found, a tiny, hard, slightly shriveled core of disappointment floating in a room whose one window gave on identical, other windows. The picture had the sadness of a Magritte. So it would startle him, confronting one of his daughters in actuality, to find her large and hearty and solicitous toward *him*; he was aging, he would read in her eyes" (176). He cannot re-create even these women, in other words. He is instead re-created by their expectations and their view of him.

His strange interaction with an insane woman at a dinner party drives the point home. He later reports "that she wasn't *there*, in the way that people normally are" (180). He is kind to her, and in his kindness finds himself trapped in a world of her devising: "The vague human appeal that always hangs gaseously in the air of parties had become suffocating solid; the ceiling of the room seemed to be lowering and chasing him from corner to corner, from group to group, as the woman circled in her hunt" (179). This is language that Updike commonly assigns to male lust; that it is here assigned to a woman suggests just how topsy-turvy Morison's world has become in his old age. He has gone from heroic re-creator of the world of *l'être-en-soi* to an example of *l'être-en-soi* to be re-created by a woman's consciousness.

It is difficult to exactly determine Updike's attitude toward the increased female power present in these pieces. Certainly in a story like "The Stare" it is played for pathos almost to the point of horror, but "Slippage" and "Living with a Wife" both border on comedy. An essay first published as "Venus and Others" but collected as "The Female Body" (1990) may provide a clue. The essay begins the way we might expect it to, with praise (straight from the biblical *Song of Solomon*) of the female form. "A naked woman," Updike writes, "is, for most men, the most beautiful thing they will ever see. On this planet, the female body is the prime aesthetic object, re-created not only in statuary and painting but in the form of door knockers, nutcrackers, lamp stands, and caryatids."[16] He approaches the subject through the lens of the male gaze and the male imagination, re-creative in its force: "An interesting thought-experiment, for an adult male, is to try to look at a prepubescent girl, one of ten or eleven, say, with the eyes again of a boy the same age. The relative weakness, the arresting curves, the female fastidiousness are not yet in place, but the magic is—the siren song, the strange simultaneous call to be kind and to conquer, the swooning wish to place one's life *beside* this other" (71). And yet, at the very least, he recognizes the latent (or blatant) sexism of this attitude: "And naturally modern women feel a personal impatience with being mythologized, with being envisioned (talk about hysteria!) as madonnas and whores, earth-mothers and vampires, helpless little girls and implacable dominatrices, and with male inability to see sex simply for what it is. What is it? A biological function and procedure, presumably, on a plane with eating and defecation, just as women are, properly regarded, equally entitled human beings and political entities with minds of their own" (71).[17] Thus, he suggests that men need to ask women for forgiveness for our mythologizing them, and that a correction can take place through "appeal to their own sexuality, which is different but not basically different, perhaps, from our own" (72). And he points out that *Song of Solomon* has a female speaker, who also uses stretched metaphors to re-create the body of her lover. "For male and female alike," Updike concludes, "the bodies of the other sex are messages signalling what we must do—they are glowing signifiers of our own existence" (72). In other words, the solution to the problem of male idealization of women—which is indeed a problem, as the *Scarlet Letter* trilogy so deftly demonstrates—is to allow women their own imaginative space. (It is not a coincidence that Updike praises the feminist novelist Margaret Atwood in this essay.) And if women must be responsible for their own aesthetic creations in general, Updike nevertheless attempts to imagine the female imagination, as it were, in both the short pieces examined in this chapter and in *The Witches of Eastwick*.

Notes

1 Updike, *Couples*, 464.

2 Updike, "Marching through Boston," 223. Hereafter cited in-text.

3 de Beauvoir, *The Second Sex*, xxxv.

4 Donne, "A Valediction," ll. 25–28.

5 Ibid., ll. 35–36.

[6] Hamilton and Hamilton, *The Elements of John Updike*, 70–71.

[7] Updike, "The Stare," 58–59. Hereafter cited in-text.

[8] Updike, "Midpoint," ll. 4.442–43.

[9] Crews, "Mr. Updike's Planet," 172.

[10] Updike, "Report of Health," ll. 1.8–12.

[11] Ibid., ll. 2.17–19.

[12] Updike, "Living with a Wife," ll. 15–19.

[13] Ibid., ll. 32–36.

[14] Many of the stories from this era feature older men, tired and decaying, surrounded and controlled by younger women who identify with the feminist movement. No doubt this trope was influenced by his second marriage to Martha Ruggles Bernhard, who was several years younger than him (though the age difference was not as significant as "Slippage" and several other stories would have us believe).

[15] Updike, "Slippage," 175. Hereafter cited in-text.

[16] Updike, "The Female Body," 70.

[17] His language here recalls a passage from *Rabbit, Run*. Rabbit is horrified by the thought that Ruth has had many lovers before him. "It's like asking how many times you've taken a crap," she replies. "O.K. I've taken a crap" (159).

13: *The Witches of Eastwick*

ALEXANDRA SPOFFORD, THE HEROINE OF *The Witches of Eastwick* (1984), is not Updike's first female protagonist. *Couples* occasionally presents the thoughts of its female characters, especially Foxy Whitman and Janet Appleby; *Rabbit, Run* periodically, and sympathetically, enters the consciousnesses of Janice Angstrom and Ruth Leonard; and another Ruth, Ruth Conant, takes over *Marry Me* for nearly half of its length. But *The Witches of Eastwick* is the first novel in which Updike solely follows female consciousness. He does so, at least in part, in order to examine the flip side of the sort of lusty male imagination limned so expertly in the *Scarlet Letter* trilogy and in many of his short stories of the 1960s and 1970s. That is, *The Witches of Eastwick* is a novel about female power, a power that is explicitly presented as a form of imagination, a projection of the female mind on the natural world. But this projection is itself projected on by the male imagination, in the form of the disruptive and dismantling presence of Darryl Van Horne, which systematically interrupts and destroys the power of the novel's heroines.

The power of the witches in this novel is heavily connected with the natural world. We are told early on that "this air of Eastwick empowered women."[1] Updike often describes the magic of the natural world in feminist terms. For example, he hints that there is something special in Rhode Island that will foster natural female power: "Once you cross the state line, whether at Pawtucket or Westerly, a subtle change occurs, a cheerful dishevelment, a contempt for appearances, a chimerical uncharing. Beyond the clapboard slums yawn lunar stretches where only an abandoned roadside stand offering the ghost of last summer's CUKES betrays the yearning, disruptive presence of man" (9). The word *man* does double duty in this passage—it suggests, on the one hand, all of humanity, suggesting that much of Rhode Island is a world apart from human civilization. But on the other hand, it suggests a specifically masculine humanity and suggests that women can prosper in an uncivilized world to a degree that men simply cannot. Women are thus in tune with nature at its smallest and most intricate level;[2] for example, as she looks at a cabinet door, Alexandra is "conscious of the atomic fury spinning and skidding beneath such a surface, like an eddy of weary eyesight" (4). Witches have access to a deeper reality than normal mortals, but witchcraft is an open category in this novel, a club to which, it is heavily implied, all women have access at times of emotional distress.

The Witches of Eastwick takes place, vaguely, in the late 1960s or the early 1970s, an era that would seem to be ripe for female ascendency. And yet Alexandra is skeptical of the sexual revolution that promised to liberate women: "Female yearning was in all the papers and magazines now; the sexual equation had become reversed as girls of good family flung themselves toward brutish rock stars, callow unshaven guitarists from the slums of Liverpool or Memphis somehow granted indecent power, dark suns turning these children of sheltered upbringing into suicidal orgiasts" (11). The real power of the sexual revolution, then, is masculine; no wonder Alexandra, a powerful and authentically liberated woman, has "a sense of herself as a pathetic onlooker" (11) of its civilization-shaking events. She is involved instead with something much more potent, a genuine feminism of a sort largely unknown to the Helen Gurley Browns of the world. It is a feminism that owes precious little to the youth culture fostering, and fostered by, the sexual revolution: "So many of Alexandra's remarkable powers had flowed from this mere appropriation of her assigned self, achieved not until midlife. Not until midlife did she truly believe that she had a right to exist, that the forces of nature had created her not as an afterthought and companion—a bent rib, as the infamous *Malleus Maleficarum* had it—but as the mainstay of the continuing Creation, as the daughter of a daughter and a woman whose daughters in turn would bear daughters" (14). Men are, quite simply, an afterthought to the genuinely feminist imagination that Alexandra possesses.[3] What matters are relations among women and girls.

Female power, in this world, is built on balance rather than assertion: "Things fall into threes. And magic occurs all around us as nature seeks and finds the inevitable forms, things crystalline and organic falling together at angles of sixty degrees, the equilateral triangle being the mother of structure" (5). Female power simultaneously lets things happen as they will naturally happen and nudges them with one's emotional imagination—a remarkably difficult task: "This female struggle of hers against her own weight: at the age of thirty-eight she found it increasingly unnatural. In order to attract love must she deny her own body, like a neurotic saint of old? Nature is the index and context of all health and if we have an appetite it is there to be satisfied, satisfying thereby the cosmic order. Yet she sometimes despised herself as lazy, in taking a lover of a race so notoriously tolerant of corpulence" (6).[4] Here, too, the male imagination is influencing her own. As a girl, she had decided to love her body, but marriage changed all that; after being married for a few years, "her own body disgusted her, and Ozzie's attempts to make love to it seemed an unkind gibe" (70). Her solution is for her spirit to leave her body and join "the body outside, beyond the windows, that light-struck, water-riddled, foliate flesh of that other self the world to which beauty still clung" (70). The merger is not literal, of course, but an imaginative exercise, albeit one that has an effect on the world around her. Her divorce allows the merger: "The morning after the decree, she was up at four, pulling up dead pea plants and singing by moonlight, singing by the light of that hard white stone with the titled sad unisex face—a celestial presence, and dawn in the east the gray of a cat. This other body too had a spirit" (70)—a spirit with which her own must commune.

Witchcraft takes place, then, when a woman's subjective interior merges and balances with the objective exterior world around her—when her *l'être-pour-soi* merges with *l'être-en-soi*. When Alexandra prepares to create a thunderstorm to vacate a public beach, we are told that "one's inner weather always bore a relation to the outer; it was simply a question of reversing the current, which occurred rather easily once power had been assigned to the primary pole, oneself as a woman" (14). To create the storm, Alexandra must will "this vast interior of herself," figured as the entire natural history of the world, "to darken, to condense, to generate an interface of lightning between tall walls of air" (14–15). The exterior world then changes to a version of her interior life, albeit an interior life that has been refigured as the real substance of the world. In this magic, "The very medium of seeing was altered, so that the seaside grasses and creeping glassworts near Alexandra's fat toes, corned and bent by years of shoes shaped by men's desires and cruel notions of beauty, seemed traced in negative upon the sand, whose tracked and pitted surface, suddenly tinted lavender, appeared to rise like the skin of a bladder being inflated under the stress of the atmospheric change" (15). The female and the natural have been set off against the masculine and the artificial—but it is not as if female imagination involves merely letting nature alone. Alexandra creates this storm, genuinely creates it, although she probably could not have done so if certain natural conditions were not already in place.

If female power in this novel is deeply connected with nature, male power—represented most prominently by the diabolic Darryl Van Horne—is starkly artificial: "When he spoke, his voice resounded in a way that did not quite go with the movements of his mouth and jaw, and this impression of an artificial element somewhere in his speech apparatus was reinforced by the strange slipping, patched-together impression his features made and the excess of spittle he produced when he talked" (35). Part of his artifice is his sophistication, for "he had the confidence of the cultured and well-to-do" (35). And while he is interested in art, he has no space for reproductions of nature or even natural materials (like Alexandra's own clay sculptures of more-or-less human forms). Instead, he is a devotee of Pop Art, the most artificial of all twentieth-century movements. His very sophistication is thus demeaning and dehumanizing; his home, filled to overflowing with Pop Art, is a dump: "All that we wish to use and discard with scarcely a glance was here held up bloated and bright: permanized garbage" (87). Likewise, his interest in science is limited to chemical plastics. "The point is," he boasts, "this century's just the infancy; synthetic polymers're going to be with us to the year one million or until we blow ourselves up, whichever comes sooner, and the beauty of it is, you can *grow* the raw materials, and when you run out of land you can grow 'em in the ocean. Move over, Mother Nature, we've got you beat" (45–46). This, too, is an imaginative imposition on the world—but it is much more violent than Alexandra's brand of magic. It is not surprising that his tastes are vaguely misogynist. His favorite work of art is a Kienholz statue, "an especially ugly assemblage, a naked woman on her back with legs spread; she had been concocted of chicken wire, flattened beer cans, an old porcelain chamber pot for her belly, pieces of chrome car bumper, items of underwear stiffed with lacquer and glue" (86). Kienholz—and Darryl Van Horne with him—has literally turned womankind into garbage in an imaginative reworking that is as disturbing as anything in *A Month of Sundays* or *Roger's Version*.

It would be tempting, then, to set up a simple dichotomy: feminized nature is good, and masculinized artifice is bad. But Updike complicates such a dichotomy. Nature, at times, is no friend to humanity. Cancer terrifies Alexandra, who sees "its emblem everywhere in nature—in clusters of blueberries in the neglected places by rocks and bogs, in the grapes ripening on the sagging rotten arbor outside her kitchen windows, in the ants bringing up conical granular hills in the cracks in her asphalt driveway, in all blind and irresistible multiplications" (24). Nature hides cancer like a dagger up its sleeve: "Irritation, psychic as well as physical, was the source of cancer. Those get it who leave themselves open to the idea of it; all it takes it one single cell gone crazy" (24). The language of cancer is remarkably similar to the language used to describe female magic—cancer, like magic, involves an adaptation and expansion of what is already there, hidden away. Thus, cancer is a kind of runaway imagination—and indeed, Alexandra's imagination runs wild in her fears about it. Cancer, like the storm that Alexandra summons early in the novel, is the product of human projection on a natural world that is already primed for that projection.

The female imagination, in this novel, is an aesthetic imagination, and Updike frequently connects female power with traditionally feminine social and artistic roles: gardening, cooking, clay sculpture, music, gossip, and so forth. For example, Alexandra's recipe for spaghetti sauce is described like a magical potion; it "called for no onions, two cloves of garlic minced and sautéed for three minutes (no more, no less; that was the magic) in heated oil, plenty of sugar to counteract acidity, a single grated carrot, more pepper than salt; but the teaspoon of crumbled basil is what catered to virility, and the dash of belladonna provided the release without which virility is merely a murderous congestion" (5–6). Here, too, Alexandra's imagination projects itself upon the natural world without utterly re-creating that world; these properties lurk hidden in the herbs and vegetables until she unlocks them. Jane Smart's cello playing is perhaps a bit more forceful. Her

> vibratory melancholy tones, pregnant with the sadness of wood grain and the shadowy largeness of trees, would at odd moonlit hours on warm nights come sweeping out of the screened windows of her low little ranch house where it huddled amid many like it on the curved roads of the Fifties development called Cove Homes. Her neighbors on their quarter-acre lots, husband and wife, child and dog, would move about, awakened, and discuss whether or not to call the police. They rarely did, abashed and, it may be, intimidated by the some-thing naked, a splendor and grief, in Jane's playing. (20)

Jane's artistic expression moves what is figuratively inside her—her emotions, perhaps even her inmost self—to the outside world, and in so doing projects her imagination on all who hear the strains. The effect is hypnotic. Updike says, "It seemed easier to fall back to sleep, lulled by the double-stopped scales" (20). Alexandra's and Jane's power lies, at least in part, in their artistic talents. Sukie Rougemont, the third mem-ber of their coven, lacks these sorts of gifts, but as a gossip columnist she devotes herself to the social world of Eastwick, where an odd men-tion of her two friends "thrilled her like a glint of beach glass in the sand or a quarter found shining on the dirty sidewalk—a bit of code buried in the garble of daily experience, a stab of communication between the inner and outer world" (21). This, too, is a sort of magic; Updike's language here echoes his earlier evocation of Alexandra's thunderstorm and Jane's music. Gossip, after all, involves the creation of order from relative chaos and is as much a projection of human consciousness as any other meaning-making process.

The powerful women of this novel have, as we might expect, a com-plicated relationship to the men in their lives. Alexandra, for her part, distrusts men. When Jane tells her that "a man can be just a person," her response is telling: "I know that's the theory, but I've never met one who thought he was. They all turn out to be men, even the faggots" (56). Sukie echoes this sentiment when she thinks back to "her old life, before sheer womanhood had exploded within her and she realized that the world men had systematically made was all dreary poison, good for noth-ing really but battlefields and waste sites" (135). These sentiments should not be surprising; after all, Updike's work frequently features a rapacious male imagination overpowering and controlling the imagination of the women in its vicinity; certainly much of the power these women have springs from their freedom from legal and spiritual ties to men. But on occasion a man can be beneficial for female power. For example, Alexan-dra's lover, Joe Marino, makes her gardening unbelievably fertile: "ever since, two summers ago, Joe Marino had begun to come into her bed, a preposterous fecundity had overtaken the staked plants, out in the side garden where the southwestern sun slanted in through the line of willows each long afternoon" (6). Joe, however, is scarcely a character in the novel. It is difficult to imagine his personality and imagination overpowering Alexandra, who looms large both in life and in fiction. His presence benefits Alexandra's magic specifically because he is overpowered by her.

At times, Updike hints that even this diabolical female power was set in place to aid men. The narrator says that

> Healing belonged to their natures, and if the world accused them of coming between men and wives, of tying the disruptive ligature, of knotting the aiguillette that places the kink of impotence or emotional coldness in the entrails of a marriage seemingly secure in its snugly roofed and darkened house, and if the world not merely accused but burned them alive in the tongues of indignant opinion, that was the price they must pay. It was fundamental and instinctive, it was womanly, to want to heal—to apply the poultice of acquiescent flesh to the wound of a man's desire, to give his closeted spirit the exaltation of seeing a witch slip out of her clothes and go skyclad in a room of tawdry motel furniture. (67)

We see this urge to heal particularly in Sukie's attraction to weak men like Ed Parsley and Clyde Gabriel. Her ex-husband, Monty, was done in by aggressive misogyny: "He had hated uppity women—female governors, hysterical war protestors, 'lady' doctors, Lady Bird Johnson, even Lynda Bird and Luci Baines. He had thought them all butch" (7). Appropriately enough, Sukie flattens him out and uses him as a placemat. But after his death, she seeks to aid men who need her. When Clyde Gabriel complains to her about his harridan wife, "Sukie's nipples had gone erect beneath her sweater in awareness of her healing powers, of being for any man a garden stocked with antidotes and palliatives" (75). This language brings to mind Miriam Angstrom's self-conception in *Rabbit Redux*. Miriam, Rabbit's little sister, has in her twenties moved to Las Vegas to be a prostitute. As she explains to her brother, men are

> soft, . . . like slugs under fallen leaves. Out there, Harry, there are no leaves. People grow these tan shells. . . . You never see them out in the sun but they're all tan, with flat stomach muscles. Their one flaw is, they're still soft inside. They're like those chocolates we used to hate, those chocolate creams, remember how we'd pick through the Christmas box they'd give us at the movie theater, taking out only the square ones and the caramels in cellophane? The other ones we hated, those dark brown round ones on the outside, all ooky inside. But that's how people are. It embarrasses everybody but they need to be milked. Men need to be drained. Like boils. Women too for

that matter. You asked me my specialty and that's it, I milk people. I let them spill their insides on me.[5]

A woman's job, then, is to purge a man, literally and figuratively. A woman—at least a woman like Miriam and Sukie—in taking a man's semen, removes what is poisonous and damaging in him and replaces it with something beneficial. This action requires a great deal of imaginative effort from Sukie. As she ministers to Clyde Gabriel, she thinks about Alexandra, who "believed that nature, the physical world, was a happy thing. This huddling man, this dogskin of warm bones, did not believe that. The world for him had been rendered tasteless as paper, composed as it was of inconsequent messy events that flickered across his desk on their way to the moldering back files. Everything for him had become secondary and sour" (139). Her job becomes to take this man who has surrendered to the despair of *l'être-en-soi* and to project meaning into his life. It is not an easy task, and "Sukie wondered about her own strength, how long she could hold these grieving, doubting men on her own chest and not be contaminated" (139). Still, she has been called to this vocation.

At other times, however, female power destroys the men who encounter it. This is the case with Alexandra's hapless ex-husband, Ozzie. When they moved to Eastwick, "her powers had expanded like gas in a vacuum and she had reduced dear Ozzie as he made his daily trek to work and back along Route 4 first to the size of a mere man, the armor of patriarchal protector falling from him in the corrosive salt air of Eastwick's maternal beauty, and then to the size of a child as his chronic needs and equally chronic acceptance of her solutions to them made him appear pitiful, manipulable. He quite lost touch with the expanding universe within her" (6–7). We are meant to take this shrinking literally; Alexandra keeps what remains of Ozzie in a jar. But it is also the language of a housewife who has ceased to think of her husband at all—he is not overpowered by her imagination so much as he escapes it and loses his existence. Her adultery helps him along into oblivion: "As Alexandra accepted first one and then several lovers, her cuckolded husband shrank to the dimensions and dryness of a doll, lying beside her in her great wide receptive bed at night like a painted log picked up a roadside stand, or a stuffed baby alligator" (7). Ozzie quite literally needs Alexandra's imagination to be focused on him in order to exist—when other men distract her, he shrinks almost to nothingness. But even so, the novel often speaks of female power as passive; Updike's use of the word *accepted* suggests that Alexandra is receiving these men rather than seeking them out. And whereas the male imagination, as we have seen, is bound up in lust, female lust is directed at the female body as seen, imaginatively, through the eyes of a man. Alexandra notes "how much of love, when you thought about it, was not of the other but of yourself naked in his eyes: of that rush, that little flight, of shedding your clothes, and being you at last" (83). The formulation is complicated: Women are powerful, and it is their imagination that makes them powerful. Yet they need men for their imagination to function, even though these same men are often destroyed by the imaginative work they enable.

The Witches of Eastwick has the rhythms of a comedy, but at its heart is a tragedy—at least if we are to take the lives and viewpoints of its central trio seriously. It is a novel about outrageous female power that is nonetheless wiped out by a male imagination. We see this from the earliest moments of the book; when Jane tells Alexandra that a man has bought the old Lenox mansion, the latter feels "off-center, her peaceful aura that morning splayed by the assertive word *man*" (3). Even the rumor of masculinity, it seems, can undermine female power. And the more power a man has, the less power the women close to him are allowed. Thus Marge Perley is "a heavily made-up, go-getting woman who, if one at all, was a witch on a different wavelength from Jane, Alexandra, and Sukie. There was a husband, a tiny fussy Homer Perley always trimming their forsythia hedge back to stubble, and this made a difference" (4). The central trio has broken free, at least partially, of male dominance in destroying or divorcing their husbands. Even so, the masculine imagination maintains its power over even them to some extent. As soon as Alexandra hears about Darryl, "she saw that she would meet and fall in love with this man and that little good would come of it" (4), as if Darryl were controlling her thoughts. But she does not resist that control; when Updike tells us about her vision, she is "already dilating, diffusing herself to be invaded" (5). In this way—through his imaginative projections into the minds of the women—Darryl disrupts the coven before he even meets its members. Alexandra

> was jealous of this man, that the very shadow of him should so excite her two friends, who on other Thursdays were excited simply by her, her regally lazy powers stretching there like a cat's power to cease purring and kill. On those Thursdays the three friends would conjure up the spectres of Eastwick's little lives and set them buzzing and circling in the darkening air. In the right mood and into their third drinks they could erect a cone of power above them like a tent to the zenith, and know at the base of their bellies who was sick, who was sinking into debt, who was loved, who was frantic, who was burning, who was asleep in a remission of life's bad luck; but this wouldn't happen today. They were disturbed. (33)

Jealousy is a way in, the tiny grain of sand that disrupts the delicate balance of female friendship. The three realize almost immediately that "they were themselves under the spell, of a greater" (34). And the impression is confirmed when Alexandra finally meets Darryl, who informs her that he has bought a local store's entire collection of the clay figurines that constitute her livelihood. When she first heard that he bought the mansion, she prepared "to be invaded"; his capitalist intrusion now "felt like a rape" (36). She is thrown out of alignment: "The pressure his personality set up had intensified her cramps, which she had woken with that morning, days ahead of schedule" (36). At his house, she feels "splayed and out of focus, in tune with the moment— a gliding sensation, the world passing through her or she moving the world, a cosmic confusion such as when the train silently tugs away from the station and it seems the platform is sliding backwards" (87). Darryl disrupts her imaginative magic; he controls her imagination just as his buying all her figurines forces her "to run another batch through the kiln now earlier than she had planned" (36). The power belongs to him, almost immediately. Likewise, he distracts Sukie from her vocation of ministering to broken-down men. When she meets Darryl, she is in the midst of an affair with the Unitarian minister, Ed Parsley, but over time "she was shrinking Ed Parsley in her mind, so that when the call came she could travel sufficiently lightened across the flooded marsh to Darryl Van Horne's island. That's where the action was, not here in town" (75). But such a voyage would move Sukie from an imaginative agent in her own right to a mere receiver of Darryl's imagination.

Even more sinisterly, Darryl's controls the witches by letting them think that their sexual escapades with him are ways of communing with each other. He tricks them into seeing him as a mere medium for their imaginations: "On the black velour mattresses Van Horne had provided, the three women played with him together, using the parts of his body as a vocabulary with which to speak to each other" (119). But under this veneer of female community lurks a controlling male imagination: "It was Van Horne's kindness to subsume their love for one another into a kind of love for himself. There was something a little abstract about his love for them and something therefore formal and merely courteous in the obeisances and favors they granted him" (118). Darryl thus takes their attraction—sexual and otherwise—to one another and diverts it to himself. When Sukie is with him, she talks a good deal about Jane and Alexandra. The impulse is not new: "With other men also Sukie had noticed this urge of hers to talk about the other two witches, to seek coziness conversationally in evoking the three of them, this triune body under its cone of power being the closest approach to a mother she had ever had" (133). But Van Horne's reaction is different than other men's, who "minded when her thoughts and tongue gravitated to the coven and its coziness and mischief" (133). For Darryl, on the other hand, her talking of her friends "was his meat somehow, he was like a woman in his steady kindness, though of course terribly masculine in form: when he fucked you it hurt" (133). He is a predator here, despite his kindness—in fact, his kindness is a mental trick that lures his prey into a false sense of shelter and belonging.

He is misogynist in his egotism and demands, if not in his language: "Like all men Van Horne demanded the women call him king, but his system of taxation at least dealt in assets—bodies, personal liveliness— they did have and not in spiritual goods laid up in some nonexistent heaven" (118). Later, talking to Sukie, Darryl will feel "a surge of possessive pride in her beauty, her vital spirit. His. His toy" (131). He does not, in other words, cede them nearly as much power as they imagine, and in fact he controls almost every aspect of their trysts, which "usually arose as if spontaneously, without the deigning of his personal invitation, but through a telepathic, or telephonic, merge of the desires of his devotees. They would find themselves there without quite knowing how they came to be there" (220–21). The narrator frames this as the result of the witches' collective desires, but the phrase *as if* should clue us into the fact that those desires spring from Van Horne, not originally from the witches—he controls their imaginations psychically, and they are helpless in the face of his telepathic summons.

Ironically, while he controls their imaginations, he also feeds off of them. Unlike the witches, he is not a terribly creative person. As he plays the piano for the coven, for example, Alexandra hears in it "a wizardry . . . of theft and transformation, with nothing of guileless creative engendering about it, only a boldness of monstrous combination" (224). Even so, as his relationship with the trio progresses, he deepens their interest in their own respective artistic fields. Updike tells us that "since Van Horne had come into her life, Jane was more passionate than she had ever been about music, that golden high-arched exit from this pit of pain and ignominy" (161). Under his tutelage, Alexandra branches out into papier-mâché sculptures, and Sukie reports that "he was saying to me when I lose my job at the *Word* I should try a novel" (161). But he does not grant power to these women. He attempts to control them by controlling their imaginative worlds. All roads lead back to him: "Alexandra's thoughts did fly to Darryl Van Horne at all hours: his overeager face with its flecks of spit, and certain dusty corners of his home awaiting a woman's touch, and such moments as the frozen one after he had laughed his harsh brittle bark, when his jaw snapped shut and the world as it were had to come unstuck from a momentary spell. These images did not visit Alexandra's brain by invitation or with a purpose but as one radio station overlaps another as we travel on a winding road" (197). And while he draws the thoughts of the three witches into his own imagination, he separates them from one another. Sukie tells Alexandra that Jane "thinks she has the inside track with Darryl and is fighting to possess it," and Alexandra replies, "That's one of his diabolical arts, to give each of us that impression. I'm really quite sure it's me he loves" (161). The coven no longer meets together on Thursdays—instead, they all play tennis with Darryl and have orgies. Separated from the "cone of power" that their meetings brought them, the love they once felt for one another begins to disintegrate: "Alexandra used to love her, Sukie knew. That first night at Darryl's, dancing to Joplin, they had clung together and wept at the curse of heterosexuality that held them apart as if each were a rose in a plastic tube. Now there was a detachment in Alexandra's voice" (165). Darryl has quite literally come between them.

The irony, given each woman's steadfast belief that Darryl loves her most of all, is that Darryl actually loves none of them, and the novel's dénouement reveals that, after inviting the adult children of Clyde and Felicia Gabriel (dead in a grisly murder-suicide) to live with him, he has married Jenny and then, after the witches' jealousy destroys her body with cancer, he has run away with her brother, Chris. These events serve as the harsh reality that interrupts Alexandra's month-long daydream: "The hope that the dark stranger would eventually claim her cowered in its corner of her imagining; could it be that her queenly patience would earn itself no more reward than being used and discarded?" (219). Stripped of her illusions and her imagination, meaning flees her universe: "How short life is, how quickly its signs exhaust their meaning" (219). The trio's magic has been cut off—not entirely destroyed, given that it reappears twenty-five years later in *The Widows of Eastwick*,[6] but chastened. What was once a female paradise of imaginative labor has been undermined by a diabolical male imagination—and the final burst of magic in the novel is the destruction of Jenny Gabriel Van Horne, the most malicious action we see any of the witches commit.[7] This in turn suggests that their own imaginations have been so warped by Darryl's that they, too, have become diabolical. *The Witches of Eastwick* thus functions as an inverse of the three *Scarlet Letter* novels—whereas those books feature a re-creative male imagination that is ultimately conquered by a subtler but more powerful female imagination, *Witches* sees the subtleties of the female imagination undermined and undone by male power. But, as Jeff Campbell points out, Darryl is not necessarily any more powerful than the witches; he is merely more manipulative: "He is not the source of the feminine powers of the witches, even though he would like to use those powers to his own ends and pretend that he was their source."[8] He emerges victorious at the end of this novel by the subtlety of his deceptions, not the overwhelming strength of his imagination.

Notes

[1] Updike, *The Witches of Eastwick*, 8. Hereafter cited in-text.

[2] For more on the many connections in Updike's work between femininity and nature, see Verduin, "Updike, Women, and Mythologized Sexuality."

[3] Of course men are an afterthought, since the male imagination is frequently connected in Updike's work with prolonged adolescence. Ace Anderson and Rabbit Angstrom cling to their mothers and to their high-school triumphs; Joey Robinson's development is as arrested as his childish forename suggests; in "Sublimating," Richard Maple becomes obsessed with raw cabbage, his favorite childhood snack; Jerry Conant is frequently described as an immature man attempting to live in a child's fantasy world; Piet Hanema tries to return to infancy by suckling at his lover's breast; there is more than a hint of child and mother in Tom Marshfield's relationship with Ms. Prynne; Roger Lambert seeks a younger lover as a means of returning to his own adolescence; and Art Steinmetz's vision of sexuality involves a nursing man and a motherly woman. The female imagination has to be mature specifically because the male imagination is immature. However, female maturity also has the unpleasant side effect of enabling male immaturity.

If female power arises out of freedom from male-controlled institutions like marriage, it is worth noting, as James Plath does, that the witches of Eastwick also "experience sexual power after being freed . . . from the constraints of religion that regards marriage as holy" ("Giving the Devil His Due," 213). In this, they have successfully enacted the break with patriarchal Christianity yearned for by Sarah Worth—and instead of retreating to an Eastern religion also controlled by men, they have created their own female-centered religion.

[4] The narrator refers to Alexandra's Italian American lover, Joe Marino.

[5] Updike, *Rabbit Redux*, 313.

[6] I will not examine *The Widows of Eastwick* in this chapter because it does not share the themes of its predecessor; instead, *Widows*, like many books of Updike's final two decades, is about the aging process and the general loss of power that old age brings.

[7] The witches do, after all, commit a number of minor injustices in the early sections of the novel, perhaps capped by the major injustices they inflict on their loathsome ex-husbands. But the novel itself stands behind him with these actions; it is not until their destruction of Jenny Gabriel—a destruction brought on by Van Horne to serve his own purposes—that the novel and its readers are genuinely horrified by the coven.

[8] Campbell, *Updike's Novels*, 202.

Part V. The Remembering Imagination

14: "In Football Season," "First Wives and Trolley Cars," "The Day of the Dying Rabbit," "Leaving Church Early," and "The Egg Race"

MOST PEOPLE PROBABLY THINK of memory more or less the way Plato describes it in the *Theaetetus* (ca. 369 B.C.E.). Socrates paints the picture for the titular mathematician:

> Let us make in each soul a sort of aviary of all kinds of birds; some in flocks separate from the others, some in small groups, and others flying about singly here and there among all the rest. . . . Then we must say that when we are children this receptacle is empty; and by the birds we must understand pieces of knowledge. When anyone takes possession of a piece of knowledge and shuts it up in the pen, we should say that he has learned or has found out the thing of which this is the knowledge; and knowing, we should say, is this.[1]

A given act of memory, then, involves a person's reaching into the aviary and trying to pull out the bird that corresponds to the fact or concept or event that she or he wants to remember. Some birds resist being pulled out, of course, and so people cannot always remember the things they want to remember; other times, they will misremember by pulling the wrong bird out of the aviary. But the overall image, perhaps, corresponds to our experience of memory (or at least to our interpretation of our experience of memory): memories are abstract objects that we retrieve from our minds more or less intact. To use a more up-to-date analogy, we might think of memory working "the way a computer works: you use some sort of search cue (a time, a key word, a title) and find the memory waiting in some corner of the brain, in somewhat the way you might use a word to search for a document in your computer files."[2] The popular notion of a "photographic memory" says much the same thing using different imagery: The miraculous rememberer, we are told, can look at a scene and instantly memorize every single detail of it, perfectly recalling it later (often on the command of a television detective). Most of us, it is admitted, do not have this level of recall—but it is merely an extreme version of the process we all undergo in our every act of remembering.

Philosophers and scientists have known for decades, however, that these are not accurate models of human memory. Almost all of our memories are fragmentary and indefinite and must therefore be filled in with information and images from other sources—"most typically," says Edward S. Casey, "to *other memories* from the same general period of my life—and to simple inductive and deductive modes of inference." And what is more, the process happens almost automatically, or at least so close to it that "in the act of remembering itself I did not choose to employ these reasoning procedures, nor was I even aware of their operation."[3] As Susan Engel points out, the computer model of memory retrieval is strikingly inadequate; in fact, memory "is almost always more a process of construction that one of simple retrieval. One creates the memory at the moment one needs it, rather than merely pulling out an intact item, image, or story."[4] The word *image* in this explanation demonstrates the degree to which memory is a specialized act of the imagination and thus subject to the same sorts of idealist constructions and falsifications as any other act of the imagination. As Mary Warnock explains, "whether we are imagining or recalling, we are thinking of something that is not before our eyes and ears, and of something that has meaning for us, and may be imbued with strong emotions."[5] Memory is likely involved in every act of the imagination, just as imagination is likely involved in every act of memory. Like other acts of the imagination, the memory is closely tied to the material world; the difference between it and other imaginative functions comes in our perception that, in our rememberings, we owe a fidelity to that world in a way that we simply do not in our imaginings. Sartre explains the difference between memory and other acts of the imagination in the conclusion of his *L'imagination* (The Psychology of Imagination, 1936): "If I recall an incident of my past life I do not imagine it, I *recall* it. That is, I do not posit it as *given-in-its-absence*, but as *given-now-as-in-the-past*. The handshake of Peter of last evening in leaving me did not turn into an unreality as it became a thing of the past: it simply *went into retirement*; it is always real but *past*. It exists *past*, which is one mode of real existence among others."[6] Compare this memory to my imagination of Peter when he is in Berlin and not in the room with me; in imagining him, "I grasp an object which is not at all given to me or which is given to me simply as being beyond reach. There I grasp *nothing*, that is, I posit *nothingness*. In this sense the imaginative consciousness of Peter in Berlin . . . is very much closer to that of the centaur (whose complete inexistence I proclaim), than the recollection of Peter as he was the day he left."[7] The very nature of the imagination, for Sartre, is that it posits unreality—but this leads to problems when we see memory as a function of imagination, specifically because memory requires fidelity to the real world in a way that mere imagination does not. As Warnock puts it, "insofar as memory consists of images, these are *not* wholly created by ourselves, or rather, we cannot create them in any way we like. Being concerned with the real, memory images *dictate* to us. We are, in a sense, bound by them, even passive before them, as we are passive in the perception of the world."[8] But this formulation is quite similar to the overall imaginative formula I have pointed out in Updike's work: *l'être-pour-soi* imposes itself on the world of *l'être-en-soi*, only to be corrected by the material facts of that world, beginning the cycle anew. In this sense, memory in Updike's work is another form of imaginative re-creation that must by turns reinvent and be reinvented by the reality of existence. In other words, our relationship with the past is on a continuum with our relationship with the present— dredging up events that happened decades or years or even minutes ago merely requires more of an imaginative labor than relating to the world in which we find ourselves at this moment.

Updike's work has always been concerned with the author's past. Many of his best-loved short stories—along with the novels *The Centaur* and *Of the Farm*—are explorations of his early life in Shillington, Pennsylvania. Adam Begley reports that Updike's early editor at the *New Yorker*, Katharine White, "discouraged him from indulging in wistful reminiscence," suggesting "that he should avoid stories in which 'a young man looks back nostalgically on his basketball-playing days.'"[9] The irony is clear: nostalgic looking-back "turned out to be one of his most fruitful fictional modes" (113), and his career as a novelist was made by *Rabbit, Run*, which begins with just such a glance back at a youth spent playing basketball. Many of Updike's most beloved early stories—including most of those collected as the *Olinger Stories* in 1964—are gauzy glances back at Updike's childhood. Updike himself had a special fascination with his story "The Happiest I've Been" (1959), the writing of which gave him "a sensation of breaking through, as if through a thin sheet of restraining glass, to material, to truth, previously locked up."[10]

But to my eyes, "In Football Season" (1962) is a more interesting, and representative, example of Updike's treatment of nostalgia. The story begins with a direct question to the reader: "Do you remember a fragrance girls acquire in autumn?"[11] The question establishes the story's directionality; it is situated in the present, as it were, and pointed toward the past. This is, in fact, the very essence of nostalgia, which, as Fred Davis points out, is an attitude or a stance that the present takes toward the past. Nostalgia is a method of making meaning; it "has less . . . to do with how recent or distant these events are than with the way they contrast—or more accurately, the way we make them contrast—with the events, moods, and dispositions of our present circumstances."[12] Even more so than other forms of memory, then, nostalgia is connected with the imagination; it creates a past that has much less responsibility to the material facts of lived past experience. The narrator of "In Football Season" asks the question because he has found himself—like so many

narrators of Updike's nostalgic mode—cut off from the magic of his adolescence and dropped into a world in which the signifiers still exist but do
not quite attach to their signifieds anymore. Even the female body arouses
in him not lust so much as a sense of loss: "The other day, in a town far
from Olinger, I passed on the sidewalk two girls utterly unknown to me
and half my age, and sensed, very faintly, that flavor from far-off carried
in their bent arms like a bouquet" (7). Needless to say, he does not sense
this flavor so much as he projects it. He remembers high-school football
season as bringing a special kind of grace to the world and especially to
the smell of the girls at his school. He admits that this smell was "perhaps
imaginary and certainly elusive" (3), but connects it to something larger,
something perhaps mystical and divine; the odor presents itself "when
the cloudless fall sky like the blue bell of a vacuum lifts toward itself the
glad exhalations of all things" (3). This language suggests some sort of
religious ritual, a suggestion that he doubles a few paragraphs later: "And
of course I remember the way we, the students, with all of our jealousies
and antipathies and deformities, would be—beauty and boob, sexpot and
grind—crushed together like flowers pressed to yield to the black sky a
concentrated homage, an incense, of cosmetics, cigarette smoke, warmed
wool, hot dogs, and the tang, both animal and metallic, of clean hair"
(4). This was a world, however briefly, in which time did not matter, in
which fifteen- and sixteen-year-olds were free to dawdle in their youth,
to make of the distance between Olinger and Alton what they would.
But, nostalgia being what it is, none of these qualities existed in the
1940s—not even the fictional 1940s represented in the story. Instead,
the narrator reads them into his adolescence as a way of making sense
of his disappointment in adult life. The unreality, the timelessness of the
situation, could not have been a function of the actual time period; who
among us feels the current moment as timeless? These Friday nights
seem unreal only in retrospect, when their very unreality can serve as
a balm to the disenchanted reality of the narrator's life. And in fact,
when he passes those two teenage girls in a "town far from Olinger," he
imagines himself "sink[ing] into a chasm deeper than the one inverted
above us on those Friday nights during football season" (7). He has
found himself on the outside of the enchanted world of youth, even
though it is age itself that enchants it. The grace once bestowed by
the autumn evening now exists only in memory, but it is more than
likely that the notion of autumnal grace would never have occurred to
the narrator when he was a teenager. The falling-off is less a definable
moment in his past than a means by which he can make sense of his
present unhappiness.

This process of meaning-making is made more clear in the minor story
"First Wives and Trolley Cars" (1982).[13] Like the nameless narrator of "In

Football Season," William Farnham misses something from his past. But in this story it is made clear that the sensation of loss belongs to the present imagination rather than to the past event. William admits that the thing he misses—the titular trolley car—was less than an ideal at the time. He was consistently made nauseated by his repeated voyages on the trolley, which went in two directions from his hometown of Wenrich's Corner: toward Alton, the comparatively large city familiar to readers of the Olinger stories, and toward "a town so small and rural that its mere name, Smokeville, was enough to make the boy Farnham and his flip pals laugh."[14] The irony of his personal history is that "it was the ride toward Smokeville that lingered sentimentally in his memory" (18). He remembers his childhood—as many of us do, and as almost every Updike hero does—as a better and more innocent time, "these far-off days before television and R ratings, when Hollywood's fantasies were as safe as the family living room" (19). Those days, like all glory days, have vanished. But his emotional and nostalgic impressions of his boyhood linger on, like the stain smoke leaves on white cement. His childhood, as he remembers it, was enchanted. The trolley car is the best example:

> The streetcars had negotiated this corner with much plaintive friction of metal on metal and sometimes a shower of sparks that indicated the trolley had lost its electrical connection overhead. The motorman, generally a rude and overweight Pennsylvania Dutchman, would shove off from his high metal stool, let himself out of the clattery folding doors, step on a step that flopped magically into place, and run to the rear of the stalled car, where with a single angry thump he would set things right. The motor resumed its throb, that incessant mechanical pulsing as of a heart trapped beneath the long, dirt-blackened floorboards. (19)

This is not a pretty picture, but, viewed through the haze of middle-aged nostalgia, it is a magical one in which machines had a life and feelings of their own—feelings that are, of course, projections of the human imagination.

His nostalgia for these long-gone conveyances is twinned by another; he is fascinated by fictional representations of first wives, which figure as "marginal obstacles to the narrator's slowly unfolding, obscurely magnificent quest; as tremulous rainbows cast by the prism of his ego, bound at a cloud's passing to pale and wink out. Yet they return, vividly" (21). The vivid return of the discarded first wife, like that of the once-hateful trolley car, allows her to take her full revenge in the haze of nostalgia. She gains an incredible power simply by no longer being present: "In memory's telephoto lens, far objects are magnified. First wives grow in power and size, just as the children we have had by them do. They knew you when, and never let that knowledge go. Their very ability to survive the divorce makes them huge, as judges and public monuments are huge" (21). When a man leaves his first wife, Farnham believes, he gets the sensation that she was the key to his own personality: "We sat light on the world once; the keys to this lightness first wives have taken with them" (22). But this cannot possibly be true—the lightness he remembers is actually lightness that he imagines, because the weight of the collapsing marriage must have weighed on him more than he allows. Like the narrator of "In Football Season," he projects a past happiness to make sense of his present unhappiness, and though he seems to realize that this is so, he cannot quite bring himself to dismiss the illusion. The day his first wife remarries, he has a dream about her, and when he awakes, "The woman asleep beside him was pale and, like a ghost, transparent. Everything was black and white. Only his dream had been in color" (22). The nostalgized past has become the only real thing—even though, by its very definition, a nostalgized past cannot be real. Farnham is blocking his access to the enchantments of his present life by his insistence that his former life was Garden of Eden from which he has been barred forever.

"The Day of the Dying Rabbit" (1969) is even more reflexive, as its narrator can feel the fall from grace happening in the present rather than locating it in an imagined or remembered past. But because he is an artist—a photographer—his vision of the present is a distinctly aesthetic one. He notes at the outset a peculiar quality of children; they are, he says, "delicate as film, wrapped in bunting instead of lead foil, but coiled with that same miraculous brimming whatever-it-is: *susceptibility*, let's say."[15] His imagery here reveals him to be an unreliable narrator. In comparing children to film, he has suggested that they are, in effect, *l'être-en-soi*—that is, they are a blank space on which to imprint an image of whatever the camera is pointed at. The very "susceptibility" that he finds in children suggests that the visions he has of them, the visions he presents to us, are projections. *Ceci n'est pas une pipe*, after all—a photograph of a tree does not literally turn the film into a tree. The film is the canvas onto which an image of the tree is, through the magic of technology, stamped. To view the photograph is to ignore the film, or perhaps to have the image stand between you and the film. The same goes for his children; the qualities he reads into them, the exemplars of human reality that he turns them into through the magic of imagination, do not actually exist within them.

The narrator is melancholic because he feels that the golden hour of childhood is passing for his children. His oldest daughter, Linda, lets loose with "a collection of those four-letter words that come out of her face more and more. The more pop out, the more angelic her face grows" (27). This radical discrepancy between the sorts of things Linda says and does and the idealized face her father sees suggests, like his photographic language, that he is not quite looking at Linda but at a form that he has stamped on top of her. He knows this, instinctively, and notes: "She is thirteen, and in a few years I suppose it will be the liquor and drugs, going in" (27); at that point, needless to say, the angel image will have been rubbed off the human film. The aging of his children and their loss of innocence form the macrocosm of which their vacation is the microcosm. It, too, is slipping away: "In the sky, the clouding over from the west that often arrives around noon. The level of light moved down, and the hands of the year swept forward a month. It was autumn, every blade of grass shining. August has this tinny, shifty quality, the only month without a holiday to pin it down" (32). Time is an inexorable march that will take his children away from him and into the adult world, just as it will drag him away from his vacation house and back to his own job. Thus he is driven, as a photographer, to fix time into a still photo: "What was it in the next twenty-four hours that slowly flooded me, that makes me want to get the day on some kind of film? I don't know exactly, so I must put everything in, however underexposed" (29). This is an impossible task, however—a work of the imagination can never capture reality, which ultimately must elude it. And so art is strangely unpredictable in its effectiveness. The narrator talks about his friend Jenny Pingree, whom he finds beautiful and charming: "I could look at her forever, she's such fun for the eyes. Which isn't the same as being photogenic. The few shots I've taken of her show a staring woman with baby fat, whereas some skinny snit who isn't even a name to me comes over in the magazine as my personal version of Eros. The camera does lie, all the time. It has to" (30). This observation brings to mind Henry James's short story "The Real Thing," whose painter-narrator notes that not everyone can be a model for art. He tries to paint a formerly aristocratic couple, but decides in the end that he prefers the personality-free Cockney girl who has been sitting for him: "After I had drawn Mrs. Monarch a dozen times I felt surer even than before that the value of such a model as Miss Churm resided precisely in the fact that she had no positive stamp, combined of course with the other fact that what she did have was a curious and inexplicable talent for imitation. Her usual appearance was like a curtain which she could draw up at request for a capital performance."[16] Reality, it turns out, does not translate very well into art, which requires the imagination. That the art in question is photography rather than painting adds an additional dimension in that photography requires less imaginative input than other disciplines, though it does require imagination to set a shot up properly. Thus the photographic proof of a person or an event is not pure l'être-en-soi, not a pure representation of physical reality, but neither can it match up to the photographer's imaginative projections. The photograph hangs halfway between *l'être-en-soi* and *l'être-pour-soi*, and the narrator's explanations and reminiscences must bridge the gaps. Thus it is not the pictures that preserve the day but a vague feeling felt in retrospect. "This day," the narrator tells us at the end of the story, "was singular in its, let's say, *gallantry*" (40). This gallantry exists neither in the bare material world nor in the photographic proof of it—it exists in the narrator's memory, which is to say, his imagination.

In other places, Updike points out the degree to which we experience the past as a garment full of holes—a garment that must be patched by the imagination, if at all. In his poem "Leaving Church Early" (1977), for example, he tries to remember a morning from his childhood in which his entire family exited their church before the service was concluded. He finds, however, that he cannot remember very many of the details. For example, he remembers that his grandmother was waiting for them when they got home,

> her frame
> hung in my memory between two tasks,
> about to do something, but what? A cream
> jug droops in her hand, empty or it would spill—
> or is it a potato-masher, or
> a wooden spoon?[17]

There is a lacuna here—the image of his grandmother is not crystal clear, but fades out in certain of its details. Unsurprisingly, Updike resorts to archetypes in his reminiscence of the day:

> "Jesus," my father cried, "I hate the world!"
> "Mother," my mother called, "you're in the way!"
> "Be grateful for your blessings," Grandpa advised,
> shifting his feet and showing a hairless shin.
> "Ach," Grandma brought out in self-defense,
> the syllable a gem of German indignation. (ll. 79–84)

These utterances are familiar to any reader of Updike's Olinger fiction, but there is no reason to suppose that they all took place in rapid succession the day the family left church early. Instead, Updike is filling in the details with impressions that have become generalized (even mythologized) through repetition in both time and memory. The poem ends with a recognition of the impossibility of a memory purified of imagination:

> We know the truth of it, the past, how strange,
> how many corners wouldn't bear describing,
> the "rubbing elbows," how busy we were forgiving—
> we had no time, of course, we have no time
> to do all the forgiving that we must do. (ll. 134–38)

The spiritual business of the present always colors and controls our memories of the past, then, and we cannot hope to present things precisely.

"The Egg Race" (1977) makes a similar point. This story about memory and nostalgia begins with a question that immediately throws the efficacy and fidelity of memory into question: "Or was it called the Spoon Race?"[18] And yet Ferguson, the protagonist, cannot avoid his own memories; he is called to them, drawn to them, forced into them. He had forgotten the titular picnic pastime, but in his middle age, all sorts of memories have come flooding back to him. Memory becomes a way of dealing with death. As Ferguson talks to a dying colleague, he sees "the other man's face as something already lost in the earth, and an onrush of pity and joy quelled the triumphant racing of his heart; he wanted to save his colleague from the crushing mass of forward time when the man would not be here" (236). Memory could accomplish such a purpose, and in fact, as an archaeologist, Ferguson is a professional rememberer, "a seeker of lost cities" (231). His vocation, as he explains it to a former classmate, is "to bring what was hidden back into the light" (239). Updike's implication, then, is that Ferguson's archaeology is imaginative rather than scientific. His dying colleague tells him that his last paper was "a little less than rigorous. You posited a new stratum on the basis of a single shard" (235). If such a stratum existed, it would mean a major upheaval in the work of professional archaeology—unlikely. This new stratum, then, does not emerge from the simple facts of the civilization, long buried in the ground and exhumed by the heroic archaeology; it is largely a product of the archaeologist's mind. Realizing this truth causes Ferguson a great deal of professional and existential anxiety.

What is more, Ferguson feels himself to be locked out of the past, even his own personal past. At the Smithsonian, he sees "an antique classroom" and realizes, horribly: "He had studied in such a classroom. If it were not for the glass, he could walk in . . . and take his seat" (234). As he ages, he finds himself belonging to the past rather than to the present, and yet because his memory is tightly bound to his imagination, he has no real access to the past. The closest he comes to accessing it is his twenty-five-year high-school reunion, where, he hears a number of songs from the 1940s; as he listens, "Ferguson through a veil of bourbon perceived that amid these old children, these accents, and these melodies he had experienced Paradise" (238). The realization is a familiar one—it takes place in "In Football Season," "First Wives and Trolley Cars," and a number of other stories. But here, Ferguson's former classmate Linda Weed—and her body in particular—becomes a physical embodiment of his nostalgia. Her low-cut dress seems to him "to advertise that her breasts had survived two Asian wars, six Presidents, five recessions, and four children" (239). Ferguson thus connects with the past in a profoundly Updikean way, by watching Linda Weed's breast pop out of her dress. He has wanted to see this woman naked for thirty years, and the moment has at last presented itself: "Her breast was perfect, more candid and ample than he had dreamed, weighty yet buoyant in its shadowy cup of cloth, as perfect as an egg" (240). He has returned, however briefly, to the past.

This blissful return is twinned by an anxious return a few pages later, when Ferguson walks around Hayesville. It is not a pleasant experience: "On all sides, Ferguson was known. The tilting front porches knew him, and the twitching window curtains. The horse-chestnut trees would have known him, had they not been cut down. The alleys seemed brighter, the sky barer, since the days when he had sneaked the back way home from school to avoid bullies" (242). Here he finds himself being trapped by the past, and thus losing himself; the residents of his hometown consistently mistake him for his father. Ultimately, then, his experience returning home convinces him of the importance of his present life; he realizes that "all was nestled like a spoon beneath his life, his only life, his incredibly own, that he must not drop" (244). His imaginative encounters with the past, be they blissful (Linda Weed) or horrific (the sense that the town "knows" him), have allowed him to make sense of his present. At least they have put him on that road; we get no particular sense that he knows *how* not to drop the egg of his life.

Notes

1 Plato, *Theaetetus*, 197d–e.

2 Engel, *Context Is Everything*, 6.

3 Casey, *Remembering*, 22.

4 Engel, *Context Is Everything*, 6.

5 Warnock, *Memory*, 75–76.

6 Sartre, *The Psychology of Imagination*, 263.

7 Ibid.

8 Warnock, *Memory*, 35.

9 Begley, *Updike*, 113. Hereafter cited in-text.

10 Updike, "How Does the Writer Imagine?" 135.

11 Updike, "In Football Season," 3. Hereafter cited in-text.

12 Davis, *Yearning for Yesterday*, 12.

13 This piece is presented as fiction, and its narrator has a name that is not "John Updike," and yet it is collected under the subheading "Fairly Personal" in *Odd Jobs*, alongside another short story, a piece of long-form journalism, a one-act play version of "Your Lover Just Called," and a number of shorter autobiographical

pieces. The degree to which we are meant to take "First Wives and Trolley Cars" as straight autobiographical is thus difficult to ascertain.

14 Updike, "First Wives and Trolley Cars," 18. Hereafter cited in-text.

15 Updike, "The Day of the Dying Rabbit," 26. Hereafter cited in-text.

16 James, "The Real Thing," 366.

17 Updike, "Leaving Church Early," ll. 43–48. Hereafter cited in-text.

18 Updike, "The Egg Race," 231. Hereafter cited in-text.

15: *Memories of the Ford Administration*

*M*EMORIES OF THE FORD ADMINISTRATION (1992) is a strange hybrid of a novel, as its split cover—half of Gerald Ford's face, and half of James Buchanan's—suggests. The novel is formatted as a response to a query on the part of the Northern New England Association of American Historians for "Memories and Impressions of the President Administration of Gerald R. Ford (1974–77) for Written Symposium on Same to Be Published in NNEAAH's Triquarterly Journal, *Retrospect*."[1] Its author is Alfred L. Clayton, a professor of history at a women's college in New Hampshire, and he turns in a much longer text than the NNEAAH must have expected. What is more, it has little to do with what we think of as *history*, and what history there is has little to do with Gerald Ford's administration. Instead, he talks about his own life, which was in an absolute shambles in the mid-70s, interspersing his personal memoirs with sections from a book he was at the time trying—and failing—to write about James Buchanan. As he sees it, the editors of *Retrospect* cannot possibly want the bare political details of the period, "which any sophomore with access to a microfilm reader that hasn't broken its fan belt can tote up for you. You want *living* memories and impressions: the untampered-with testimony of those of who fortunate enough to have survived . . . the Ford Administration" (9). Living memory, however, is by definition always being tampered with, always being rewritten as the present influences the past and the past influences the present. And in fact, the major theme of *Memories of the Ford Administration* is the unreliability of the discipline of historiography in dredging up the facts of history. History, it turns out, is *l'être-en-soi*, and historiography is the imaginative projection of *l'être-pour-soi*. Historiography thus imagines a past that history constantly tears down.

The novel opens with Alf, freshly separated from his wife, babysitting his children and watching Nixon's resignation. He lives, at the time, in something of an imaginative world, in that he cannot quite believe that his old life has come to an end; he has "the illusion that the house we were in, a big Victorian with a mansard roof, a finished third floor, and a view from the upper windows of the yellow-brick smokestacks of the college heating plant, was still mine" (7). He feels, delusionally, that "I had left my wife but not our marriage, its texture and mind-set" (8). Time will show him the ugly truth that the house he sits in, the home that once was his, is "gone, cast off, as lost to my life as my childhood home in the hamlet of Hayes, my college rooms in Middlebury, our graduate-student quarters in Cambridge in a brick apartment building down Kirkland Street from the then-Germanic Museum, or the little apple-green Cape-and-a-half, our first bona-fide house, with a yard, a basement, and a letter slot, that the university rented to us in Hanover, right off Route 120, a stone's throw from the Orozco murals" (8). This progression through the homes he has lost suggests that time is swallowing his life, just as it swallows the life of the protagonist of "The Brown Chest" (1992), who spends his boyhood afraid of the titular storage unit. The chest holds familial memorabilia and thus functions as a "well of time, with its sweet deep smell of things unstirring, waiting, taking on the moldy flavor of time, not moving unless somebody touched them." Eventually the protagonist is "shocked to discover, glancing in, that at some point the chest had come to contain drawings he had done as a child, and his elementary-school report cards, and photographs . . . of him when he was five."[2] In the same way, Alf is horrified to discover that his once-bucolic life is now itself history, irretrievable history. As he asks the editors, "Enough time slides by, we're all history, right? And if you want to feel *really* sick, NNEAAH, think of the time that will keep sliding by after you're dead. After *we're* dead, I should say" (9). Time is more powerful than human life, more powerful than human memory, even more powerful than history and historiography themselves.

Alf sees this same destructive time in the bodies and faces of his lover Genevieve's daughters, who "were still unformed and traces of their parents eddied within a pure potentiality that confronted me with a strong sense of separate identity, of genetic synthesis hurled forward into a world that would eventually leave me behind" (96). The presence of the next generation proves that part of us belongs to the past and that eventually our entirety will belong to the past. The passing away of the earlier generation has the same effect. "Who now," Alf wonders when his mother dies, "would remember me as a Keds-shod boy padding along the brick sidewalks of our tinted, maple-shaded downtown? Who was left to share cinnamon doughnuts with me as if they were, far from 'junk food,' a gourmet treat? The dear soul had left me alone with my eventual death. The dead teach this great lesson, which we are loathe to learn: we too will die" (160). And yet historiography attempts eternality, attempts to bring history into the present. Thus past and present collapse in on each other in Alf's book on Buchanan. He speaks of his protagonist's traveling "toward the cemetery known as Woodward Hill, where, a half-century hence, Buchanan would be laid, with a civic pomp that he had specifically forbidden in his will, a document in which he also exactly designed and inscribed his own tombstone. But today he was alive, alive, and Ann, too, who would lie not long hence in St. James Episcopal Churchyard at Orange and Duke streets" (42). At least three periods coexist within these two sentences: Buchanan's traveling, Ann's death, and Buchanan's own death. And we can add two more in the context of the novel: Alf's writing the scene in the 1970s and his reproducing it in this essay in 1992. The more time spreads itself through past and present, the more the dead survive—but the more the living begin to look dead. Historiography thus both cures death-anxiety and exacerbates it.

Historiography is difficult, however, for some the same reasons that any project based on memory is. As Alf puts it, "Memory has a spottiness, as if the film was sprinkled with developer instead of immersed in it. And then as in an optical illusion the eye makes what it can of the spots" (9). Imagination is thus involved in every act of memory, since it has to fill in the gaps. But because of the role of the imagination in memory, "historical truth is forever elusive" (14). Alf will put it in scientific terms later: "As in physics, the more minutely we approach them, the stranger facts become, with leaps and contradictions of indecipherable quanta. All we have are documents, which do not agree" (75). Additionally, memory and historiography have the tendency to idealize the very un-ideal reality of the past:

> For we forget, as we tote up our lives in terms of copulations, how framed and squeezed the act is by less exalted realities—by appointments and anxieties, by the cooking smells arising from the floor below and the rumbling of one's hungry stomach, by the changes of light and obscure pressures of the day as the afternoon ebbs on the yellowing wallpaper into the gray fuzz of lost time. The day is shot, we say, as of a lackadaisical execution. And all the while behind the sun-dried brown shade near one's head (subdivided like a graham cracker by the sash rails and mullions) the great sky brims with its unnoticed towers of luminous, boiling cloud. No, only in retrospect, Retrospect, are our amorous encounters ideal, freed of inconvenience. (20)

Through the magic of memory, Alf can be suave and debonair in the past—but in the present spirit of honesty, he has to draw attention to the potential disparity: "'Well, in for a penny, in for a pound,' I said, or should have said, or seem now as I write this to have said, debonairly" (23). Alf's honesty, however, only makes the line between real and ideal less clear.

Alf's abandoned book on Buchanan further proves that memory—and with it, historiography—ultimately fails us. He cannot work on the book after arriving at "history's outer darkness" (35). But an encounter with poststructuralist literary theory gives him, for a time, the strength he needs: "For a long time, on the safe excuse of further research, I circled, fiddled, held fearfully back, until a deconstructionist arrived in the English department." Alf learns from this deconstructionist, Brent Mueller,

whom he will later cuckhold, that "all history consists simply of texts."
The historian has access to history only through these texts, which are
"inevitably indefinite, self-contradictory, and doomed to a final aporia"
(35). Alf has received the permission he wanted to abandon historiography as an ideal altogether, and thus much of his book on Buchanan is
imagined rather than researched, let alone remembered. In other words,
he sets his imagination free from the strictures of memory: "So why not
my text, added to all the others? I leaped in. I began, I should say, to
leap in, to overcome my mistaken reverence for the knowable actual ver-
sus supposition or fiction, my illusory distinction between fact and fancy"
(35). Updike means us to see this as a serious error, but as an under-
standable error. As Edward P. Vargo argues, "*Memories* pulses between
Updike's ingrained tendency toward the representation of things as they
really are and his sensitivity to late twentieth-century views on the inde-
terminacy of facts."[3] Certainly memory and imagination are so closely
related that there can be no clear separation of them, but Updike's aesthetic project has always involved fidelity to material reality even as it rec-
ommends a projection of meaning and imagination on the top of it. Alf
has only projection here—or at least he does in theory, since he cannot
quite bring himself to abandon history for fiction. His correction that "I
began, I should say, to leap in," suggests that the actual still matters to
him, even if it is an unattainable actual.

In fact, what he remembers about the days of his affair with Genevieve Mueller is the events themselves, not his interpretation of them:
"she and I had suddenly, recently managed, under cover of the bustle
of an academic community, to make contact, to confess our mutual
discontents, to make love, to fall in love, to exchange feverish pledges
whose exact meaning and circumstantial redemption remained cloudy in
my mind" (50). This is the opposite of what we would expect from his
stated devotion to deconstruction—there the interpretation takes prece-
dence over the events themselves, whereas in his memory of his affair it
is the event that is important. He also finds himself devoted to the actual
facts of Wayward, the city he lives in. In an aside to the editors, he writes
that "I would write, 'She stepped off the curb and came around to the,
etc.' except that the informal town of Wayward, like the Lancaster of my
imagining, was short on curbs and sidewalks, and had none here, where
the elm tree's roots would in any case have posed a problem for the pav-
ers" (51). Here his commitment to the actual and the workings of his
imagination combine: He insists on the actual street layout of the town
at the same time that he admits his understanding of his historiographical
subject is primarily imaginary. It seems that he holds a different standard
for the historical imagination than he does for the personal imagination,
which suggests in its turn that he does not really believe in his stated historiographical orientation.

Deconstruction would be, for Alf, a cleaning-up of the messy facts of the world. For example, he tries to use poststructuralist language to escape the ramifications of his own actions in an attempt to escape his guilt for breaking up two families. Such language emerges most clearly in his confrontation with Brent Mueller. As he argues with Brent, the entire situation becomes unreal: "The buried escapade with ample and appetitive Ann Arthrop—it seemed quite possible, as nonchalant, know-nothing Norma [Alf's wife] joined us, that it had never happened. After all, doesn't history demonstrate over and over how hard it is to say what actually *did* happen, so that even the Nazis' fanatically documented experimentation of six million Jews and Lee Harvey Oswald's broad-daylight shooting of John F. Kennedy and (let's not forget) Patrolman J. D. Tippitt are still seriously debated?" (254). If his transgressions against his family are swept clean by deconstructionist fantasy, then he will not have to face himself for what he is. His desire for this sort of purity echoes throughout the novel. He frequently refers to Norma as "my Queen of Disorder" (10), and he tells her that "I'm trying to lead an orderly life" (11). The problem is that order is fundamentally opposed to the domestic life, just as it is fundamentally opposed to history. And Updike generally presents domesticity as the site of virtue.[4] For example, as the Stallworths, a local moving-company family, move his belongings out of the Clayton home, Alf finds himself "suppressing my desire to cry out something like, 'No, *stop*, it's all a mistake, a crazy overreaching, I belong *here*, these things belong here, embedded in the mothering disorder, gathering dustballs and cat hair, blamelessly sunk in domestic torpor and psychosexual compromise!" (25). Human life is fundamentally disordered, and Alf's desire for perfect order is a species of idealism. It is no wonder that he refers to Genevieve Mueller as "the Perfect Wife" (49) and admires her perfectly structured household:

> She had managed to instill in her household a European sense of children as graceful adornments to the parents, as opposed to our ugly American democratic style, with even an infant given his noisy vote in all proceedings. As to décor, in my own house there was simply too much—too many pictures on the wall, too many worn-out rugs overlapping on the floor, too much carelessly inherited furniture, too many shawls and cats shedding threads and hairs on the sofa cushions, too many half-empty bottles in the pantry and half-read books piled up everywhere, even in the bathrooms—whereas here there was just enough of books, tables, vases, chairs, a cool sufficiency with poverty's clean lines, a prosperity short of surfeit. (54–55)

Even her genitals are a model of order; Alf tells us that their lovemaking "was quick, firm, adventurous, definitive. There was none of that female male and endocrinal grievance I had to work through with the Queen of Disorder. I pictured my wife's psychosexual insides as a tidal swamp where a narrow path wound past giant nodding cattails and hidden egret-nests, with a slip into indifference gaping on both sides; Genevieve's entrails were in comparison city streets, straight, broad, and zippy" (55). There is thus something unreal about Genevieve—Alf's relationship with her seems the product of his imagination more than something existent in reality. He tells us that "our lovemaking melted us into one, one with the dark, a mass of blind sensation, her dear flexible and seven times receptive body firm and graceful, like curves my mind kept drawing in the pitch-black back of some cave, perhaps Plato's" (176). His language here suggests the degree to which Genevieve's perfection is an imaginative projection on his part. He has a sense when they are in bed of his "body being the only one present, Genevieve transformed for this interval into pure fierce spirit" (176). She has been in some sense deconstructed—she no longer exists at the level of physical reality.

Accordingly, Alf rationalizes his infidelity by saying that he is "leaving this marriage as a tribute to marriage, to create a perfect marriage. Not the most uxurious Methodist deacon in Hayes would be a stricter adherent of the old vows, once I got the right wife. I was a fervent supporter of marriage, just not of *my* marriage, my present marriage" (142). But this is clearly bad faith, clearly a weak rationalization of an action that he himself knows to be unsupportable, if irresistible. His rationalization resembles his adoption of deconstruction—it is less a lifestyle than an attempt at a lifestyle, an attempt to ignore the facts of existence in favor of an imaginative re-presentation of them. Genevieve recognizes this fact long before Alf does. When he tells her that she's perfect, she replies, "Nobody's perfect. It makes me sad to hear you say that. It's as if I'm not real to you, the way Norma is" (173). He will eventually agree with her; speaking of their sexual frenzy during a three-day trip to New York, he remarks, "For her to be so transported by passion, so much a maenad, she had to have had an *idea* of me, like a groupie blowing a rock star. The longer we know another, the less of an idea we have; eventually all we have are facts" (176). The ideal will eventually shatter on the hard ground of reality.

Unsurprisingly, then, Alf is thrown off when Genevieve tells him that she and Brent are getting a divorce and that Brent expects her to marry Alf: "The world had changed complexion; in an instant, the intoxicating spring air had become a wet hot washrag pressed against my face—the pressure of the actual, the mortal, the numinously serious" (55). Such an expectation requires a radical reordering of his life; he realizes he must "dispose of my own wife and children. They had been deconstructed, but didn't know it yet" (52). This sort of "deconstruction" imposes order on the world by removing its messier elements. The problem is that human beings are messy, and Alf eventually realizes that "the order [Genevieve] would create in my life depended upon reifying people, reducing them to their uses" (178). We are given the choice between order and relationship—both are not possible.

By the end of the novel, Alf has cheated on Genevieve too many times for him to count, and both he and Genevieve have returned to their families and Alf has given up on writing his imagination-assisted book on Buchanan. Furthermore, in an astounding scene, Brent Mueller—the diabolic, Derridean deconstructionist—has revealed himself to be, of all things, a defender of traditional family values:

> "Brent is willing to forgive me everything," Genevieve was saying.
> "Big deal," I said. "What's to forgive? A post-structuralist bastard like that has no right to talk about forgiveness as if it has meaning. . . ."
> Her smile had become less sad; a twinkle brimmed in her eyes like a new kind of tear. "Don't be so competitive. Brent's much more of a traditionalist than you think. He believes in family. I'll tell you a secret. His own true parents got a divorce when he was three, then his mother married her lover and they became ardent Lutherans. He swore he'd never do it to his own children. Get a divorce. He said if I'd come back he'd even let me have lovers, if he wasn't adequate for me sexually." (296–97)

As it turns out, a person cannot live deconstruction as a life philosophy— Brent Mueller deconstructs ideas for a living but clings desperately to traditional family structures when he leaves the classroom. Likewise, it does not work as a historiographical practice; Alf has to abandon his imaginative reconstruction of Buchanan's life. The novel restores us to the dialectic posited by Updike's other novels: We project our imagination onto material reality, and material reality corrects our imaginative projections. The same is true with historiography and history:

> The texts are like pieces of a puzzle that only roughly fit. There are little irregular spaces between them, and through these cracks, one feels, truth slips. History, unlike fiction and physics, never quite jells; it is an armature of rather randomly preserved verbal and physical remains upon which historians slap wads of supposition in hopes of the lumpy statue's coming to life. One of the joys of doing original research is to observe how one's predecessor historians have fudged their way across the very gaps, or fault-lines that one is in turn balked by. History in its jaggedness constantly tears at our smooth conceptions of human behavior. (165–66)

In other words, yes, history is impossible to reconstruct, but that doesn't leave us free for a deconstructionist free-for-all. Instead, we must fill in the gaps with our imaginations, with the understanding that history itself will constantly wear away the mortar. Historiography is a discipline that is always necessary because it is always being corrected, just like the imagination.

Notes

1 Updike, *Memories of the Ford Administration*, 3.

2 Updike, "The Brown Chest," 227.

3 Vargo, "Updike, American History, and Historical Methodology," 112.

4 For more information, see Schiff, "The Pocket Nothing Else Will Fill."

16: "The Dogwood Tree," "A Soft Spring Night in Shillington," and "On Being a Self Forever"

I T IS NOT SURPRISING THAT Updike continues his interest in the intersection of memory and imagination in his memoirs; autobiography would seem to be the natural place for such ideas. His earliest biographical statement of note is "The Dogwood Tree: A Boyhood," composed for Martin Levin's *Five Boyhoods* (1962). Updike attempts to draw a picture of Shillington, Pennsylvania, in the 1940s and notes near the outset both the success and failure of such a project: "Though I cannot ask you to see it more clearly than I myself saw it, yet mentioning it seems to open the possibility of my boyhood home coming again to life. With a sweet damp rush the grass of our yard seems to breathe again on me."[1] The disclaimer that makes up the initial clause suggests both the impossibility of retrieving the material reality of his childhood and the difficulty of communicating even a subjectively remembered version of that reality to his readers. The rest of the sentence, however, suggests that through the union of memory and imagination he can resurrect a version of his childhood, if only temporarily and imperfectly and if primarily only for himself. (For the reader, of course, his childhood remains purely in the realm of the imagination.) Here, too, his imagination must fill in the gaps left by his memory. He tells us about his grandmother's chickens, which she "beheaded . . . with an archaic efficiency that I don't recall ever witnessing" (122). And yet he feels confident in referring to the "archaic efficiency" of these beheadings, a clear indication that the memories in this memoir are deeply connected to imagination.

In some ways, "The Dogwood Tree" is as much a reflection on imagination as it is an exercise of it. Updike's boyhood was, as we might expect from a future author, filled with acts of the imagination—acts that he increasingly came to see as fragile as he aged. He speaks, for example, about the poorhouse at the end of his street, which was surrounded by a wall with "a drop of twenty or thirty feet." As an adult, Updike cannot understand this dangerous drop, "but at the time it seemed perfectly natural, a dreadful pit of space congruent with the pit of time into which the old people . . . had been plunged by some mystery that would never touch me." This safety was, needless to say, an illusion built on a child's sensation of invincibility: "That I too would come to their condition was as unbelievable as that I would really fall and break my neck" (125). Later in the essay he discusses a memorable day in which, playing with other children, he saw a huge cloud whose "size seemed overwhelming; it was more than a portent, it was the fulfillment of one. I had never seen, and never saw again, such a big cloud" (137). As an adult, he recognizes that the enormity of the cloud was a child's projection, since "clouds have no size. Moving in an immaterial medium at an indeterminate distance, they offer no hold for measurement, and we do not even judge them relative to each other" (137). And yet this imaginative projection has stuck with him for two decades, suggesting that our imaginative projections, especially as children, form in some part our identity.

As so many of his characters later will, the young Updike had a sense of himself as the Cartesian origin of the universe:

> My geography went like this: in the center of the world lay our neighborhood of Shillington. Around it there was greater Shillington, and around that, Berks County. Around Berks County there was the State of Pennsylvania, the best, the least eccentric state in the Union. Around Pennsylvania, there was the United States, with a greater weight of people on the right and a greater weight of land on the left. For clear geometrical reasons, not all children could be born, like me, at the center of the nation. But that some children chose to be born in other countries and even continents seemed sad and fantastic. There was only one possible nation: mine. (130)

This sort of ethnocentrism is common among children and is, needless to say, much more insidious among adults.[2] But for children it is an important part of self-discovery or self-invention; one needs to discover oneself at the center of the world before one can expand that world to include other intelligences, other souls. Thus Updike says that he has a terrible time describing the scenes of his childhood "because they are so fundamental to me, they enclosed so many of my hours, that they have the neutral color of my own soul" (135). He is literally constituted of his memories; as such he cannot possibly imagine that they are entirely accurate to the bare facts of 1940s Shillington. His soul infuses any look back. For example, he talks about the woods on the edge of town, through which "my parents often took me on walks. Every Sunday afternoon that was fair, we would set out. Sun, birds, and treetops rotated above us as we made our way" (126). He has the same sense that all of us sometimes do, especially as children, that the world has been benevolently placed around us to tend to our needs. The feeling continues as he enters adolescence, since Shillington boys brought their girlfriends to this spot to fool around. Updike's description of his own presexual dalliances in the woods suggests both a repudiation of his family's walks and a continuation of their meaning: "We walked, the girl and I, down the path where I had smashed so many branches, and sat down on a damp broad log—it was early spring, chilly, a timid froth of leaves overhead—and I dared lightly to embrace her from behind and cup my hands over her breasts, small and shallow within the stiffness of her coat, and she closed her eyes and tipped her head back, and an adequate apology seemed delivered for the irritable innocence of these almost forgotten hikes with my parents" (127). As he enters sexual maturity, then, he outgrows his simple familial activities—and yet these amorous encounters also allow him to feel like the center of the universe. In his memory, after all, "this broad crescent of woods is threaded with our walks and suffused with images of love" (126). The bare material reality has been stamped with the imagination.

His childhood landmarks thus become ideals for his present life, just as "reading is the master of cities, the one at the center that all others echo" (129). The imagination stamps the memory, but the memory stamps the imagination, which then stamps the material world. In the same way, Updike feels his remembered childhood self, and especially his artistic ambitions, to be more real than his present reality: "The boy continues to smile at the corner of the room, beyond me. That boy is not a ghost to me, he is real to me; it is I who am a ghost to him. I, in my present state, was one of the ghosts that haunted his childhood." And from his childhood self he inherits his famous sense of the purpose of art: "To transcribe middleness with all its grits, bumps, and anonymities, in its fullness of satisfaction and mystery" (147). But the material world resists our attempts at transcription, to the point where Updike acknowledges that this goal may be impossible. And yet, he says, "the horse-chestnut trees, the telephone poles, the porches, the green hedges recede to a calm point that in my subjective geography is still the center of the world" (147). Material reality, in other words, is important because it is the canvas on which we paint—but it is also important because it is the model from which we paint. As he puts it, "Blankness is not emptiness; we may skate upon an intense radiance we do not see because we see nothing else. And in fact there is a color, a quiet but tireless goodness that things at rest, like a brick wall or a small stone, seem to affirm. A wordless reassurance these things are pressing to give" (147). We must project, with our imaginations—and in many cases, with our memories—but we must recognize that the things of the world are going to speak back to us and correct our projections, our interpretations, and our transcriptions.

These tensions continue in the first and last chapters of Updike's 1989 memoir, *Self-Consciousness*: "A Soft Spring Night in Shillington" and "On Being a Self Forever." In these memoirs, we see clearly the role that memory and imagination must take in making meaning for human life, but correspondingly how fragile meaning must be when it is built on such shaky foundations. In "A Soft Spring Night in Shillington," Updike remembers a series of photographs documenting his childhood and says that "without those accumulating photographs my past would have vanished, year after year. Instead, it accumulated, loose in a set of shoe-boxes, in no order, and because of its randomness ever fresh, ever stunning: shuffled windows into a sunlit abyss."[3] His language here suggests that the bare facts of life—the events and memories captured by these photographs—must be constantly put into order by the imagination. In themselves, they have no particular meaning. It is only when they are put into an order, only when they are imaginatively made into a story, that they mean anything. But the order itself does not belong to them, and after a given story is told, they will be returned to the "sunlit abyss" of the shoebox. The imagination brings the memory to life—and memories, once instilled with meaning, make up the substance of human existence. In fact, the flood of memory that is "A Soft Spring Night in Shillington" is set loose by Updike's meaning-making imagination, his "walking the sidewalks of Shillington, Pennsylvania, searching for the meaning of my existence as once I had scanned those same sidewalks for lost pennies" (3). The process is necessary because the world of material reality, the *l'être-en-soi*, is oppressively meaningless: "How circumstantial reality is! Facts are like the individual letters, with their spikes and loops and thorns, that make up words: eventually they hurt our eyes, and we long to take a bath, to rake the lawn, to look at the sea" (4). The solution to this oppression is meaning-making, enacted through the powerful force of the human imagination.

Memory is an important part of this process, and as Updike wanders the streets of Shillington, the past and the present collapse into a single imaginative space. The emblem of this process is the awning that once decorated the town: "It was common, in pre-air-conditioning days, to intensify the cool of the deep porches of Shillington with awnings, usually green; these houses still wore on their pillars and pasciae the attached hardware needed to hook up an awning, but painted over, disused, like some religious custom whose significance has been forgotten" (10). In the same way, there are traces of the 1940s town in its 1980s incarnation, but they are visible only to an observer who, like Updike, has the eyes to see them. But under the sway of his memory, parallel universes exist simultaneously: "The soft warm air had turned humid again, and I craved rain, remembering how one could walk and stay dry under trees that no longer existed" (19). Often, too, the real shares its space not just with the remembered but also with the imagined and the ideal. For example, Updike remembers "a curious little stone hut where grown-ups paid their electric bill" (8). This building exists only in his memory, and yet his writing it down projects it into our collective imagination as readers: "This quaint structure, long since replaced by a drive-in bank, was intertwined in my childish mind with German fairy tales, with spidery illustrations in books that beckoned me to look deep into the past, into mankind's communal memory, abysmally deeper than my own" (8). These ideals have as strong, or stronger, a hold on the real present as the remembered past does: "Illustrations affected me more strongly than reality; a picture of falling snow, for example, whether in black-and-white line drawing or blurry four-color reproduction, moves me more than any actual storm. An ideal world was projected by my childish yearning onto commercial Christmas art, and it lies forever embedded there" (8–9). But if this is true—if the remembered, the real, and the imagined are mixed this thoroughly—memory is inherently untrustworthy as an actual chronicler of the past, however useful it might be as an interpreter of the present. In reporting an afternoon in which he stayed after class to draw, Updike has "a sensation that one of these two teachers came over and ruffled my hair, as if we had become a tiny family; but it may be simply that one of them stood close, to see how far along I was, because when I was finished we could all go to our separate homes" (17). Memory, that is, sentimentalizes itself into nostalgia. And even when it does not, it imposes a meaning on the world of bare facts. Updike, for example, remembers the man who lived next door, who "always wore dark clothes and, fifteen years after we had moved away, was found murdered in his feed store in Reading. Did he really always wear dark clothes, or has my memory, knowing of his grisly end, dressed him appropriately?" (22). There is no way to give a sure answer to this question, because the past is fundamentally inaccessible—or, what it amounts to the same thing, it is accessible only through memory, which is accessible only through the imagination.

Sometimes the distinction between memory and reality is disenchanting, or at least disappointing; in cases like these, the material reality corrects the imaginative/memorious vision of it, just as it corrects other imaginative projections onto the world. Updike stands on his old street, "waiting, self-consciously, to feel something, and felt less than I had hoped. The street, the house where I had lived, seemed blunt, modest in scale, simple." His memories readjust, however, and he finds meaning in this smaller scale whose "deceptive simplicity composed [the street and houses'] precious, mystical secret, the conviction of whose existence I had parlayed into a career, a message to sustain a writer book after book" (24). A few pages later, meaning again floods out of the world. He looks "back up the straight sidewalk in the soft evening gloom, looking for what the superstitious old people of the county used to call a 'sign.' The pavement squares, the housefronts, the remaining trees receding in silence and shadow" (30). Meaning has retreated back into the bare facts of existence, which wait in silence for *l'être-pour-soi* to fill them with meaning again. This imaginative emptying and refilling is fundamental to Updike's vocation as a writer: "A writer's self-consciousness, for which he is much scorned, is really a mode of interestedness, that inevitably turns outward" (24). And when it does, it is (at times) refreshed by the material reality that (at other times) depletes it. Updike looks at the houses that once belonged to his neighbors: "There was a dove grayness to their united mass in my memory, and the reality, however often revisited, never failed to improve upon memory with a fresh enchantment" (25). We have here, then, a double motion: The memory enchants the reality, but the reality also enchants the memory. To lose this double re-enchantment is to remove ingress and egress from the pond of the mind. It will grow scummy, and a person will succumb to despair.

The final essay in *Self-Consciousness*, "On Being a Self Forever," is in many ways an attempt to avoid despair. Updike's fiction has always shown a concern with and a fear of death—perhaps most notably in "Pigeon Feathers," in which David Kern has a horrible vision of himself as a corpse, thrusting him into an intense religious crisis that is relieved only by a vision of his own eternal survival. The hope for the afterlife, then, is itself a kind of self-consciousness, a hope that I, my self, will survive my death. In "On Being a Self Forever," Updike presents the dominant secular view, which is that such a hope is self-centered and childish: "isn't it terribly, well, *selfish*, and grotesquely egocentric, to hope for more than our animal walk in the sun, from eager blind infancy through the productive and procreative years into a senescence that, by the laws of biological instinct as well as by the premeditated precepts of stoic virtue, will submit to eternal sleep gratefully?"[4] In other words, it would be selfish to expect anything beyond the barest material reality. Updike clearly takes this viewpoint seriously even as he finds it lacking; it is part of "the power of materialist science to explain everything" that he affirms, partially, in his "This I Believe" essay.[5] But it is clear from David Kern's terror in "Pigeon Feathers" that Updike cannot accept this vision of human death on an existential level; he needs an afterlife—which by its very nature can be accessed only through the imagination—to ground his present existence in something other than despair and nihilism. The problem is that the afterlife is, in a real sense, entirely unimaginable. Christian orthodoxy does not provide any real solution because it insists "no less firmly than modern materialism that the body *is* the person, and [leaves] us with a tenet, the resurrection of the dead, that has become unthinkable, though it remains part of the Apostles' Creed professed in chorus by millions every Sunday" (215).[6] The popular vision of the afterlife, on the other hand, is heretical: "the escape of something impalpable—the essential 'I'—from this corruptible flesh, occurring at the moment of death and not at 'the last trump' as Paul stated and as hundreds of medieval sculptors tried to imagine on church tympani" (215). Thus Updike suggests that we should not try to imagine the afterlife so much as we realize that "it is the self as window on the world that we can't bear to think of shutting" (217). His longing for eternal life is not so much theological as it is existential.

It is true, then, that this longing is fundamentally opposed to modern materialism, but it is not an attempt to escape from material reality. Thus it "is the opposite of selfish: it is love and praise for the world that we are privileged, in this complex interval of life, to witness and experience" (217). It is an affirmation of the material world through a projection of the imagination on it: "Our self is thrust into a manifold reality that is thoroughly gratuitous, and the faith in an afterlife, however much our reason ridicules it, very modestly extends our faith that each moment of our consciousness will be followed by another—that a coherent matrix has been prepared for this precious self of ours" (217). And God, in whom our hope for eternal survival is grounded, "is the self projected onto reality by our natural and necessary optimism. He is the not-me personified" (218). In this sense, faith is the ultimate act of the imagination—an audacious act, perhaps, of wishful thinking—but one without which Updike and his fellow believers could not live without sliding into the darkest kind of despair. We project God to make meaning, and we hope that God nevertheless exists as a presence hovering above the material world that we both love and fear. Updike's faithless characters, unsurprisingly, tend to be his least imaginative. The clearest example is *Marry Me*'s Richard, whose jaundiced materialism is best expressed by his glass eye, which makes the world two-dimensional: "Things were just so flat, with nothing further to be said about them; it was the world, [Jerry] realized, as seen without the idea of God lending each thing a roundness of significance. It was terrible."[7] Faith is a form of imagination: It may falsify the material world, but it is the only way that Updike has found to maintain the third dimension of meaning that sustains human life. Without imaginative faith, the world collapses into pure *l'être-en-soi*, and human life is unlivable. The afterlife, by extending the present life, makes present life meaningful. As Updike puts it, "Religion allows us to ignore nothingness and get on with the jobs of life" (228).

Faith is thus intimately concerned with the production and maintenance of the human self. It is the future's corollary to memory, and both of these faculties are united in the imagination, which ties together the selves that we were and the selves that we hope to be forever. In some sense, to let go of the remembered past is to let go of the eternal future—and to let go of the eternal future is to let go of the experienced present. Updike admits that we sometimes dislike our past selves, "these disposable ancestors of ours. For instance, my high-school self—skinny, scabby, giggly, gabby, frantic to be noticed, tormented enough to be a tormentor, relentlessly pushing his cartoons and posters and noisy jokes and pseudo-sophisticated poems upon the helpless high school—strikes me now as considerably obnoxious." And yet he cannot let go of this remembered self because it has helped create the self he currently imagines himself to be: "I owe him a lot: without his frantic ambition and insecurity I would not now be sitting on (as my present home was named by others) Haven Hill" (221). Updike also dislikes his self from the sexually promiscuous early 1960s, who 'seems another obnoxious show-off, rapacious and sneaky and, in the service of his own ego, remorseless" (222). The self he describes here, it must be noted, is the self who wrote "The Dogwood Tree"—perhaps two decades later, a twenty-first century Updike came to despise the self who wrote "On Being a Self Forever." Contempt can therefore not result in repudiation: "But, then, am I his superior in anything but caution and years, and how can I disown him without disowning also his useful works, on which I still receive royalties?" (222). Our memories of our past selves thus—as we have seen in Updike's fiction—help us to position our current selves, and the imagination that is our faith in the afterlife does the same thing. As Updike explains, "one believes not merely to dismiss from one's life a degrading and immobilizing fear of death but to possess that Archimedean point outside the world from which to move the world" (232). Faith, a form of imagination, also frees us up for other imaginative acts, other rearrangements of *l'être-en-soi* into meaningful patterns.

Material reality will thus always be in a productive and destructive tension with the imaginative/memorious/faithful projection. Thus, in "A Soft Spring Night," Updike admits that other residents of Shillington "will see that I haven't described it very well, for I haven't described *their* town—only mine, lost luggage by and large, a few scraps preserved by memory and used more than once, used to the point of vanishing like the wishing hide in the fairy tale, used up and wished away in the self-serving corruptions of fiction" (40). But what else is there? To approach material reality without the imagination is to submit oneself to despair; to approach it with the imagination is to falsify it to one extent or another and certainly to retreat into subjectivity. What other option do we possibly have? We must make meaning out of our lives, and the memory and the imagination are our two sharpest tools for doing so. Writing becomes a form of faith: "Even the barest earthly facts are unbearably heavy, weighted as they are with our personal death. Writing, in making the world light—in codifying, distorting, prettifying, verbalizing it—approaches blasphemy" ("On Being," 226). Faith and writing both presume to peel back *l'être-en-soi* and to find something meaningful beneath it: "Habit and accustomedness have painted over pure gold with a dull paint that can, however, be scratched away, to reveal the shining underbase" (230). But the possibility always exists that it is the dull paint that is real, the gold being the product of our imagination. Even so, the process works, at least heuristically and partially: "I had expected to be told who I was, and why, and had not been entirely disappointed. The raindrops made a pattern on the street like television snow, or like the scrambled letters with which a word processor fills the screen before a completed electric spark clears it all into perfect grace. I studied the drops, feeling fulfilled and suspended" ("Soft Spring," 41). But each of us must make the drops into our own pattern, a pattern that tells us who and why *we* are. And each of us must face the fact that the material reality is the "completed electric spark" that will continually disrupt and reset that pattern, leaving us to form a new one.

Notes

[1] Updike, "The Dogwood Tree," 121. Hereafter cited in-text.

[2] Updike, it must be noted, was always a partisan for American culture and values—but he clearly strove to be as cosmopolitan as a relatively conservative American novelist could be. His trips to Eastern Europe and Africa are well-documented in his nonfiction and (in the case of Eastern Europe) in his stories about Henry Bech. And several of his novels attempt to portray lives quite different from his own: *The Coup*'s representation of sub-Saharan Africa, for example, or *Terrorist*'s portrayal of an Arab American life. That neither of these novels is quite satisfying on the aesthetic level suggests that perhaps Updike maintained, to some degree or other, that child's notion of geography into adulthood.

[3] Updike, "A Soft Spring Night in Shillington," 12. Hereafter cited in-text.

[4] Updike, "On Being a Self Forever," 214. Hereafter cited in-text.

[5] Updike, "This I Believe," 671.

[6] Updike himself notably affirms the Apostle's Creed as the essence of his Christian faith; as he puts it in "The Dogwood Tree," his faith is summed up by "an obdurate insistence that at the core of the core there is a right-angled clash to which, of all verbal combinations we can invent, the Apostles' Creed offers the most adequate correspondence and response" (144).

[7] Updike, *Marry Me*, 225.

Conclusion: Updike, Realism, and Postmodernism

REALISM IS ALWAYS A complicated concept for fiction. From the time of Flaubert and Henry James realism has furnished fiction writers with a set of tools for re-presenting the world—tools that authors tended to either use (William Dean Howells, Stephen Crane, John Cheever) or to define themselves by not using (James Joyce, Susan Sontag, David Foster Wallace). Even today, and despite the best efforts of more than a century of technical experiments, correspondence to reality (and its corollary, relatability of character) tends to be the most important aesthetic criterion for most lay readers, at least in America. The problems with the category of "realism" are manifold; the most convincing critique to my eyes is Ian Watt's in *The Rise of the Novel*. Watt argues that "formal realism" is essentially a literary convention among other literary conventions. Formal realism demands that the novel be "a full and authentic report of human experience, and is therefore under an obligation to satisfy its reader with such details of the story as the individuality of the actors concerned, the particulars of the times and places of their actions, details which are presented through a more largely referential use of language than is common in other literary forms." But Watt says that readers and theorists alike run into trouble when they assume that "the report on human life which is presented by" realism is "any truer than those presented through the very different conventions of other literary genres."[1] If fidelity to what is "real" is the criterion of literary realism, after all, then every work of literature is realistic; no author sets out to portray something that she or he feels is false, and even speculative and fantastic works of fiction are "realistic" in the sense that they point to some idea that their authors feel is intrinsic to human life. Even Plato's allegory of the cave is realistic in this broadest sense, since it is meant to alert us to the unreality of the physical world that formal realism takes for granted.

But if formal realism is concerned with vivid characters and particular details, as Watt suggests, then there can be little doubt that John Updike is, by and large, a formal realist. This is true even of his novels that take place in fantastic or semifantastic worlds—*The Centaur*'s mythological framework is laid over an intensely observed representation of Shillington, for example; the magical worlds of *The Witches of Eastwick* and *Brazil* are grounded, as all magical realism is, in a more-or-less familiar modern world; and *Toward the End of Time* is science fiction only in the broadest sense. Updike's work is frequently formally experimental; despite his popular reputation as a one-trick pony chronicler of suburban adultery, he was rarely satisfied to rest on one mode of storytelling for very long. But that formal experimentation always takes place within the context of formal realism. When John Barth classes Updike with John Cheever, Wallace Stegner, and William Styron under the heading of "more consistently traditionalist American writers,"[2] we probably should not argue with him, though we might object to the slight sneer that seems to accompany this phrase. As Updike tells us late in "The Dogwood Tree," his aesthetic goal is "to transcribe middleness with all its grits, bumps, and anonymities, in its fullness of satisfaction and mystery."[3] These are the goals of the formal realist.

But two of Updike's most important influences—Marcel Proust and James Joyce—are not formal realists, and though I do not think it is accurate to call Updike a modernist, the modernist influence on his work is considerable. In particular, Updike seems to have inherited from the 1920s a different approach to realism. As James Wood points out, "poets and novelists repeatedly attack one kind of realism only to argue for their own kind of realism,"[4] and the modernists are no exception. To the degree that we can call Proust, Joyce, Faulkner, Woolf, and the like realists, we are speaking about a psychological rather than a physical realism. To read *A Portrait of the Artist as a Young Man* is to experience the world the way Stephen Dedalus experiences it, or would experience it; the stream-of-consciousness technique that recurs in *Portrait*, dominates *À la recherche du temps perdu* (1913–27; *In Search of Lost Time*, 1922–31), and surfaces from time to time in Updike's fiction[5] makes its claim on reality not by its fidelity to the physical world but by its fidelity to our emotional and existential experience of the physical world. In this sense, too, Updike's fiction is realistic because the process he describes again and again in his fiction—the process of the human projection of the imagination onto the bare material reality—is the process by which all of us make sense of the world around us. He goes beyond formal realism in this sense, which in its purest form strives to present the bare material reality itself. In a 1987 lecture, Updike connects that realist striving with William Dean Howells, who saw three virtues in fiction: "naturalness of manner, a tract of presentation that allows the story to seem to tell itself, and a willingness to deal with common material and to suppress the author's personality, which yet makes itself felt in the 'essential friendliness' of style—the virtues, in short, that Howells was himself to manifest."[6] But Updike sees a desperation beneath these virtues: "One wonders if Howell's tenacious artistic clinging to the surface of things doesn't show a fear of falling back into an abyss" (177). His ultimate problem with Howells is a lesser version of his problem with Alain Robbe-Grillet—the bare presentation of reality is of limited value because it lacks the input of the human imagination. For Howells, "plot is justifiable only to the extent that reality itself can be said to have a plot, a design," and thus "his fiction is formless, and was sensed as such by his contemporaries" (185). If fiction only presents reality rather than re-presenting it, there is nothing to keep author and reader alike from "falling back into an abyss." One difference between Updike's fiction and Howells's, as James Schiff argues, is "Updike's desire to depict states of transcendence within the ordinary. Updike often endows ordinary scenes with 'something extra.'"[7] That something extra is the meaning that the human imagination projects onto the bare facts of reality, and it is this meaning that keeps Updike and his readers from falling into the abysses that frequently open up beneath his novels.

It is tempting, given the focus I have given to the projections of the human imagination, to position Updike within a postmodernist tradition extending back at least to Friedrich Nietzsche's "Über Wahrheit und Lüge im Außermoralischen Sinn" (On Truth and Lies in a Nonmoral Sense, 1873). Nietzsche's argument in this disturbing essay is that human language is the great falsifier of material reality (which is the only reality). The problem is that human beings think in language, not before it, and thus we have no access to the world except through language, which falsifies the world it ostensibly describes. The language through which we approach the world categorizes the entities in that world by abstraction, and so "each word immediately becomes a concept, not by virtue of the fact that it is intended to serve as a memory (say) of the unique, utterly individualized, primary experience to which it owes its existence, but because at the same time it must fit countless other, more or less similar cases, i.e. cases which, strictly speaking, are never equivalent, and thus nothing other than non-equivalent cases. Every concept comes into being by making equivalent that which is non-equivalent."[8] For example, if I create the category "leaf," I can fill it with real objects from the world. But to do so, I have to ignore the myriad differences between each of the leaves—and this ignoring is always going to be arbitrary on some level. The process is even more evident when we invent abstract qualities like "honesty." We have to fill such a category with actual events from the real world, and by doing so we ignore their differences and fabricate the quality. And the categorizing does damage to the events themselves.

Truth thus does not exist: "What, then, is truth? A mobile army of metaphors, metonymies, anthropomorphisms, in short a sum of human relations which have been subjected to a poetic and rhetorical intensification, translation, and decoration, and which, after they have been in use for a long time, strike people as firmly established, canonical, and binding; truths are illusions of which we have forgotten that they are illusions, metaphors which have become worn by frequent use and have lost all sensuous vigor, coins which, having lost their stamp, are now regarded as metal and no longer as coins."⁹ We invent truth through our language, and then we apply it to the world. Then we quickly spin around, find that same truth in the world, and pretend we have discovered something. This is, in fact, the characteristic human activity, the thing we do that no other animal does. But it means that we can never know things as they are; all we can know is our linguistic projections on them. Jacques Derrida is getting at something similar when he famously says, in *De la grammatologie* (Of Grammatology, 1967), "*il n'y a pas de hors-texte*"—not so much "there is nothing outside the text," as it is sometimes translated, as "there is no outer-text."¹⁰ In other words, everything we receive is interpreted; no matter how many levels of interpretation we peel back, another level awaits us. It is interpretation all the way down, with no connection to a noninterpreted reality.

Updike's modus operandi, as I have described it in the preceding chapters, does have some things in common with these postmodernist approaches, but his lampooning of Derridean deconstruction in *Memories of the Ford Administration* should warn us that he does not see himself as a fellow traveler with the poststructuralists. His approach is more conservative, more "realistic" in that Flaubertian sense. Updike presents a world in which the human imagination always projects—or at least always should project—itself onto a blank material reality, a world in which *l'être-pour-soi* is constantly expected to project meaning onto the essentially meaningless *l'être-en-soi*. But this projection is self-correcting in a way that Nietzsche and Derrida do not, I think, allow. For Updike, in other words, there is an outer-text, and the author's responsibility "to transcribe middleness with all its grits, bumps, and anonymities, in its fullness of satisfaction and mystery" is in part a method of keeping the human imagination honest: we may not be able to have perfect access to the material world, but the material world periodically, perhaps even constantly, makes itself known by tearing down the imagination constructions we build on its back. The author's fidelity to the world is thus held in dialectical tension with his imaginative project; the two are always in dialogue, and the human self is always moving between the two of them—forever building, forever destroying.

Notes

1 Watt, *The Rise of the Novel*, 32.

2 Barth, "The Literature of Replenishment," 195.

3 Updike, "The Dogwood Tree," 147.

4 Wood, *How Fiction Works*, 239.

5 One of the earliest and most notable uses of stream of consciousness in Updike's fiction comes from *Rabbit, Run*, when the narration suddenly shifts to Ruth's

perspective: "It's just like when she was fourteen and the whole world trees sun and stars would have swung into place if she could lose twenty pounds just twenty pounds what difference would it make to God Who guided every flower in the fields into shape? Only now it's not that she's asking she knows now that's superstitious all she wants is what she had a minute ago *him* in the room who when he was good could make her into a flower who could undress her of her flesh and turn her into sweet air Sweet Ruth he called her and if he had just said 'sweet' talking to her she might have answered and he'd still be between these walls" (166). The technique is realist in the sense that it effectively portrays Ruth's state of distress; this is especially true in a novel in which most of the narration is not stream-of-consciousness.

6 Updike, "Howells as Anti-Novelist," 175. Hereafter cited in-text.

7 Schiff, "Updike and Howells," 75.

8 Nietzsche, "On Truth and Lie," 767.

9 Ibid., 768.

10 Derrida, *Of Grammatology*, 158.

Bibliography

Allen, Mary. "John Updike's Love of 'Dull Bovine Beauty.'" In Bloom, *John Updike*, 69–95.

Augustine. *City of God*. Translated by Henry Bettenson. New York: Penguin Books, 2003.

Barth, John. "The Literature of Replenishment." In *The Friday Book*, 193–206. New York: G. P. Putnam's Sons, 1984.

Barth, Karl. *The Epistle to the Romans*. Translated by Edwyn C. Hoskyns. London: Oxford University Press, 1968.

———. "The Problem of Ethics Today." In *The Word of God and the Word of Man*, 136–82.

———. "The Righteousness of God." In *The Word of God and the Word of Man*, 9–27.

———. *The Word of God and the Word of Man*. Translated by Douglas Horton. New York: Harper Torchbooks, 1957.

Beauvoir, Simone de. *The Second Sex*. Translated by H. M. Parshley. New York: Vintage Books, 1989.

Begley, Adam. *Updike*. New York: Harper, 2014.

Bellis, Jack. *The John Updike Encyclopedia*. Westport, CT: Greenwood, 2000.

Berryman, Charles. "Faith or Fiction: Updike and the American Renaissance." In Yerkes, *John Updike and Religion*, 195–207.

Bloom, Harold. "Introduction." In Bloom, *John Updike*, 1–7.

———, ed. *John Updike: Modern Critical Views*. New York: Chelsea House, 1988.

Bordo, Susan. "The Cartesian Masculinization of Thought and the Seventeenth-Century Flight from the Feminine." In *From Modernism to Postmodernism: An Anthology*, edited by Lawrence Cahoone, 354–69. Malden, MA: Blackwell, 2002.

Boswell, Marshall. "Updike, Religion, and the Novel of Moral Debate." In Olster, *Cambridge Companion to John Updike*, 43–57.

Campbell, Jeff H. *Updike's Novels: Thorns Spell a Word*. Wichita Falls, TX: Midwestern State University Press, 1987.

Casey, Edward S. *Remembering: A Phenomenological Study*. Bloomington: Indiana University Press, 2000.

Cixous, Hélène. "The Laugh of the Medusa." Translated by Keith Cohen and Paula Cohen. In Leitch, *Norton Anthology of Theory and Criticism*, 1942–59.

Cooper, John M., ed. *Plato: Complete Works*. Indianapolis, IN: Hackett, 1997.

Crews, Frederick. "Mr. Updike's Planet." In *The Critics Bear It Away: American Fiction and the Academy*, 168–86. New York: Random House, 1992.

Crowe, David. *Cosmic Defiance: Updike's Kierkegaard and the Maples Stories.* Macon, GA: Mercer University Press, 2014.

Davis, Fred. *Yearning for Yesterday: A Sociology of Nostalgia.* New York: Free Press, 1979.

Derrida, Jacques. *Of Grammatology.* Translated by Gayatri Chakravorty Spivak. Baltimore: The Johns Hopkins University Press, 1976.

Detweiler, Robert. "*The Same Door*: Unexpected Gifts." In Thorburn and Eiland, *John Updike*, 169–77.

Donne, John. "The Sun Rising." In Smith, *The Complete English Poems*, 80–81.

———. "A Valediction: Forbidding Mourning." In Smith, *The Complete English Poems*, 84–85.

Engel, Susan. *Context Is Everything: The Nature of Memory.* New York: W. H. Freeman, 1999.

Farmer, Michial. "An Existentialist *Ars Moriendi*: Death and Sacrifice in John Updike's *The Centaur*." *Literature and Theology* 29, no. 3 (2015): 335–447.

Fisher, Alden L., ed. *The Essential Writings of Merleau-Ponty.* New York: Harcourt, Brace, and World, 1969.

Galloway, David. *The Absurd Hero in American Fiction.* Austin: University of Texas Press, 1981.

Greiner, Donald J. *John Updike's Novels.* Athens: Ohio University Press, 1984.

Hamilton, Alice, and Kenneth Hamilton. *The Elements of John Updike.* Grand Rapids, MI: Eerdmans, 1970.

Hawthorne, Nathaniel. *Tales and Sketches.* Edited by Roy Harvey Pearce. New York: Library of America, 1984.

Heddendorf, David. "The Modesty of John Updike." In Rodgers, *Critical Insights*, 320–32.

Heidegger, Martin. *The Origin of the Work of Art.* In *Poetry, Language, Thought*, translated by Albert Hofstadter, 15–87. New York: Harper and Row, 1971.

———. *Hugging the Shore: Essays and Criticism.* New York: Vintage, 1984.

Hunt, George W. *John Updike and the Three Great Secret Things: Sex, Religion, and Art.* Grand Rapids, MI: Eerdmans, 1980.

Iwamoto, Iwao, and John Updike. "A Visit to Mr. Updike." In Plath, *Conversations with John Updike*, 115–23.

James, Henry. "The Real Thing." In *The Norton Anthology of American Literature*, shorter 2nd ed., edited by Nina Baym, 2: 356–74. New York: Norton, 2008.

Kant, Immanuel. *Prolegomena to Any Future Metaphysics.* Translated by James W. Ellington. Indianapolis, IN: Hackett, 2001.

Karl, Frederick R. *American Fictions, 1940–1980: A Comprehensive History and Critical Evaluation.* New York: Harper and Row, 1983.

Kierkegaard, Søren. *Concluding Unscientific Postscript to "Philosophical Fragments."* Edited and translated by Howard V. Hong and Edna H. Hong. Princeton, NJ: Princeton University Press, 1992.

———. *Either/Or: A Fragment of Life.* Translated by Alastair Hannay. New York: Penguin, 1992.

———. *The Sickness unto Death: A Christian Psychological Exposition for Edification and Awakening.* Translated by Alastair Hannay. New York: Penguin, 1989.

———. *Søren Kierkegaard's Journals and Papers.* Edited and translated by Howard V. Hong and Edna H. Hong. Princeton, NJ: Princeton University Press, 1978.

———. *Training in Christianity and the Edifying Discourse Which "Accompanied" It.* Translated by Walter Lowrie. Princeton, NJ: Princeton University Press, 1941.

Leitch, Vincent, ed. *The Norton Anthology of Theory and Criticism.* New York: W. W. Norton, 2010.

Merleau-Ponty, Maurice. "Cézanne's Doubt." Translated by Hubert L. Dreyfus and Patricia Allen Dreyfus. In Fisher, *Essential Writings of Merleau-Ponty,* 233–51.

———. "Eye and Mind." Translated by Carleton Dalley. In Fisher, *Essential Writings of Merleau-Ponty,* 252–86.

———. *Phenomenology of Perception.* Translated by Colin Smith. Delhi: Motilal Banarsidass, 1996.

Miller, D. Quentin. "Updike, Middles, and the Spell of 'Subjective Geography.'" In Olster, *Cambridge Companion to John Updike,* 15–28.

Nabokov, Vladimir. *King, Queen, Knave.* Translated by Dmitri Nabokov. New York: McGraw-Hill, 1968.

Neary, John. *Something and Nothingness: The Fiction of John Updike and John Fowles.* Carbondale: Southern Illinois University Press, 1992.

Newman, Judie. "Guru Industries, Inc." In Yerkes, *John Updike and Religion,* 228–41.

———. *John Updike.* Basingstoke, England: MacMillan, 1988.

Nietzsche, Friedrich. "On Truth and Lying in a Non-Moral Sense." Translated by Ronald Speirs. In Leitch, *Norton Anthology of Theory and Criticism,* 764–74.

Olster, Stacey, ed. *The Cambridge Companion to John Updike.* Cambridge: Cambridge University Press, 2006.

Orr, John, and John Updike. "Interview with John Updike." In Plath, *Conversations with John Updike,* 159–63.

Pascal, Blaise. *Pensées.* Roslyn, NY: Black's Readers Service, 1941.

Plath, James, ed. *Conversations with John Updike.* Jackson: University of Mississippi Press, 1996.

———. "Giving the Devil His Due." In Yerkes, *John Updike and Religion,* 208–27.

Plato. *Meno.* Translated by G. M. A. Grube. In Cooper, *Plato,* 870–97.

———. *Phaedo.* Translated by G. M. A. Grube. In Cooper, *Plato,* 50–100.

————. *Republic.* Translated by G. M. A. Grube and C. D. C. Reeve. In Cooper, *Plato,* 971–1223.

————. *Symposium.* Translated by Alexander Nehamas and Paul Woodruff. In Cooper, *Plato,* 458–505.

————. *Theaetetus.* Translated by M. J. Levett and Myles Burnyeat. In Cooper, *Plato,* 157–234.

————. *Timaeus.* Translated by Donald J. Zeyl. In Cooper, *Plato,* 1224–91.

Prince, Martin. "A Note on Character in *The Centaur.*" In Thorburn and Eiland, *John Updike,* 132–33.

Reston, Sally. "John Updike Works Three Hours and Poses as a Vacationer." In Plath, *Conversations with John Updike,* 18–21.

Rhode, Eric. "John Updike Talks about the Shapes and Subjects of His Fiction." In Plath, *Conversations with John Updike,* 46–54.

Rickless, Samuel C. *Plato's Forms in Transition: A Reading of the Parmenides.* Cambridge: Cambridge University Press, 2006.

Rodgers, Bernard F., ed. *Critical Insights: John Updike.* Pasadena, CA: Salem Press, 2012.

Rougemont, Denis de. *Love in the Western World.* Translated by Montgomery Belgion. Princeton, NJ: Princeton University Press, 1983.

Samuels, Charles Thomas. "The Art of Fiction XLIII: John Updike." In Plath, *Conversations with John Updike,* 22–45.

————. *John Updike.* Minneapolis: University of Minnesota Press, 1969.

Sanoff, Alvin P., and John Updike. "Writers 'Are Really Servants of Reality.'" In Plath, *Conversations with John Updike,* 181–85.

Sartre, Jean-Paul. *Being and Nothingness.* Translated by Hazel E. Barnes. New York: Washington Square, 1992.

————. *Imagination: A Psychological Critique.* Translated by Forrest Williams. Ann Arbor: University of Michigan Press, 1962.

————. *Nausea.* Translated by Lloyd Alexander. New York: New Directions, 1964.

————. *The Psychology of Imagination.* Translated by Jonathan Webber. Secaucus, NJ: Citadel, 1980.

————. *What Is Literature?* Translated by Bernard Frechtman. London: Routledge, 2001.

Schiff, James A. "The Pocket Nothing Else Will Fill: Updike's Domestic God." In Yerkes, *John Updike and Religion,* 50–63.

————. "Updike and Howells." In Rodgers, *Critical Insights,* 65–84.

————. "Updike's *Scarlet Letter* Trilogy: Recasting an American Myth." In Rodgers, *Critical Insights,* 258–76.

————. *Updike's Version: Rewriting* The Scarlet Letter. Columbia: University of Missouri Press, 1992.

Sidney, Philip. "A Defence of Poesy." In Leitch, *Norton Anthology of Theory and Criticism,* 254–83.

Smith, A. J., ed. *The Complete English Poems.* New York: Penguin, 1977.

Sontag, Susan. "Sarre's *Saint Genet.*" In *Essays of the 1960s and '70s,* edited by David Rieff, 93–98. New York: Library of America, 2013.

Stevens, Wallace. "The Idea of Order at Key West." In *American Poetry: The Twentieth Century*, 1: 310–11. New York: Library of America, 2000.

Tallent, Elizabeth. *Married Men and Magic Tricks: John Updike's Erotic Heroes*. Berkeley, CA: Creative Arts Book Company, 1982.

Tanner, Tony. *Adultery in the Novel: Contract and Transgression*. Baltimore: Johns Hopkins University Press, 1981.

Taylor, Larry E. *Pastoral and Anti-Pastoral Patterns in John Updike's Fiction*. Carbondale: Southern Illinois University Press, 1971.

Thorburn, David, and Howard Eiland, eds. *John Updike: A Collection of Critical Essays*. Englewood Cliffs, NJ: Prentice Hall, 1979.

Trendel, Aristi. "The Resurgence of the Repressed in John Updike's Homecoming Stories 'The Sandstone Farmhouse' and 'The Cats.'" *Psychoanalytic Review* 97, no. 1 (2010): 163–74.

Updike, John. "Accuracy." In *Picked-Up Pieces*, 16–17.

———. "Ace in the Hole." In *The Same Door*, 14–26.

———. *The Afterlife and Other Stories*. New York: Alfred A. Knopf, 1994.

———. "The Angels." In *Midpoint and Other Poems*, 56.

———. *Assorted Prose*. New York: Random House, 1965.

———. "The Astronomer." In *Pigeon Feathers and Other Stories*, 179–86.

———. "Avec la Bébé-Sitter." In *The Music School and Other Stories*, 66–75.

———. "Bech Swings?" In *Bech: A Book*, 147–84. New York: Alfred A. Knopf, 1970.

———. "The Brown Chest." In *The Afterlife and Other Stories*, 225–33.

———. "Card Tricks." In *Hugging the Shore*, 463–70.

———. "The Cats." In *Licks of Love: Short Stories and a Sequel*, 60–84. New York: Ballantine Books, 2000.

———. "Cemeteries." In *Picked up Pieces*, 56–62.

———. *The Centaur*. New York: Fawcett, 1996.

———. *Couples*. New York: Random House, 2012.

———. "The Day of the Dying Rabbit." In *Museums and Women and Other Stories*, 26–40.

———. "The Dogwood Tree: A Boyhood." In *Assorted Prose*, 121–48.

———. "Dream Objects." In *Midpoint and Other Poems*, 55.

———. "The Egg Race." In *Problems and Other Stories*, 231–44. New York: Alfred A. Knopf, 1979.

———. "English Train Compartment." In *Verse*, 42. Greenwich, CT: Fawcett, 1965.

———. "The Female Body." In *Odd Jobs*, 70–72.

———. "Fireworks." In *Midpoint and Other Poems*, 47.

———. "First Wives and Trolley Cars." In *Odd Jobs*, 18–25.

———. "Flight." In *Pigeon Feathers and Other Stories*, 49–73.

———. "The Football Factory." In *Higher Gossip: Essays and Criticism*, 16–24. New York: Alfred A. Knopf, 2011.

———. "Giving Blood." In *The Music School and Other Stories*, 18–34.

———. "Grove Is My Press, and Avant My Garde." In *Picked-Up Pieces*, 352–65.

———. "The Happiest I've Been." In *The Same Door*, 220–42.

———. "The Hillies." In *Museums and Women and Other Stories*, 18.

———. "His Mother Inside Him." In *The Afterlife and Other Stories*, 234–41.

———. "How Does the Writer Imagine?" In *Odd Jobs*, 122–37.

———. "Howells as Anti-Novelist." In *Odd Jobs*, 168–89.

———. *Hugging the Shore: Essays and Criticism*. New York: Vintage Books, 1983.

———. "Incest." In *The Same Door*, 144–62.

———. "Introduction to the Czech Edition of *Of the Farm*." In *Picked-Up Pieces*, 82–83.

———. "Leaves." In *The Music School and Other Stories*, 52–56.

———. "Leaving Church Early." In *Tossing and Turning*, 7–11.

———. "Lifeguard." In *Pigeon Feathers and Other Stories*, 211–20.

———. "Living with a Wife." In *Tossing and Turning*, 68–70.

———. "A Madman." In *The Music School and Other Stories*, 35–51.

———. "Man and Daughter in the Cold." In *Museums and Women and Other Stories*, 98–107.

———. "Marching through Boston." In *Museums and Women and Other Stories*, 221–34.

———. *Marry Me: A Romance*. New York: Fawcett, 1996.

———. *Memories of the Ford Administration*. New York: Alfred A. Knopf, 1992.

———. *Midpoint and Other Poems*. New York: Alfred A. Knopf, 1978.

———. "Midpoint." In *Midpoint and Other Poems*, 3–44.

———. *A Month of Sundays*. New York: Alfred A. Knopf, 1975.

———. "Museums and Women." In *Museums and Women and Other Stories*, 3–17.

———. *Museums and Women and Other Stories*. New York: Alfred A. Knopf, 1972.

———. "The Music School." In *The Music School and Other Stories*, 183–90.

———. *The Music School and Other Stories*. New York: Alfred A. Knopf, 1991.

———. *Odd Jobs: Essays and Criticism*. New York: Alfred A. Knopf, 1991.

———. *Of the Farm*. New York: Alfred A. Knopf, 1965.

———. "On Being a Self Forever." In *Self-Consciousness*, 212–57.

———. "On Meeting Writers." In *Picked-Up Pieces*, 3–7.

———. "Packed Dirt, Churchgoing, A Dying Cat, A Traded Car." In *Pigeon Feathers and Other Stories*, 246–79.

———. *Picked-Up Pieces*. New York: Alfred A. Knopf, 1975.

———. "Pigeon Feathers." In *Pigeon Feathers and Other Stories*, 116–50.

———. *Pigeon Feathers and Other Stories*. New York: Alfred A. Knopf, 1962.

———. "Polish Metamorphoses." In *Hugging the Shore*, 491–97.

———. *Rabbit at Rest*. New York: Fawcett, 1996.

———. *Rabbit, Run*. New York: Fawcett, 1996.

———. "Rémarks upon Receiving the Campion Medal." In *More Matter: Essays and Criticism*, 850–52. New York: Alfred A. Knopf, 1999.

———. "Report of Health." In *Midpoint and Other Poems*, 68–69.

———. "Rhyming Max." In *Assorted Prose*, 204–10.

———. "Robert Pinget." In *Hugging the Shore*, 417–23.

———. *Roger's Version*. New York: Alfred A. Knopf, 1986.

———. "Roman Portrait Busts." In *Midpoint and Other Poems*, 59.

———. *S*. New York: Alfred A. Knopf, 1988.

———. *The Same Door: Short Stories*. New York: Vintage, 1981.

———. "A Sandstone Farmhouse." In *The Afterlife and Other Stories*, 103–35.

———. "The Sea's Green Sameness." In *Museums and Women and Other Stories*, 159–64.

———. *Self-Consciousness: Memoirs*. New York: Alfred A. Knopf, 1989.

———. "Should Writers Give Lectures?" In *Odd Jobs*, 137–48.

———. "Slippage." In *Trust Me: Short Stories*, 171–81. New York: Alfred A. Knopf, 1987.

———. "A Soft Spring Night in Shillington." In *Self-Consciousness*, 3–41.

———. "A 'Special Message' for the Franklin Library's First Edition Society Printing of *Roger's Version*." In *Odd Jobs*, 856–58.

———. "The Stare." In *The Music School and Other Stories*, 57–65.

———. "Still Life." In *Pigeon Feathers and Other Stories*, 27–48.

———. "The Taste of Metal." In *Museums and Women and Other Stories*, 235–41.

———. "This I Believe." In *Due Considerations: Essays and Criticism*, 670–71. New York: Alfred A. Knopf, 2007.

———. "Three Illuminations in the Life of an American Author." In *Bech Is Back*, 3–27. New York: Alfred A. Knopf, 1982.

———. *Tossing and Turning*. New York: Alfred A. Knopf, 1977.

———. "Toward Evening." In *The Same Door*, 61–68.

———. "What MoMA Done Tole Me." In *Just Looking: Essays on Art*, 3–19. New York: Alfred A. Knopf, 1989.

———. "Whitman's Egotheism." In *Hugging the Shore*, 106–17.

———. "Why Write?" In *Picked-up Pieces*, 29–39.

———. *The Witches of Eastwick*. New York: Ballantine Books, 2008.

Vargo, Edward P. "Updike, American History, and Historical Methodology." In Olster, *Cambridge Companion to John Updike*, 107–21.

———. *Rainstorms and Fire: Ritual in the Novels of John Updike*. Port Washington, NY: Kennikat, 1973.

Verduin, Kathleen. "Updike, Women, and Mythologized Sexuality." In Olster, *Cambridge Companion to John Updike*, 61–75.

Versluys, Kristiaan. "'Nakedness' or Realism in Updike's Early Short Stories." In Olster, *Cambridge Companion to John Updike*, 29–42.

Warnock, Mary. *Memory*. London: Faber and Faber, 1987.

Watt, Ian. *The Rise of the Novel: Studies in Defoe, Richardson, and Fielding*. Berkeley: University of California Press, 1957.

Whitman, Walt. "Crossing Brooklyn Ferry." In *Leaves of Grass*, 198–207. New York: Modern Library, 2000.

Wood, James. *How Fiction Works.* New York: Picador, 2009.

Wood, Ralph C. *The Comedy of Redemption: Christian Faith and Comic Vision in Four American Novelists.* Notre Dame, IN: Notre Dame University Pres, 1988.

Wordsworth, William. "The Solitary Reaper." In *The Norton Anthology of English Literature,* vol. D, *The Romantic Period,* edited by Stephen Greenblatt, 342. New York: Norton, 2012.

Yerkes, James, ed. *John Updike and Religion: The Sense of the Sacred and the Motions of Grace.* Grand Rapids, MI: Eerdmans, 1999.

Index

Page numbers in **boldface** formatting indicate that a chapter, or a sizeable portion of one, is dedicated to the work in question.

Credits